Climbing Colorado's Fourteeners

From the Easiest Hikes to the Most Challenging Climbs

Chris Meehan

FALCONGUIDES

GUILFORD, CONNECTICUT
HELENA, MONTANA

FALCONGUIDES®

An imprint of Rowman & Littlefield
Falcon and FalconGuides are registered trademarks and Make Adventure Your Story is a trademark of Rowman & Littlefield.

Distributed by NATIONAL BOOK NETWORK

Copyright © 2016 by Rowman & Littlefield

Photos by Chris Meehan unless otherwise noted
Maps by Design Maps © Rowman & Littlefield

British Library Cataloguing-in-Publication Information available

Library of Congress Cataloging-in-Publication data is available on file.
ISBN 978-1-4930-1970-0 (paperback)
ISBN 978-1-4930-1971-7 (e-book)

∞™ The paper used in this publication meets the minimum requirements of American National Standard for Information Sciences—Permanence of Paper for Printed Library Materials, ANSI/NISO Z39.48-1992.

Contents

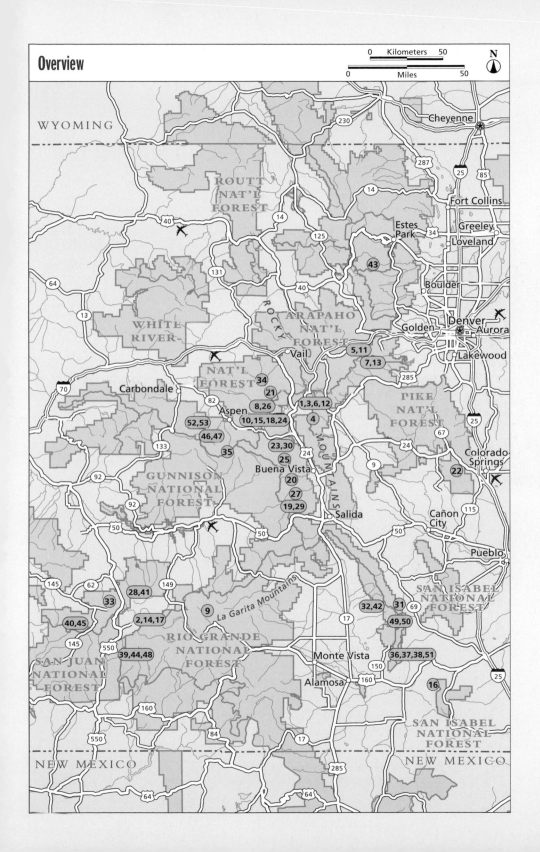

Overview

0　Kilometers　50

0　Miles　50

N

WYOMING

ROUTT NAT'L FOREST

Cheyenne

230

287

25

85

14

Fort Collins

Estes Park

Greeley

Loveland

34

125

43

64

131

40

131

40

WHITE RIVER-

13

ROCKY

ARAPAHO NAT'L FOREST

Golden

Denver

Aurora

70

NAT'L FOREST

Carbondale

82

Aspen

Vail

5,11

7,13

Lakewood

285

34

PIKE NAT'L FOREST

25

52,53

46,47

35

8,26

10,15,18,24

1,3,6,12

4

67

24

133

23,30

25

Buena Vista

20

27

19,29

Salida

9

24

22

Colorado Springs

115

92

GUNNISON NATIONAL FOREST

92

50

50

Cañon City

Pueblo

145

62

28,41

149

33

2,14,17

9

La Garita Mountains

32,42

31

69

SAN ISABEL NATIONAL FOREST

40,45

145

550

39,44,48

RIO GRANDE NATIONAL FOREST

17

49,50

50

25

SAN JUAN NATIONAL FOREST

160

Monte Vista

Alamosa

150

160

36,37,38,51

16

84

17

SAN ISABEL NATIONAL FOREST

550

160

NEW MEXICO

285

NEW MEXICO

64

64

Fourteeners Peak Bagging List by Elevation

Can you climb all of them? Record the date of each accomplishment.

1. Mount Elbert, 14,433', _____
2. Mount Massive, 14,421' _____
3. Mount Harvard, 14,420', _____
4. Blanca Peak, 14,345', _____
5. La Plata Peak, 14,336', _____
6. Uncompahgre Peak, 14,309', _____
7. Crestone Peak, 14,294', _____
8. Mount Lincoln, 14,286', _____
9. Grays Peak, 14,270', _____
10. Mount Antero, 14,269', _____
11. Torreys Peak, 14,267', _____
12. Castle Peak, 14,265', _____
13. Quandary Peak, 14,265', _____
14. Mount Evans, 14,264', _____
15. Longs Peak, 14,255', _____
16. Mount Wilson, 14,246', _____
17. Mount Shavano, 14,229', _____
18. Crestone Needle, 14,197', _____
19. Mount Princeton, 14,197', _____
20. Mount Belford, 14,197', _____
21. Mount Yale, 14,196', _____
22. Mount Bross, 14,172', _____
23. Kit Carson Peak, 14,165', _____
24. South Maroon Peak, 14,156', _____
25. Tabeguache Peak, 14,155', _____
26. Mount Oxford, 14,153', _____
27. Mount Sneffels, 14,150', _____
28. Mount Democrat, 14,148', _____
29. Capitol Peak, 14,130', _____
30. Pikes Peak, 14,110', _____
31. Snowmass Mountain, 14,092', _____

32. Mount Eolus, 14,083', _____
33. Windom Peak, 14,082', _____
34. Challenger Point, 14,081', _____
35. Mount Columbia, 14,073', _____
36. Missouri Mountain, 14,067', _____
37. Humboldt Peak, 14,064', _____
38. Mount Bierstadt, 14,060', _____
39. Sunlight Peak, 14,059', _____
40. Handies Peak, 14,048', _____
41. Culebra Peak, 14,047', _____
42. Ellingwood Point, 14,042', _____
43. Mount Lindsey, 14,042', _____
44. Little Bear Peak, 14,037', _____
45. Mount Sherman, 14,036', _____
46. Redcloud Peak, 14,034', _____
47. Pyramid Peak, 14,018', _____
48. Wilson Peak, 14,017', _____
49. Wetterhorn Peak, 14,015', _____
50. San Luis Peak, 14,014', _____
51. Mount of the Holy Cross, 14,005', _____
52. Huron Peak, 14,003', _____
53. Sunshine Peak, 14,001', _____

Unofficial Fourteeners

1. Mount Cameron, 14,238', _____
2. El Diente Peak, 14,159', _____
3. Conundrum Peak, 14,060', _____
4. North Eolus, 14,039', _____
5. North Maroon Peak, 14,014', _____

Preface

With more people than ever flocking to Colorado's fifty-three official fourteeners, this guidebook is designed as an introduction to these adventures. It's arranged differently than other fourteener guidebooks. Other guidebooks, very sensibly, are arranged by mountain range. This guidebook is arranged by relative ease and considers the distance and elevation gain required to summit each peak as well as the challenges each mountain poses to climbers. It uses a host of metrics, both objective and subjective, to rank and organize the mountains by their unique challenges and hazards. Therefore it offers something for beginners as well as for experienced mountaineers.

HELP US KEEP THIS GUIDE UP TO DATE

Every effort has been made by the author and editors to make this guide as accurate and useful as possible. However, many things can change after a guide is published—terrain can vary, regulations change, techniques evolve, land comes under new management, and so on.

We would appreciate hearing from you concerning your experiences with this guide and how you feel it could be improved and kept up to date. While we may not be able to respond to all comments and suggestions, we'll take them to heart, and we'll also make certain to share them with the author. Please send your comments and suggestions to the following address:

FalconGuides
Reader Response/Editorial Department
246 Goose Lane
Guilford, CT 06437

Or you may e-mail us at: editorial@falcon.com

Thanks for your input, and happy trails!

Acknowledgments

Colorado! Couldn't have done it without you! This state is truly awesome. The geology, the mountains, the wildlife, the wildflowers, and the people make the Centennial State an amazing place to live and play. It's been a fascinating journey in writing this book and discovering more of the human and geological history of the fourteeners.

Thanks to all the friends and family I've hiked with over the years and to those friends and family who haven't gone on a long hike or climb with me—don't worry, there's still time! Thanks to the trail buddies, the folk you meet while out climbing and end up walking and talking with for a while.

I wanted to offer special thanks to those who contributed to this book directly: Lee Mauney and Chris Seaver, thanks for your photos and our experiences together so far. Russ Sackson, thanks for your photos, for guiding with me back in the day, for hiking with me whenever you're in Colorado, and for introducing me to Granite Gear and other opportunities.

Thanks to my brother, Colin, who helped created a mountain-ranking system, and thanks to my folks, Hugh and Martha, for telling me my head was always in the clouds. This book is proof they were right!

Thanks to the amazing Andrew Hamilton, who just went out and did it—again, setting the speed record for doing all the fourteeners in record time in 2015. He thinks someone could beat him soon; we'll see.

Thanks to Skeet Glatterer and Dale Atkins for contributing safety information, and of course thanks to all the search and rescue volunteers and coordinators in Colorado. Every year they give up thousands of hours not only to rescue stranded or injured hikers and climbers throughout the state but also to train and stay in mental and physical shape to provide aid in unique and often challenging situations.

Thanks to the Colorado Mountain Club, Colorado Fourteeners Initiative, Conservation Colorado, and all the other organizations and their supporters throughout the state that are helping to keep Colorado's mountains wild and as pristine as possible for future generations. Also, thanks for creating partnerships to allow access to private lands and for purchasing lands that make accessing these amazing peaks possible.

Thanks also to the National Park Service and the Bureau of Land Management for allowing access to the scores of roads and trails that wend deep into the heart of the mountains.

A special thanks to the pioneers we'll never meet, from Native Americans who trapped eagles on the top of fourteeners or placed stones on mountaintops—surprising explorers hundreds, perhaps thousands of years later; to the early miners; to the pioneering climbers of the late 1800s and early 1900s—men and women alike.

Introduction

There's something special about climbing a fourteener (14er) in Colorado. It's a singular and challenging experience that becomes addicting to some. It's easy to see why. Nothing is as spectacular as beginning a trip engulfed in a lush forest of pines, aspens, and firs, surrounded by a surprising palette of wildflowers, greenery, and scampering forest creatures, coming to a small clearing to see a high-altitude peak—the mountain you'll soon be on top of—then taking that final step or crux move to gain that peak and marveling as you look down on that same forest and that same meadow you spied the peak from earlier. That's the start of fourteener fever for many. But opening your senses to the thin, crisp air, the solitude, the sweeping panoramas and seeing peaks and valleys and high plains stretching to the curvature of the horizon—it's awesome! So is sharing that adventure with friends, family, and loved ones—even the ones you have to push, pull, or prod to the top. Then again, the well-earned ice cream or pizza or beer afterwards is pretty sweet too!

Every fourteener is a unique journey, whether you're going just outside a city like Colorado Springs or Denver and driving to a parking lot before heading up the mountain or you're finding your way on ever-shrinking dirt roads after dark with no signage, hoping you made the right turn at FR 214—or was it 214B?—this book should help with that! The climbs themselves are the real gems. Fun, challenging and humbling, they invigorate, inspire, and astound (and sometimes confound). Then there's that crux move or a singular vista or a moment of achievement for you or someone on the same journey that you and your friends will talk about years later.

The seeds of this book were planted when I was mountain guide at the turn of the millennium—you don't have too many opportunities to say something like that! Taking people young and old—I was a guide at a Boy Scout base—on their first fourteener was an amazing experience, something I will always relish. It deepened my love of Colorado's mountains and its wild places. I'll forever be grateful for that.

Over time and through countless conversations with friends and random folk alike, I've realized that the fourteeners guidebooks out there, excellent as they are, aren't geared toward those first-time adventurers or those looking for an easy way to identify which challenges they want to take. This book aims to change that by setting that as the organizing point.

Most everyone can climb a fourteener—I've seen kids as young as 6 and folks in their 80s atop Colorado's peaks. I've seen wounded veterans and (supposedly) disabled folk on the peak, and hopefully I'll see you up there.

With careful planning and knowledge of your own and your groups' skills, most fourteener adventures are great, but sometimes you have to be realistic and turn around. Weather, unrealistic expectations—whether the mountain is tougher than expected or its challenges take longer than expected—injuries, illnesses; all of these can be contributing factors to making the wise decision for some or all of a group or a solo peak bagger to turn around. After all, as many experienced mountaineers say, you can always live to climb another day. This should be your mantra in adverse situations.

A trip where you had to turn back because of thunder hail (yes, that's a thing in Colorado) can make for a much better story than someone getting hurt or even killed because of a stupid mistake.

Remember: Adventure is what you set out for. Adventure is what you get. But the expectations and realizations are often not the same; after all, it wouldn't be much of an adventure if they were!

Colorado's Fourteeners (Ranges and Locations)

All of Colorado's fourteeners fall within one of six mountain ranges. Each range is distinct from the others, and within some of the ranges the mountains are from different geologic eras and consist of different rock types.

The Front Range is the longest range of fourteeners entirely in Colorado. It snakes south from the Wyoming border for 175 miles, ending in Pueblo. It is the fort wall of the Rockies, jutting up from the Colorado Plateau and bookended by Longs Peak to the north and Pikes Peak to the south. It has six fourteeners, and most are easier mountains to climb and can be climbed within a day. The bookends are the most challenging peaks in the range.

The Ten Mile / Mosquito Range is an interesting range because it is divided by the Continental Divide. Its five fourteeners are in the high country of Colorado, and all have remnants of mining activity. Most of the five fourteeners in the range are accessed from the east. These mountains are relatively easy to access from the interstates, as the range ends at I-70 near Frisco, Colorado.

The Sawatch Range is the only Colorado range with fourteeners that takes its name from a Native American word. The Ute word, also spelled Saguache, means "blue-earth spring." The range is called the backbone of the Rockies—and the continent. With fifteen fourteeners, it has the highest concentration of fourteeners anywhere in the United States. All of California has fewer fourteeners than this range in the heart of Colorado. It also has Mount Elbert and Mount Massive, the highest peaks in the state. These are beautiful mountains, and they aren't too hard. They're pretty easy to get to, but they're not as accessible as the Front Range and Ten Mile / Mosquito Range. This 100-mile range starts at Vail and I-70 and ends in, appropriately enough, Saguache.

The Sangre de Cristo Range is wilder, with nine fourteeners. It has some of the most difficult fourteeners in the state, including the Crestone Group and Little Bear. It also has the southernmost fourteener in the state, Culebra Peak. Access to these mountains is generally more difficult, as they are tougher climbs and in less-populated areas. Sangre de Cristo is Spanish for "Blood of Christ." At 220 miles long, starting where the Sawatch Range ends, this range is actually longer than the Front Range but spills over into New Mexico.

The Elk Range hosts many of Colorado's most iconic fourteeners, including the Maroon Bells. Like a siren song, these are also among the most deadly and difficult fourteeners in the state. The range includes Capitol Peak and its infamous Knife Edge, as well as the notoriously rotten rock of the Maroon Bells. However, the composition of these peaks is entirely different. The Maroon Bells are reddish sedimentary rock, while Capitol is composed of young granite. These mountains are mostly hidden from civilization and, while a long way from the state's population center on the Front Range, aren't the hardest to get to.

The San Juan Mountains are clusters of handsome fourteeners in the southwestern part of Colorado, closer to Durango. These thirteen mountains offer a little something for everyone, from the easy-to-access, easy-to-climb, winsome Handies Peak to the devilish tooth of El Diente—a sub-peak of the difficult Mount Wilson that's not an official fourteener but widely respected for its challenges and beauty.

History

Colorado's popular—and true—history is full of cowboys and miners and Native Americans. But the land that is Colorado today saw its first humans long before modern Native Americans. Relics at the Lindenmeier Site near Fort Collins in northern Colorado place members of the Clovis Culture in Colorado as early as 11,000 years ago. The cliff dwellings in Mesa Verde National Park were built sometime in the 1190s. It's possible that members of the Clovis Culture were the first to climb some of Colorado's fourteeners, and some of these peaks are still regarded as sacred places by Native Americans.

The first Europeans to reach Colorado came via the southeast, naming places like Culebra Peak and Pueblo—heck, Colorado is a Spanish word for red! After the Spaniards came trappers and traders. The first known American to come to Colorado was James Pursley, who wintered with the Ute Nation in South Park in 1805. He found gold flakes in a stream there. President Thomas Jefferson sent Lt. Zebulon Montgomery Pike in 1806 to survey what's now the southern United States, including Colorado. They named a fourteener for him. You might have heard of it.

The gold rush of 1859 brought settlers hoping to find their fame and fortune in the plains and on the mountains. These settlers and prospectors were the first to ascend some of the fourteeners; they definitely named some of them, such as Handies Peak, even if they didn't climb them.

Following the Civil War the federal government began a more earnest effort to understand Colorado and the West. The two federal surveys that really explored Colorado's high country and made the first ascents of fourteeners were the Hayden Survey, led by Dr. Ferdinand Vandeveer Hayden, and the survey led by Lt. George Montague Wheeler, both in the 1870s.

Geology

Colorado is truly the United States' high country. That's not a reference to the legalization of marijuana, either. There are eighty-nine peaks across all the states, Alaska and Hawaii included, that surpass 14,000 feet; fifty-three (60 percent) are in Colorado.

These aren't even the first Rockies. Though some of the rock that makes up Colorado's fourteeners today is more than 1 billion years old, the Ancestral Rockies are long gone, eroded to rubble. Rocks in Kansas trace back to those extinct monoliths, borne on the backs of glaciers.

Today's Rockies are a complex mix of time: Longs Peak, for instance, is made of 1.4-billion-year-old granite. Quite a grandfather compared to the granite uprising that formed Capitol Peak and Snowmass just 35 million years ago. The mountains were and are being carved by erosion—all those scree fields are clear evidence of that. Glaciers—most now melted—also played a huge part in sculpting the bowls and basins of Colorado's fourteeners, as well as the moraines that stretch to the foothills.

The same conditions that created the Rockies in Colorado also deposited countless minerals and ores in them, which Native Americans have used in their jewelry for centuries.

Word of gold in 1859 brought people from far and wide to Colorado's vast high country. The mountains have been exploited for minerals ever since. Ranging from uranium to gypsum, gold to copper to lead—it's all in the Rockies. This section could go on for quite some time but will end before getting into a discussion of the Precambrian era's deposits and the Laramide orogeny. There are other books about that!

Ranking the Fourteeners

There is no absolute objective way to rank the difficulties of each mountain. This guidebook used the most objective information available in developing the rankings. That includes elevation, elevation gain, trip length, slope angle, route surface, and more. That information was compiled from personal experiences, observed data from the author and others who have offered rankings of the fourteeners to create a comprehensive ranking system.

Still, a 6-foot-tall person will generally have an easier time striding over large rocks than someone who is 5 feet tall. On the other hand, that 5-foot person may be able to wriggle through a tight spot more easily, be able to climb on rotten rock with more ease, or see hand and footholds in a chimney better than a taller person.

Weather

Colorado's weather is tempestuous and unpredictable. There's a well-known adage in Colorado: "If you don't like the weather wait 10 minutes." At altitude and above tree line, it's more of an inverse. If the weather looks bad, it's probably going to get worse. A blue sky can swarm with clouds in mere minutes.

The Rockies and Colorado's fourteeners are the first major breakers that clouds encounter between the West Coast and the Midwest. Their water-heavy bellies scrape against the peaks and release rain, sleet, snow, thunder and lightning, wind—sometimes all at the same time. The rain and sleet can turn solid dirt and rock into slick surfaces in minutes. Snow can turn into whiteout conditions.

Thunder and lightning above tree line are nerve-wracking distractions that—at best—can impair decision making as you scramble to get down. At worst they're deadly. In June 2015 fifteen people and a dog were struck by lightning on Mount Bierstadt at the same time. The people were lucky; all survived. The dog did not. And in July 2015 a newlywed couple was struck by lightning on Mount Yale. It took other climbers 45 minutes to reach a location where they could get cell reception to call 911. It took more than 2 hours for rescuers to reach the couple. (In a more remote area, everything could have taken a lot longer!) The 31-year-old bride died.

Common advice for all fourteeners is to start early, summit early, and get down. Storms generally roll in during the afternoon in late spring and summer, when the risk is highest, but lightning can happen at any time up there—even during sleet and snow. To learn more about how to deal with lightning in the mountains, check out the "Safety" section, where search-and-rescue experts offer advice.

All that having been said, most of the time the weather in the mountains is lovely. The visibility from the top of fourteeners can stretch for 100 miles or more on sunny days. At lower altitudes, afternoon storms are a welcome respite on hot summer days—and Colorado has plentiful rainbows.

Not only are Colorado's high places subject to rain, they're also colder. For every 1,000 feet of elevation gain, the temperature drops about 4°F. On a sunny summer day when it's 90°F in Denver, it could still be in the 50s on top of a fourteener. So, even in the heat of summer, always bring rain/wind wear and some insulation.

Despite the cooler temperatures, you're more at risk of sunburn at altitude. The sun's rays are 26 percent stronger at 14,400 feet than at Denver's famous 5,280 feet. Sun protection is a must. Places you don't think about protecting as much need attention too. That means the underside of your forearms, under your chin, your nostrils, and your earlobes. Sunlight reflecting off bright rocks, snow, and water can burn the inside of your nose. It's quite uncomfortable!

This guide is intended to cover the warmer months as winter routes are much different. Winters in Colorado close many alpine roads. Wolf Creek Pass on the Continental Divide can receive more than 300 inches of snow annually. Still, more people are venturing into the mountains in winter now than ever before, to snowshoe, ski, or snowboard.

Snow poses unique dangers, such as avalanches and moats close to rocks and trees. Winter adventures also require more gear, which means more weight. Additionally, road closures mean longer treks into the backcountry. All together that means it takes more time to summit these mountains in winter months. So this is a quick warning that the times and mileages given are only for spring through fall.

Spring in the fourteeners begins later than at lower altitudes. Most fourteeners will have snow on them into June. Some still have glaciers and year-round snow patches, despite the effects of climate change.

No two years are alike in the high country. Climbing these peaks can be a muddy, slippery mess well into July some years. In other years the mountains can be dry in June.

Flora and Fauna

Climbing a fourteener in Colorado means gaining significant altitude, which means crossing through multiple biomes and microclimates. It's one of the amazing draws of the mountains. In one day on a climb, you're likely to travel through forests of ponderosa pine and Douglas fir before reaching lodgepole pine and aspen and then spruce, fir, and limber and bristlecone pine—all this interspersed with mountain meadows, willow marshes and wetlands, and alpine lakes and streams. Finally you'll reach the alpine tundra, where stubby plants like club moss and moss campion are merely inches tall but decades old. These plants are weather hardy but not boot hardy, so please stay on-trail to minimize impact. Walking on rocks instead of plants is even better!

Wide swaths of evergreen forests have been decimated in the past twenty years, owing largely to drought and climate change. Pine and spruce beetles are at the heart of this epidemic and have killed more trees than forest fires. While pine and spruce are healthy in much of the state, sadly you will come across some of these de-vegetated lands. Thus far, land managers haven't been able to remedy the problem, and shorter, warmer winters have exacerbated the problem by allowing the beetles to reproduce at record rates.

Colorado also is famous for its quaking aspens. Aspen groves are some of the largest living organisms on earth and reproduce chiefly by root sprouts—every tree in an aspen grove can be a clone. Aspens are usually found in moist, protected areas. They grow and spread aggressively and live at elevations of up to 12,000 feet. In Colorado they're more commonly found at lower elevations. Trunks of aspens are often scarred. Elk, bears, and other animals will eat aspen bark and shoots in winter.

Speaking of elk, these lumbering quadrupeds are found in alpine meadows throughout Colorado. White River National Forest has the largest elk herd in the world, numbering nearly 40,000 by some estimates, so it should be no surprise that the Maroon Bells and other mountains in the forest are called the Elk Range.

Other wildlife in the mountains includes moose—still rare but growing in number—mule deer, black bears (there are currently no known grizzlies in Colorado) and mountain lions. Mountain lions are elusive and are much more likely to spot you than you are to spot them. The high forests are also full of chipmunks and ground squirrels.

Mountain goats and bighorn sheep graze at high elevations and are likely to be the biggest mammal you'll see high up on a fourteener. The animals you're most likely to see—or hear—at higher elevations are marmots and pikas. The best way to spot them is by letting your ears guide your eyes. Listen; then look.

Marmots, which look like a mix between beavers and groundhogs, are larger and easier to see. They like to sun on rocks. Pikas blend in with the rocks and often scamper underfoot on more-remote trails.

Please don't feed the wildlife—no matter how cute! Don't leave your stuff around. If camping, hang your food and anything else that smells—toothpaste, lotion, etc.—in bear bags at least 10 feet off the ground and preferably suspended between two trees. Certain parts of Colorado now require the use of bear canisters for overnight stays.

It's not just the bears you have to worry about. Chipmunks, squirrels, and mice can gnaw through that nice new $400 tent to get at your tasty treats. Marmots love rubber, and many people who leave their trekking poles behind to climb a rocky summit come back to find the rubber chewed off their grips. Also, don't throw food away; instead, pack out what you don't consume. The more handouts and trash animals get from humans, the more likely they are to chew through tents in search of food, eat wrappers or other trash, and get sick.

Colorado is a birder's paradise. Crows, magpies, blue Steller's jays with their black crowns, and pesky Clark's nutcrackers and gray jays (nicknamed camp robbers) are found throughout Colorado. You can also hear hummingbirds whirring near flowers and alpine water sources. Ptarmigans are masters of disguise on snow or rock and gravel and often surprise unsuspecting hikers and snowshoers. Eagles were caught and trained by Native Americans on Longs Peak, and today you'll occasionally see birds of prey at the state's highest altitudes.

Alpine lakes and creeks are amazing spots for cutthroat trout. Anglers can also find stocked sport fish such as rainbow and brown trout in much of the state.

Wilderness Restrictions/Regulations

Colorado is a wild place! The state has two national grasslands, eight national wildlife refuges, twelve national forests, forty-three wilderness areas (not counting wilderness study areas), and a growing number of national parks and monuments; Browns Canyon National Monument was established in 2015. The majority of fourteeners are in USDA Forest Service and/or national wilderness areas. Parts of some fourteeners are on private land.

Regardless of land ownership, please respect laws, regulations, and requirements. That means don't camp too close to water sources, pack your trash out, don't take alpine souvenirs, and make campfires only where allowed. Leash your dogs as required. Check out the landowner or manager listed for each hike to learn about local requirements and regulations before heading out. It's up to us to protect these lands.

Sign trail registers and, if offered, use wilderness tags. These could be required in the future, and fines could be assessed for not using them. Both help land managers understand how many people are accessing Colorado's mountains and backcountry and help government entities allocate funds.

Leave No Trace

Leave No Trace ethics help protect wild places. These principles ask users of the back-country to leave things as they've found them, to not scar the land with fires or trash, to travel on known or established trails, and to camp at least 200 feet from streams, lakes, and trails. Learn more about Leave No Trace ethics at LNT.org.

Peak Celebrations/Respecting Wilderness

You just climbed a fourteener and now want to celebrate. Do it; you've earned it! Peak celebrations come in many forms. Show the world; do it with style and your own unique flair. One group did keg stands on top of Mount Princeton. Some people do headstands, or yoga poses, or bring a stuffed animal, or something personal with them. I haven't seen any garden gnomes up there yet though.

Probably the most common celebration photograph includes a sheet of paper with the elevation and peak name written on it—kind of boring, you can do better! There's also a problem with those signs: A lot of people leave them up there. A four-teener is not a trash can. You pack it up, you pack it out. With minimal effort you can make sure the peak is in as good or better shape for everyone who comes after you. Scores of responsible, albeit bitter, climbers carry out trail trash all the time, including those thin, lightweight, compaction-friendly signs. Woodsy Owl never made it to 14,000 feet, but his message holds true: "Give a hoot, don't pollute!"

Please don't spend the whole time trying to call someone on your cell phone from the peak. You're not really appreciating the moment if you're trying to call your pal back in Beantown or San Fran and walking around the peak looking for a signal. If you must call someone, keep it short and quiet. No one else wants to hear you yapping on the phone for a couple of minutes in the wilderness.

Along the same lines, leave those Bluetooth speakers at home or in your vehicle. "Flight of the Valkyries" is an amazing piece of music; it's inspiring, it's victorious, but no one wants to hear it or the latest Katy Perry song blasting away when they're hiking through the mountains. When you play music on a speaker in the mountains, you lose the chance of hearing birdsong or marmot and pika chirps, and you lessen your and everyone else's chance of seeing wildlife.

Again, please be respectful of wildlife; you're a visitor in their home. And be respectful of nature's other guests—your fellow climbers.

Winter Climbing/Winter Mountaineering

This book is aimed toward warmer adventures. The wilderness is open year-round, and more people are taking advantage of the backcountry in winter. But winter poses additional dangers like avalanches, turning some trails that are perfectly fine in summer into veritable death traps in winter.

Ice climbing and couloir climbs are fun winter activities. In the Rockies avalanches are winter's version of lightning, deadly and surprising. Learn more about avalanches and how to avoid such dangers by educating yourself or taking classes. At the very least check the Colorado Avalanche Information Center at avalanche.state.co.us for current conditions and basic safety information.

If a road is closed by a snow berm, respect that closure. Many, many feet of snow can pile up in winter, and even if a road looks relatively clear, don't trust it. It's closed for a reason. Enjoy more time adventuring with your snow gear, and plan for longer hiking, snowshoeing, or cross-country skiing times.

Hiking with Dogs

Some people take their dogs up fourteeners. Dogs can climb most of them, but consider the impact of particularly rocky trails and peaks on their paws. Booties can help. On the most difficult pitches, it's not advisable to bring your dog. Your pup may not be able to climb across an exposed ridge or rock face, and trying to carry your pal over these hazards puts both of you at higher risk. Wilderness rules and private landowners may require leashes to protect both your dog and wildlife in the area. Certain areas, such as the Rock of Ages Trail to the Wilson Group of fourteeners, don't allow dogs. Please check with the landowner or manager to learn more about hiking with dogs for each of these climbs.

Climbing Classifications

This guidebook uses widely accepted climbing classifications: Classes 1–5, with Class 5 the most difficult. Only a few of the standard routes on Colorado fourteeners have moves that can be considered Class 5; even then, those are usually weather dependent.

Class 1: The easiest level of climbing; basically walking on a trail or path.

Class 2: More-difficult hiking on or through terrain that can require bushwhacking or scrambling on scree. With the exception of pushing branches away, Class 2 climbing rarely requires the use of hands.

Class 3: Climbing gets quadrupedal. You may need to use hands to climb up over rocks or up into chimneys that have very little exposure. You're relatively safe on Class 3 climbs, although some may require helmets.

Class 4: Things start to get dangerous. Class 4 climbs involve significant exposure, in that a fall could cause significant injury, or other elements, such as loose scree on a very steep slope that could fall on your head. This is semi-technical climbing, and you're using your whole body to climb up or down.

Class 5: This is technical climbing. At Class 5 you should definitely be wearing a helmet and should be on rope. While the Rockies abound with Class 5 routes, the routes described in this book don't reach this level, with the exception of one or two moves on mountains like Little Bear and Sunlight Peak.

Safety

Being safe at altitude is much different than normal hiking. FalconGuides reached out to search-and-rescue experts for their advice in the hopes of helping reduce accidents at altitude. Here's what they had to say:

People who venture up Colorado's fourteeners get into trouble because they underestimate weather, underestimate terrain, underestimate their ability to navigate, and overestimate their ability to get out of trouble when trouble happens.

Prepare

Do all the research you can to ensure safe travel in the mountains. Try to climb with people who have more experience than you, and learn from them. Understand your skill and risk levels, and choose routes you're comfortable with climbing. Map out travel plans ahead of time, and familiarize yourself with your planned route. Be reasonable and conservative in your estimate of how much time you need to complete a climb. Start early. If traveling with a group, which is always preferable, stay together, have a leader, be aware of peer pressure, and know when to turn back.

Share

Always let someone responsible know your itinerary. This could be family or a responsible friend. Other people who hike or climb are more likely to be accountable because they know what's at stake. Make a list explaining:

- Where you are going and how you're getting there.
- Vehicle description and license plate number.
- What you plan to climb and which route you're taking, as well as any alternative trips or side trips.
- The colors of your jacket, pack, helmet, and, if camping, tent.
- Your planned return time. This includes a reasonable time estimate of return to the trailhead and when help should be contacted. Remember that in the backcountry and even in small towns, cell reception might be limited or unavailable. It may take longer than expected to let your contacts know you're OK if you can't ring them from the trailhead itself.
- Emergency contact information. Each route lists the number for local sheriffs' offices, which contact search and rescue when needed, as well as the land manager to coordinate with in an emergency.

Learn Mountaineering Skills

Take a mountaineering class to get a good foundation; then start climbing with those who have more experience and learn from them.

Get the Gear

It can be a long process to acquire all the gear you will eventually need or want. Be sure to have at least the Ten Essentials (see page 14).

Check the Weather, Adjusting Your Plans as Necessary

In the days before you plan to head out, check the weather where you plan to climb to make any necessary changes to your trip—including rescheduling. Also check it the day or morning you leave. A great site for general forecasts is weather.gov, and 14ers.com has a link to the weather forecast for each peak.

Physical Conditioning

Don't underestimate the route. Keep in mind that climbing a mountain means vertical gain, and reaching altitudes with thinner air means exercise capacity is reduced. Give yourself time to acclimate to altitude, and be aware of the symptoms of acute mountain sickness (altitude sickness). Training will help you have enough physical reserve to handle emergency issues like weather, medical problems, and route finding.

Lightning

During summer, lightning is the main hazard on Colorado's fourteeners. Lightning and thunderstorms are most common in the late morning and through the afternoon, but lightning can strike any time of day or night. Sage and oft-repeated advice is: Climb early, and turn back if a thunderstorm is brewing. To minimize risk of being caught in a storm, study weather forecasts where you plan to climb before setting out. Learning to read the clouds for signs of danger is also important.

Turning back early is the biggest key to avoid being in the wrong place at the wrong time, but turning back or descending from high points as a storm is looming does not guarantee safety. Lightning can strike anywhere, even objects—like you—that are much shorter than close-by objects such as trees, ridges, or even summits.

A lightning strike can start miles away. It's not seeking a target from the start but is attracted to an object within the last 50 to 150 feet of its range. This is why a dog can be struck while walking next to a human. Crouching down does not make you safer or less likely to be struck.

Most climbers are concerned about a direct lightning strike, but most injuries and deaths are due to ground currents and side flashes, not direct strikes. That's because lightning can hit a tree or boulder and then spread along the ground.

To minimize the risk of lightning strikes, keep at least 6 miles and preferably at least 8 miles from a storm. The "Flash-to-Bang" method of estimating the distance of lighting is the best way to get an idea of how far away lightning is. A delay of 5 seconds between a flash and the sound of thunder is equal to about a mile. A delay of 40 seconds means lightning is about 8 miles away. At best, thunder can be heard about 10 miles away, but even a slight wind can muffle the sound.

Hikers and climbers move much more slowly than thunderstorms. Even a slow-moving thunderstorm can travel 8 miles in the time it takes a hiker to cover 1 mile.

Fast-moving storms can cross that distance in much less time. So if a thunderhead is moving toward your direction, especially if you can see lightning and hear thunder, it's time to get moving.

Avoiding Lightning

- Pay attention to towering and building clouds. They may quickly develop into storms capable of producing lightning.
- Hail storms often produce lightning at altitude.
- The best clues of lightning danger are visible flashes and audible thunder. Remember: If you can hear thunder, you're already in danger.
- There are no obvious clues to the immediate threat of lightning danger until the first flash occurs.
- Just because a storm has just passed, do not assume safety. According to the National Oceanic and Atmospheric Administration (NOAA), 50 percent of lightning deaths occur after a storm has passed.
- Turn around early. It's better to turn around early and not be faced with lightning danger than to be faced with lightning danger and wish you had turned around.

If Caught in Lightning

- Immediately get off elevated areas such as hills, mountain ridges, or peaks.
- Don't try to race to the summit just because you're close.
- Move down the mountain and keep walking.
- Never lie flat on the ground.
- Never shelter under an isolated tree.
- Never use a cliff or rocky overhang for shelter.
- Immediately get away from ponds and lakes.
- Stay away from objects that conduct electricity, such as barbed-wire fences, power lines, and windmills.
- If in a group, spread out so that you increase the chances for survivors who could come to the aid of any victims from a lightning strike.
- Wait at least 30 minutes after you hear the last sound of thunder before heading toward a summit.

Don't let summit fever overcome good judgment. One of the hardest things to do is turn around, especially when in sight of your goal. But many lightning accidents occur because climbers do not turn around. These are often avoidable situations. Dedicating yourself to reach a summit, no matter what, may appear admirable but can lead to deadly decisions. When in doubt, turn around; the mountain will always be there.

Avalanche

Most climbers consider avalanches a winter problem; however, on Colorado's four-teeners and other high peaks, those above 12,000 feet, deadly avalanche accidents happen year-round. Since 1990 avalanches have killed twelve climbers, and half of those deaths occurred in June, July, and October. As winter climbing of fourteen-ers grows, so too, sadly, will avalanche accidents. Compounding the problem is that popular summertime routes are not always safe routes in winter and spring.

Avoiding avalanche danger requires learning to recognize where and when ava-lanches can occur so that you can avoid dangerous slopes. Learning where and when avalanches occur is a blend of art and science that takes time and experience. Fortu-nately, it's not rocket science.

Slope angle is critical as to whether terrain can produce an avalanche. Most ava-lanches occur on slopes between 30 and 45 degrees, which are also perfect for climb-ing, skiing, and glissading.

Complicating matters is that avalanches can be triggered from shallow slopes at the bottom of steep slopes. With so much to know, the best way to learn about ava-lanches is to take avalanche courses and travel with those who are experienced with avalanches. Keep in mind, however, that while education teaches the rules, nature teaches the exceptions.

The American Avalanche Association (avalanche.org) is the best source for high-quality local instruction.

Mountain Rescue

There will always be risk associated with outdoor activities, but this information will help to decrease these issues. Nevertheless, anyone can have a "bad day in the moun-tains." When that time comes, it is better to call for help sooner rather than delay your call. Your situation, and the weather, is likely to get worse.

Mountain search-and-rescue activities in Colorado are performed by volunteers whose services are free of charge. However, if you require medical transport (ambu-lance or helicopter), you will be billed for those services. When you do need help, it's important to let rescuers know about any medical conditions and what issues you're having if they're not visible.

Buy a CORSAR Card

When you're hiking or climbing in Colorado, purchase a Colorado Outdoor Recre-ation Search and Rescue card. Your purchase directly contributes to the state's Search and Rescue Fund. It is not insurance. The fund helps reimburse rescue teams and sheriffs for costs incurred in your search and rescue. Funds remaining at the end of the year are used to help pay for training and equipment for these teams. You can buy an inexpensive CORSAR card from many outdoor recreation shops or online at colorado.gov/sar.

Information contributed by:

Skeet Glatterer, MD, FAWM; Alpine Rescue Team, Evergreen, Colorado (co-medical director); chairman, Mountain Rescue Association (MRA) Medical

Committee; US delegate (alternate) International Commission for Alpine Rescue (ICAR) Medical Committee

Dale Atkins, Alpine Rescue Team, Evergreen, Colorado; past chairman, Search and Rescue Committee, American Avalanche Association; past president, American Avalanche Association; past vice president, Avalanche Rescue Commission, International Commission for Alpine Rescue

The Ten Essentials

When climbing fourteeners, you should always carry necessary gear on you. This includes at a bare minimum the ten essentials for hiking and mountaineering. If hiking in a group, certain items on this list can be spread out among the members:

1. **Navigation and communication.** Map and compass are still essential despite electronics—batteries go dead, devices get wet, things break. Maps should be waterproof or kept in a bag. Global Positioning System (GPS) units and smartphones are great, but they're no fail-safe replacement for the old standbys. You can also bring a SEND (satellite emergency notification device). Also note that cell phone reception is limited in Colorado's backcountry.

2. **Proper clothing.** A rain jacket is a must, as is a layer of insulation—even in July and August. Jeans are not proper climbing/hiking clothing; most jeans are cotton, and they suck to hike in when they get wet. They stay heavy, cold, and wet, which is at best an inconvenience.

3. **Sun protection.** Sunglasses, sunscreen, hats, and clothes. Clothing can serve as sun protection, hence some outdoor companies publish the SPF levels of clothes on their tags. Remember, the sun is stronger at altitude.

4. **Illumination.** Headlights are cheap, lightweight, and great. Flashlights are good; a cell phone flash doesn't count.

5. **First aid.** Bring supplies appropriate for the trip. It doesn't have to be a big kit. You won't need antivenin on top of the mountain, for instance. It's wise to take a first-aid class and know how and when to administer care and when to make an emergency contact.

6. **Fire starter.** Make sure you have a fire starter capable of defeating the elements. Your Bic don't flick in a monsoon!

7. **Repair kit and tools.** This includes things like patches, knives, and battery backups or chargers for your devices.

8. **Extra food.** Hopefully you won't need it, but a few extra bars or some GORP may save the day for you or another climber.

9. **Water.** Bring extra water and/or water treatment. Modern filtration systems like the Sawyer Mini fit on disposable water bottles, weigh ounces, and are extremely simple to use. However, if there are no water sources nearby, you're out of luck. Carrying extra water is always a good idea.

10. **Emergency shelter.** A small, ultralight piece of protection—like a tarp, bivy sack, trash bag, or emergency blanket—can serve as a makeshift shelter or signal for search and rescue personal.

Appropriate Gear

Clothes

Jeans are not appropriate clothes for fourteeners. They soak through quickly and get heavy, they dry slowly, and they chafe uncomfortably. Probably the best leg wear for hiking fourteeners are synthetic pants or shorts, which can offer a combination of durability, water resistance, breathability, and wind resistance.

Wool or synthetic base layers are excellent insulators when hiking fourteeners in the early spring and late fall months. Many people wear or bring them in summer as well, since peak temperatures are regularly below the 70s. Whatever you choose to wear, be ready to sweat. Climbing fourteeners is hard work, and your pores show it! Good gear "breathes." You can purchase inexpensive synthetic clothing at Target or

A LONG EXPERIENCE (HOW NOT TO HIKE A DEADLY FOURTEENER)

"Hey, man, your lips are turning blue. I think you have the altitude sickness," Sarah said. It was the mid-90s—my first Colorado fourteener, Longs Peak. I wasn't sure if it was exhaustion, a hangover, or altitude sickness, but the whale of a headache I had probably kept me from being a little bit more scared about clinging to the windy, granite face of Homestretch, which I would later find out was the last pitch before reaching the summit.

In cotton jeans, a T-shirt, crappy sneakers or boots, and a light windbreaker, I was ill-prepared for the trip. Even more so considering I'd been at a party in Fort Collins until 2 a.m. and we'd begun hiking Colorado's northernmost fourteener around 4 a.m.

I don't have any photographs from that first trip to the sky back in 1995, but I'll always remember that moment, just as I'll remember watching the sun, an orange orb, pop over the curved horizon while the prairie remained in the shadows of night. I've seen other sunrises on other mountains, but never quite like that one.

I did a lot of things wrong that day. I was lucky. Longs Peak, like many Colorado peaks, can be deadly to even well-prepared and experienced climbers and hikers, let alone the ill-prepared. In the years since climbing Longs, I've been a mountain guide and a host of other things and have gained experience hiking throughout Colorado's cirques, bowls, canyons, high plateau, and of course its fourteeners. It's deepened my love for the mountains and the countryside and increased my respect for the challenges and dangers the mountains pose. Learn from my stupidity.

Walmart that will do in a pinch; however, outdoor specialty shops have a great selection of clothing designed for the outdoors that are meant to last.

Footwear

Don't go out and get some super-heavy, super-thick boot and expect to be comfortable climbing fourteeners on a hot August day. Your feet will be stuck in a soup of sweat and sock. Your feet will blister. If you're hiking in winter or mountaineering, that's the boot you'll likely need; but most of Colorado's fourteeners can be climbed in the warmer months in light hikers or trail runners.

Waterproof is nice, but waterproof doesn't always breathe that well, so your feet might get wet from sweating. And unless you're wearing good, high gaiters, if you step into a stream higher than your footwear's cuff, they're still going to get wet on the inside. I have a penchant for hiking and climbing in my modified Chacos, which might not be a popular choice but they work for me. Such sandals allow wearers to kick pebbles loose between foot soles, while shoe beds and feet dry quickly, but wearers can scrape their feet up much more and the ankle protection is minimal. A good breathable shoe, or a light hiker if you need the ankle support, is likely the best solution for hiking fourteeners. It offers a combination of grip, breathability, and comfort. Whatever style of footwear you choose, keeping your feet happy means you'll be a lot happier too.

How to Use This Guide

Each section in the guide consists of mountains with similar overall difficulty levels. No fourteener is easy unless you can drive to the top. But then what's the point! This guide is organized into four sections: Easier, Hard, Harder, and Hardest. The first two don't require extra protection, such as a helmet. Helmets are a good idea on most of the harder mountains, and on the hardest mountains they should definitely be considered and/or worn for the toughest parts of the climb. The beginning of each section offers a short overview of the difficulties the routes offer as a whole.

Each route description begins with a short overview, including what class of climbing/hiking is required and where the mountains are located.

Next you'll find the quick and dirty info: trailhead location, closest towns with services—some of the closest towns to fourteeners may not even have a gas station. This section includes the round-trip distance of each climb, average hiking time, elevation gain—some routes require re-summiting a significant peak or fourteener on the return trip—class ranking, type of terrain, trailhead elevation, camping availability, any fees or permits that might be required, best hiking season, maps, driving directions, and other relevant information. This section also includes basic information about land ownership/management as well as their contact information.

The Hike provides a more accurate description of each route, including significant route milestones, such as switchbacks, stream crossings, and challenging moves. The Miles and Directions offer a sort of tear sheet of the same information.

Note: Except for peak elevations, all figures are best estimates using actual measurements from GPS units. Elevation gain, distance, and trailhead elevation are all best estimates using actual measurements from GPS units, mapping software, and maps. Commercial GPS units are only accurate within a number of yards, and elevation information in these devices is affected by barometric changes. There are a host of unavoidable issues that limit the ability to offer precise mileage and elevation figures, from the height of the trekker to how closely or loosely switchbacks are followed. Trip times are calculated very generously. Hopefully you'll be done quicker than the estimate, but don't count on it.

Why Two Mountain Elevations?

Each route gives two mountain elevations because that's how the mountains are ranked by the US Geological Survey (USGS). Confusingly, many physical maps still rely on the older datum set, NGVD29—heck, in the case of La Plata Peak, an elevation error in the 1970s still persists on maps and websites forty years later. Meanwhile, your smartphone and GPS receiver use the newer datum set, NAVD88. Interestingly the different datums don't change any of the fourteeners' status in the rankings.

Route Map

This is a visual guide to each route. Given the distance and elevation gain of each peak, this should just be reference material.

Getting Additional Route Information

A more-detailed topo map is strongly recommended for these climbs. Detail can mean the difference between ending up at an impassible cliff or a steep, exceedingly dangerous patch of scree and a fantastic day. Before you head out, study the map and transfer routes to them with a waterproof pen, if needed. The National Geographic /Trails Illustrated maps have most of the routes described in this book, but not all. If you're using a GPS device or your smartphone, sites like 14ers.com and hikingproject.com have GPX files of the routes that you can load on your devices.

Travel Information

If you're hiking Colorado's fourteeners, you're going to have to get there. If you're taking a tour or getting a guided hike or climb, your transportation needs will likely be limited to getting to a parking lot. If you're going out on your own, you'll need reliable transportation. It's really hard to hail a taxi 20 miles from nowhere with no cell reception. The majority of fourteeners can be accessed with a car. But a passenger vehicle like a car cannot make it to most of the four-wheel-drive (4WD) trailheads listed in this book. It's a matter of clearance; even the almighty Subaru will scrape its belly on these rocky roads. Hence two-wheel-drive (2WD) trailheads and distances are explained for many of these hikes. Many of these mountain roads can be traveled in a two-wheel-drive truck in dry conditions. In wet conditions, a Jeep or SUV is a better choice.

Roads

Many Colorado backcountry roads are closed in winter. Respect these closures. Getting stuck on a high alpine road in temperatures below freezing is not fun, and whoever comes to get you out will not be happy about it. Some of Colorado's paved roads also are closed in winter. To learn more about what roads are closed, check the Colorado Department of Transportation (CDOT) website at cotrip.org. Or call them at (877) 315-7623 or 511 on your cell phone (Colorado only).

General Information

For general information on Colorado, visit the official website of Colorado travel: colorado.com. The site contains a wealth of vacation information.

Visitors to the state can find vacation information, free state maps and brochures, and clean restrooms at Colorado's welcome centers, which are located near most of the major highways as they enter the state. For more information visit colorado.com/ WelcomeCenters.aspx.

Area Codes

Colorado has four area codes: The Denver/Boulder metro area (extending out to Longmont, Idaho Springs, and Castle Rock) uses 303 and 720. The 719 area code serves the greater south-central and southeastern part of the state, including Colorado Springs, Pueblo, Buena Vista, Leadville, Alamosa, and Del Norte. The 970 area code covers the northern Front Range, Eastern Plains, and West Slope, extending east from Craig to Sterling and south from Craig to Durango and Cortez.

Wildland and Park Contact Information

The majority of Colorado's fourteeners are on public lands. You can learn more about these spaces at the following sites:

USDA Forest Service: fs.usda.gov/r2/
Bureau of Land Management: blm.gov/co/st/en.html
Colorado Parks & Wildlife: parks.state.co.us
National Park Service: nps.gov
US Fish & Wildlife Service, Mountain-Prairie Region: fws.gov/mountain-prairie/ co.html

Map Legend

══70══	Interstate Highway	✕	Airport
══24══	US Highway	≍	Bridge
══145══	State Highway	■	Building / Point of Interest
══850══	County Road	⛰	Campground
═══	Local Road	▲	Campsite
══════	Unpaved Road	○	City / Town
├─┼─┼─┤	Railroad	⚒	Mine
▬▬▬▬▬	Featured Trail	▲	Mountain / Peak
▬ ▬ ▬ ▬	Trail	**P**	Parking
▬ ∙ ▬ ∙ ▬	State Line	🚻	Restrooms
∼∼∼	Small River / Creek	📷	Scenic View / Viewpoint
∼ ∼	Intermittent Stream	⑩	Trailhead
⬭	Body of Water	≋	Waterfall
Marsh / Swamp	Marsh / Swamp		
National / State Forest	National / State Forest		
National Wilderness Area	National Wilderness Area		

Easy Fourteeners

These are the easiest fourteeners to hike and climb in Colorado. The trails are usually Class 1 hikes—essentially they're walks up a hill, a really big hill; occasionally they have some Class 2 hiking. The routes are among the shortest. These peaks are all great options for your first few fourteeners and are great if you're going on an outing as a family and hiking with kids or older adults.

Handies Peak's northeast face looms over wildflowers and a small stream in Grizzly Gulch (hike 2).

1 Mount Bross

14,172' (NGVD29), 14,177' (NAVD88), 22nd highest

Mount Bross is one of the three true fourteeners in the Democrat Group, along with Mounts Democrat and Lincoln. Mount Cameron also is in the group, but it's not considered a true fourteener because the saddle between it and Mount Lincoln does not descend the required 300 feet—even though it's taller than Bross. Each of the mountains in this tightly packed group has a distinct personality and geology. Stubby and mine-pocked Mount Bross, set to the east across an easy saddle, definitely does.

Start: Kite Lake Trailhead
Distance: 3.25 miles
Hiking time: About 2 hours
Elevation gain: 2,250 feet
Difficulty: Class 2
Trail surface: Mostly talus
Trailhead elevation: 12,000 feet
Camping: Campsites available (fee)
Fees: Parking fee
Best seasons: Summer and fall (snowshoeing in winter)

Maps: USGS Alma, Climax; National Geographic Trails Illustrated #109: Breckenridge, Tennessee Pass
Nearest towns: Alma, Fairplay
Trail contacts: Pike National Forest, (719) 553-1400; USDA Forest Service South Park Ranger District, (719) 836-2031; Park County Sheriff's Office, (719) 836-2494
Trail tips: This is a well-used trail. It's best to hike early in the day and during the week, when there's less traffic.

Finding the trailhead: From CO 9 in Alma, go west on Kite Lake Road (CR 8), a poorly marked dirt road in the middle of Alma. It's by the Alma Fire House and Mining Museum, housed in an old log cabin. Follow the road for 6 miles along Buckskin Gulch to reach Kite Lake. The last mile is rougher, but most 2WD vehicles should be able to navigate the road in summer. The road closes at Paris Mill in winter, which is 3 miles from Kite Lake. There are two parking areas. The upper area has some campsites and requires users to pay a fee; the lower area doesn't. The well-marked trailhead is near restrooms, on the south side of Kite Lake. GPS: N39° 19.67'/W106° 07.76'

The Hike

Mount Bross was named for Illinois lieutenant governor William Bross (1865–1869), who owned mining property near Alma, the closest town. Bross ascended Mount Lincoln in 1868. It's rumored Bross so enjoyed the climb that he sang a doxology on the summit. Local miners started calling it Mount Bross, which remains today.

The history of this mountain is tied to mining. The first silver claim for the Dwight Mine was filed on the mountain in 1869 by Alma's Daniel Plummer and Joseph Myers. In 1871 they filed for Moose Mine, which became the most productive silver mine in Park County.

Mount Bross from Mount Lincoln

Bross is a controversial fourteener, since its peak was closed in 2005. The Colorado Fourteeners Initiative (CFI) is working to reopen a trail to the top of Mount Bross, but part of the summit is on private land or land with claims. As of 2015 the organization hasn't been able to secure access from all landowners to permit a climb to the mountain's actual summit.

"The true summit of Mount Bross remains closed at this time due to inability to get contact with all of the landowners (100 percent consensus is needed by all landowners in order to open access). Hikers can do the full loop (up Democrat, over Cameron, to Lincoln, then around the summit of Bross) but are not granted access to the Bross summit," the organization said regarding the closure.

The organization also warns that since the lands were mined extensively, hikers are at risk of having a mine collapse under their feet if they get off-trail—so stay on-trail.

An agreement Alma made to lease the peaks for a nominal fee has minimized the risk of lawsuit to area landholders. But because of these hazards, rare plants species, and the wariness of landowners to allow people to hike, CFI recommends that people stay on the sole established trail and skirt the summit of Mount Bross following the route described here, reaching more than 14,000 feet, but not technically summiting.

The route up Mount Bross is one of the shortest and easiest in Colorado—even though it requires some Class 2 hiking across talus and loose dirt. A round-trip up and down Mount Bross via Kite Lake is only 3.25 miles—it's almost like cheating!

Mount Bross

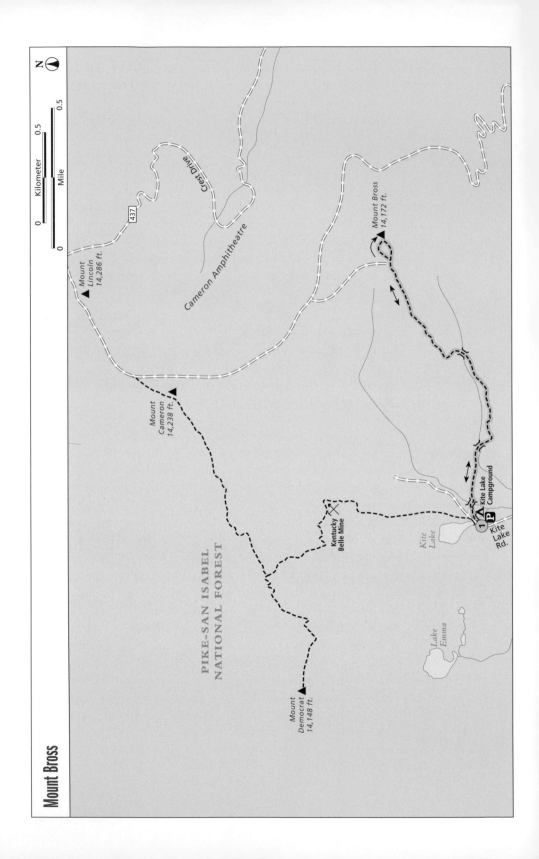

N

Kilometer
0   0.5

Mile
0   0.5

437

Crest Drive

Mount
Lincoln
14,286 ft.

Cameron Amphitheatre

Mount
Cameron
14,238 ft.

Mount Bross
14,172 ft.

PIKE–SAN ISABEL
NATIONAL FOREST

Kentucky
Belle Mine

Mount
Democrat
14,148 ft.

Kite Lake
Campground

Kite
Lake

1

Kite
Lake
Rd.

Lake
Emma

From Kite Lake Trailhead seek a trail to the right. Hike northeast then east over the basin, crossing two streambeds. Continue to a gully at 12,300 feet, crossing over another streambed, and begin the steeper ascent up the gully that separates Mount Bross from South Bross. At roughly 12,400 feet you'll encounter the last large patches of vegetation. At this point the trail veers to the left and gets steeper. At 1 mile, 13,080 feet, the trail crosses back over the gully to the left. Cross over the gully again and gain the ridgeline, ascending a little more than 200 feet in 0.1 mile.

The trail tracks to the left and then turns right at 13,300 feet, following the ridgeline. This might be a good time to take a break before ascending the ridgeline to the top of Mount Bross. At 13,600 feet the path becomes more worn and defined. At about 13,900 feet you'll begin crossing over the "S" gully. Follow the trail and all signs to reach the high point on the trail. Return the same way. Be careful on the way down. The rocks and dirt trail can be slippery, as so many people have traveled this trail.

Miles and Directions

0.0 Start at the Kite Lake Trailhead.

0.4 Cross a small streambed heading southeast and enter the gully between Bross and South Bross.

0.9 Turn left, crossing back over the streambed, and exit the gully heading north.

1.0 Turn right, ascending the northeast ridgeline toward the peak.

1.6 Reach the path below the peak. Return the way you came.

3.25 Arrive back at the trailhead.

Hiking Information

Closest Outfitters

High Alpine Sports, 525 Main St., Fairplay; (719) 836-0201; highalpinesports.com

Mountain Outfitters, 112 S Ridge St., Breckenridge; (970) 453-2201; mtnoutfitters.com

Great Pre- or Post-Mountain Spots

South Park Brewing, 297½ US 285, Fairplay; (719) 836-1932; southparkbrewingco.com

Mason's High Country BBQ, 450 US 285, Fairplay; (719) 836-3465; masonshighcountry bbq.com

Broken Compass Brewing, 68 Continental Ct., Breckenridge; (970) 368-2772; broken compassbrewing.com

Breckenridge Brewery & Pub, 600 S Main St., Breckenridge; (970) 453-1550; breck brew.com

Breckenridge Distillery, 1925 Airport Rd., Breckenridge; (970) 547-9759; breckenridge distillery.com

Downstairs at Eric's, 111 S Main St., Breckenridge; (970) 453-1401; downstairsaterics .com/new

2 Handies Peak

14,048' (NGVD29), 14,053' (NAVD88), 40th highest

Handies Peak is an enthralling peak any way you look at it. It's an easy, Class 1 hike, it's isolated, and it's spectacular. The broad, greenish-gray striation that marks its western face, as well as smaller, nearby peaks, is evidence of the volcanic activity that formed these mountain so many millennia ago and shows the process of activity that has made them the remote, monumental features they are today.

Start: American Basin 4WD trailhead; Grizzly Gulch Trailhead

Distance: American Basin 4WD trailhead: 5.2 miles; Grizzly Gulch Trailhead: 7.8 miles

Hiking time: From American Basin: about 4 hours; from Grizzly Gulch: about 6 hours

Elevation gain: American Basin: 2,430 feet; Grizzly Gulch: 3,640 feet

Difficulty: Class 1; some Class 2 near top

Trail surface: Mostly dirt trail; turns into good scree near peak, with little to no scrambling

Trailhead elevation: American Basin: 11,620 feet; Grizzly Gulch: 10,410 feet

Camping: Numerous campsites at trailhead

Fees: None

Best seasons: Year-round; access easier in late spring through fall

Maps: USGS Redcloud Peak, Handies Peak, Lake San Cristobal; National Geographic Trails Illustrated #141: Telluride, Silverton, Ouray, Lake City

Nearest town: Lake City

Trail contacts: Bureau of Land Management, Gunnison Field Office, (970) 642-4940; USDA Forest Service, Gunnison Ranger District, (970) 641-0471; Hinsdale County Sheriff's Office, (970) 944-2291

Trail tips: This is a good, stable trail with steady elevation gains.

Finding the trailhead: From the junction of 4th Street and Gunnison Avenue (CO 149) in Lake City, drive 2.5 miles on Gunnison Avenue. Turn right (south) onto Cinnamon Pass Road (CR 30) and drive 16.2 miles, following a ridgeline and eventually turning northwest and then north to the Silver Creek/Grizzly Gulch Trailheads. *Note:* After passing Lake San Cristobal, the road becomes a good dirt road that's passable by most passenger vehicles. However, the road is narrow in some places and dirt bikes, ATVs, and 4X4s may come whipping around blind corners, so drive carefully. GPS: American Basin: N37° 55.22'/W107° 30.99'; Grizzly Gulch: N37° 56.21'/W107° 27.67'

The Hike

From American Basin

The American Basin is a beautiful, verdant meadow. It's even more spectacular in late July and August, when the wildflowers are in full bloom. It's also the easiest and quickest way to climb this mountain. Sloan Lake—mere feet from the main trail—offers stunning views of American Mountain. It's home to the endangered Colorado cutthroat trout, which you can see in the shallows.

Handies Peak's southwest slope from Sloan Lake in American Basin

The American Basin Trail has two official starts, one for people with 4WD or vehicles they can get up some gnarly bits and another for those with 2WD vehicles. However, this road still requires some careful driving. Thankfully the 2WD parking starts at just a little over 0.5 mile from the 4WD trailhead on an easy-to-hike surface.

Starting from the main trailhead at 11,628 feet, the trail is only a 5.2-mile round-trip, making Handies one of the easiest and prettiest fourteeners to hike.

From the trailhead hike south on a solid Class 1 trail that's wide enough for two abreast. About 1,000 feet into the hike, there's a registry to the left.

At a little over 0.5 mile, cross the Lake Fork of the Gunnison River. To the left is a lovely waterfall. The trail continues to curl through the basin, gaining altitude relatively slowly and offering tremendous views of 13,720-foot American Peak ahead. Handies' eastern face begins to reveal itself to the left at around 12,500 feet.

At 1.2 miles the trail crosses back over the Lake Fork of the Gunnison River. After another 0.1 mile it turns right, toward Sloan Lake, which is marked with a large cairn at 1.4 miles. Sloan Lake is a great spot for a snack. The lake offers beautiful views of the peak and is home to the endangered Colorado cutthroat trout.

Handies Peak

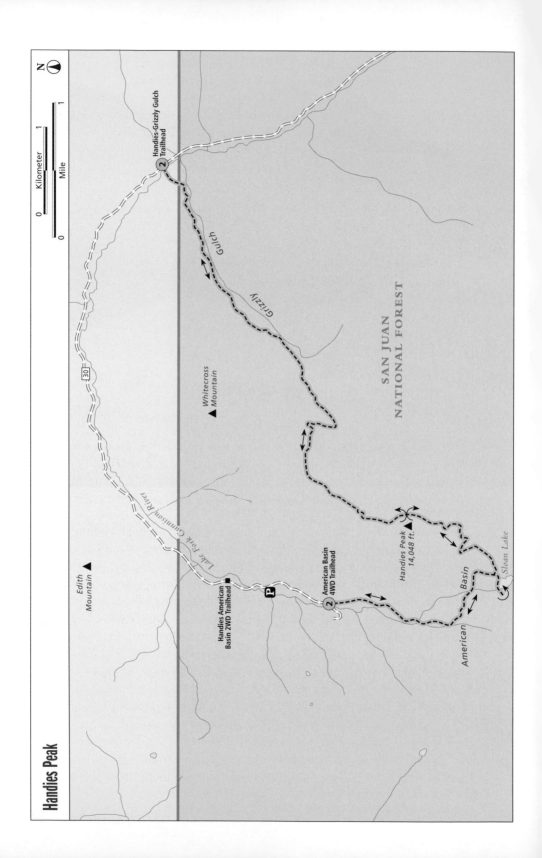

N

0   Kilometer   1

0   Mile   1

Edith
Mountain ▲

Lake Fork Gunnison River

30

Whitecross
Mountain ▲

Handies-Grizzly Gulch
Trailhead 2

Grizzly Gulch

SAN JUAN
NATIONAL FOREST

Handies American
Basin 2WD Trailhead ■

P

American Basin
4WD Trailhead 2

Handies Peak
14,048 ft. ▲

American Basin

Sloan Lake

Follow the trail to Handies to the left, about 1.5 miles into the hike, over a well-defined trail across pretty stable scree that lasts for about 0.25 mile.

Enter an alpine meadow at 1.7 miles that cuts across Handies' western face, heading north then switching back to the southwest. The trail continues to zigzag over lazy switchbacks until it reaches the saddle ridge up Handies' southwest slope at 13,490 feet. Follow the easy, well-marked trail another 0.3 mile to the peak.

Miles and Directions: American Basin 4WD

0.0 Start at the American Basin 4WD trailhead and hike south on solid trail.

0.2 Sign in at the trail registry.

0.7 Cross over the Lake Fork of the Gunnison River.

1.2 Cross over the Lake Fork of the Gunnison River again.

1.3 Follow the trail to the right toward Sloan Lake.

1.4 A large cairn marks the side trail to Sloan Lake.

1.5 Enter a large scree field with a good trail.

1.7 The scree field ends in an alpine meadow.

2.2 Gain the saddle to Handies' south ridge.

2.6 Reach Handies' summit. Return via the same route.

5.2 Arrive back at the American Basin 4WD trailhead.

From Grizzly Gulch

This stunning 7.8-mile round-trip offers awesome views of Handies' eastern face. The trail travels largely southwest before gaining Handies' northern ridge.

Cross the North Fork of the Gunnison River about 200 feet from the road. Shortly thereafter, in the middle of a meadow, find a sign-in box and register.

At 0.25 mile the trail becomes steeper and goes through some quick switchbacks to gain elevation as it comes closer to the creek and then veers away. Exit the woodland creature–filled forest at 0.5 mile and enter into another small meadow before reentering a stand of trees. Catch glimpses of cascading falls in the forest to the left.

At 0.75 mile the trail exits trees and enters meadows, offering stunning views of Handies ahead. The peak is in view for much of the hike from here. The trail continues along the western side of the gully. In another 0.75 mile the trail reenters a small stand of trees.

Cross a good stream at 2.0 miles and again at 2.4 miles. The good trail then turns to the right to begin ascending the ridge between Whitecross Mountain and the northern ridge of Handies.

The ascent mellows out until just under 3.0 miles. At this point the trail begins ascending over a short, steep rock moraine. After crossing the moraine the trail gradually arcs left toward the peak.

At 3.3 miles the trail becomes rockier as it gains the summit ridge between Whitecross and Handies. This is also the talus crux of this route. From here the trail is easily visible and ascends roughly 500 feet to a small, flat plateau. Walk south across the summit block to gain the summit, about 600 feet away.

Either retrace the same route back for a 7.8-mile trek or continue on through American Basin to make a more interesting, 6.75-mile to 11.3-mile loop out of it. With two vehicles, or a ride, you can effectively ferry your way back to the Silver Creek–Grizzly Gulch Trailhead from American Basin or catch a ride with a new hiking friend back to Grizzly Gulch.

Miles and Directions: Grizzly Gulch

0.0 Start on the Grizzly Gulch Trail at Shelf Road.

0.25 Enter into woods in a series of quick, short switchbacks.

0.5 Reach a small meadow with a creek to the left.

0.75 Come to another clearing after walking through a short forest and get your first glimpse of Handies.

1.5 Cross a small, seasonal streambed; reenter trees.

1.8 Exit the stand of trees, entering an alpine meadow.

2.0 Cross a stream and gain beautiful views of the mountain.

2.4 Cross over a small stream and follow the trail as it turns right (north).

2.6 The trail cuts back to the left as the ascent mellows.

2.9 The trail resumes a southwestern trajectory at about 12,800 feet as it crosses over a short, steep rock moraine.

3.2 Pass a decent cairn on the last flat spot before ascending to the peak.

3.3 Ascend a series of switchbacks to the summit ridge.

3.6 Reach 13,955 feet. The summit is a short jaunt and about 60 vertical feet up from here.

3.9 Reach 14,048 feet, the top of Handies. Return via the same route, or continue down to American Basin.

7.8 Arrive back at the trailhead.

Hiking Information

Closest Outfitters

The Sportsman Outdoors & Fly Shop, 238 S Gunnison Ave., Lake City; (970) 944-2526; lakecitysportsman.com

San Juan Sports, 102 S Main St., Creede; (719) 658-2359; sanjuansports.com

Great Pre- or Post-Mountain Spots

Packer Saloon & Cannibal Grill, 310 N Silver St., Lake City; (970) 944-4144

Lake City Cafe, 310 Gunnison Ave., Lake City; (970) 944-0301

San Juan Soda Company, 227 N Silver St., Lake City; (970) 944-0500; sanjuansoda company.com

3 Mount Democrat

14,148' (NGVD29), 14,152' (NAVD88), 28th highest

At 14,148 feet, Mount Democrat is the shortest mountain in the Democrat Group. It also provides a different experience than the other mountains do. It's usually the first mountain climbed when taking on the DeCaLiBron Loop—all three fourteeners and Mount Cameron in one day.

Start: Kite Lake Trailhead
Distance: 3.9 miles
Hiking time: 3 to 4 hours
Elevation gain: 2,156 feet
Difficulty: Class 2
Trail surface: Mostly talus
Trailhead elevation: 12,000 feet
Camping: Campsites available (fee)
Fees: Parking fee
Best seasons: Summer and fall (snowshoeing in winter)

Maps: USGS Alma, Climax; National Geographic Trails Illustrated #109: Breckenridge, Tennessee Pass
Nearest towns: Alma, Fairplay
Trail contacts: Pike National Forest, (719) 553-1400; USDA Forest Service South Park Ranger District, (719) 836-2031; Park County Sheriff's Office, (719) 836-2494
Trail tips: This is a well-used trail. It's best to hike early in the day and during the week, when there's less traffic.

Finding the trailhead: From Denver, take US 285 to Alma. Or, you can take CO 9 to Alma from I-70, a beautiful drive through Breckenridge and beyond. From the south, take US 24 north to Fairplay and then continue north on CO 9.

From CO 9 in Alma, go West on Kite Lake Road (CR 8), a poorly marked dirt road in the middle of Alma. It's by the Alma Fire House and Mining Museum, housed in an old log cabin. Follow the road for 6 miles along Buckskin Gulch to reach Kite Lake. The last mile is rougher, but most 2WD vehicles should be able to navigate the road in summer. The road closes at Paris Mill in winter, which is 3 miles from Kite Lake. There are two parking areas. The upper area has some campsites and requires users to pay a fee; the lower area doesn't. The well-marked trailhead is near restrooms on the south side of Kite Lake. GPS: N39° 19.67'/W106° 07.76'

The Hike

Mount Democrat was originally called Buckskin Peak, after the nearby Buckskin Joe mining camp. It got an impromptu renaming by miners from the South. They started calling it Mount Democrat when its sister peak was named for then President Abraham Lincoln. By 1883 the peak was labeled Mount Democrat on the Land Office Survey official maps.

Mount Democrat is much more of a granite peak than the others in the vicinity—a grayer, rockier mountain. It requires Class 2 hiking over some loose talus, but

Mount Democrat from slopes of Mount Bross

nothing that should require ascending on hands and feet. Descending can be a little slippery at some points where the trail is worn, but the exposure is limited.

Mount Democrat shares a saddle with Mount Cameron and Mount Lincoln. This provides the easiest and most traditional route up the mountain. However, this is a well-traveled mountain, with a series of trails etched into its eastern face.

To help minimize damage and erosion caused by the tens of thousands of feet that travel this mountain every year, stay on-trail. It's safer and easier, particularly because Mount Democrat, like other mountains in the group, is riddled with old mines. This becomes clear as you pass the remnants of the Kentucky Belle Mine, a former gold and silver mine, established in 1900.

Start climbing Mount Democrat at the Kite Lake Trailhead. The trail starts out on a closed dirt road that gradually ascends from Kite Lake until you reach the remnants of the Kentucky Belle Mine at 12,400 feet. At a little over 0.5 mile, the trail makes a sharp, short dogleg to the right (west) before resuming its northward progress to the ridge. At 0.75 mile and about 12,720 feet, the trail takes a sharp left (east) toward Mount Democrat, followed by a series of switchbacks. At about 1.0 mile, roughly 12,975 feet, the trail stops switchbacking and ascends to the saddle between the mountains. Gain the ridge at 1.3 miles and 13,415 feet, and take the trail to the left for Mount Democrat. The 14,148-foot mountain is just about 0.5 mile away. You

Mount Democrat

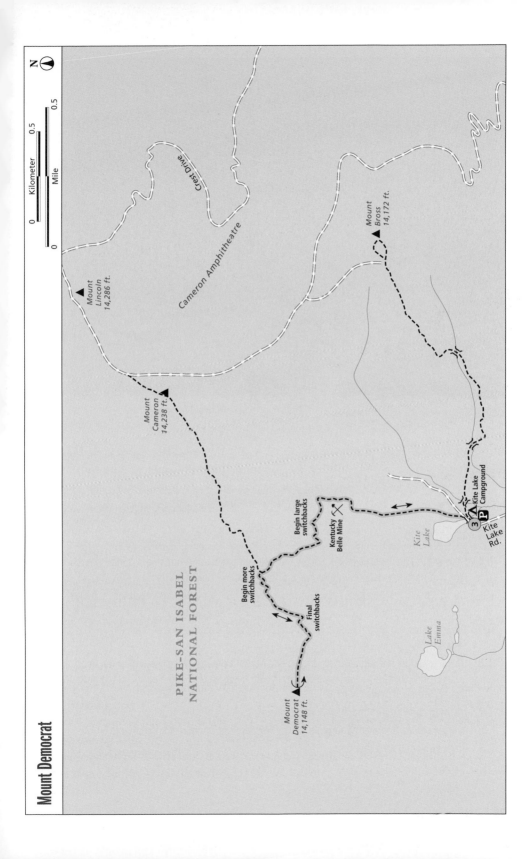

N

| 0 | 0.5 | Kilometer |
| 0 | 0.5 | Mile |

Mount
Lincoln
14,286 ft.

Crest Drive

Cameron Amphitheatre

Mount
Cameron
14,238 ft.

PIKE-SAN ISABEL
NATIONAL FOREST

Begin more
switchbacks

Begin large
switchbacks

Kentucky
Belle Mine

Final
switchbacks

Mount
Democrat
14,148 ft.

Mount
Bross
14,172 ft.

Kite Lake
Campground

Kite
Lake

Kite
Lake Rd.

Lake Emma

3

Climbing scree on Mount Democrat

won't see the true peak of Mount Democrat until you pass a false summit at 14,000 feet, about 1.7 miles into the hike. At this point the trail turns right, passing some old, flattened buildings, and you reach the true peak at 1.9 miles. Either retrace your steps to the trailhead or go back to the ridge and take on other mountains in the group.

Miles and Directions

0.0 Start at the Kite Lake Trailhead. Follow the well-established but blocked dirt road past the lake in a northerly direction to the ruins of the Kentucky Belle Mine.

0.5 The trail takes a sharp right turn for a short dogleg then turns left and resumes its trajectory up the mountain.

0.75 The trail goes left toward Mount Democrat and begins a relatively gentle accent with switchbacks.

1.3 Gain the saddle between Mount Lincoln and Mount Cameron. Take the trail to the left, following the sign to Mount Democrat and begin hiking across some small switchbacks to Mount Democrat's false summit.

1.7 The path curls around the false summit, revealing Mount Democrat's true summit.

1.9 Achieve Mount Democrat's summit at 18,148 feet. Return down the same path.

3.9 Arrive back at the trailhead.

MINERS AND PROSPECTORS

The history of Colorado's fourteeners is intimately tied to mining and prospecting. Even before the Wheeler and Hayden surveys made their way through Colorado, miners and prospectors were climbing these majestic peaks. They are responsible for many of the trails that lead to fourteeners today.

In fact, Denver started out as a mining camp. Countless towns and cities throughout Colorado, from Gypsum to Telluride to Leadville, are named for their mineral riches. Ever since then, Colorado's vast mineral resources have played a major role in the state's economy. They've also been part of some of the state's greatest environmental disasters, such as the Gold King Mine blowout in 2015.

Even today, Colorado's fourteeners have active claims. Anyone who has seen the Weather Channel's Prospector series has seen prospectors looking for their riches on the slopes of Mount Antero and other parts of Colorado's wild spaces. Love them or hate them, mines are here to stay.

Hiking Information

Closest Outfitters

High Alpine Sports, 525 Main St., Fairplay; (719) 836-0201; highalpinesports.com

Mountain Outfitters; 112 S Ridge St., Breckenridge; (970) 453-2201; mtnoutfitters
.com

Great Pre- or Post-Mountain Spots

South Park Brewing, 297½ US 285, Fairplay; (719) 836-1932; southparkbrewing
co.com

Mason's High Country BBQ, 450 US 285, Fairplay; (719) 836-3465; masonshigh
countrybbq.com

Broken Compass Brewing, 68 Continental Ct., Breckenridge; (970) 368-2772; broken
compassbrewing.com

Breckenridge Brewery & Pub, 600 S Main St., Breckenridge; (970) 453-1550; breck
brew.com

Breckenridge Distillery, 1925 Airport Rd., Breckenridge; (970) 547-9759; brecken
ridgedistillery.com

Downstairs at Eric's, 111 S Main St., Breckenridge; (970) 453-1401; downstairsaterics
.com/new

4 Mount Sherman

14,036' (NGVD29), 14,040' (NAVD88), 45th highest

Mount Sherman is among the shortest, easiest fourteeners in Colorado. It's a nearly 5-mile hike on Class 1 and Class 2 scree, all of it above tree line and on mining land. Sherman is a scarred mountain with plenty of old mine remains and roads, the latter helping make it an easy mountain to climb. The main difficulties in gaining the summit are making sure you stay on the right road and hiking the short Class 2 summit ridge. Given its ease and closeness to civilization, this is a good fourteener to start with. The mining remains should prove interesting for young minds. Children will also be interested to hear that a plane once landed on top of the mountain.

Start: Fourmile Creek Trailhead
Distance: 4.6 miles
Hiking time: About 2 hours
Elevation gain: 1,906 feet
Difficulty: Class 1, Class 2
Trail surface: Dirt, scree
Trailhead elevation: 12,070 feet
Camping: None
Fees: None

Best seasons: Year-round; road not plowed to trailhead in winter
Maps: USGS Mount Sherman, Fairplay West; National Geographic Trails Illustrated #110: Leadville, Fairplay
Nearest towns: Fairplay, Leadville
Trail contacts: San Isabel National Forest, South Park Ranger District, (719) 836-2031; Park County Sheriff's Office, (719) 836-2494

Finding the trailhead: From the intersection of US 285 and Main Street in Fairplay, drive 1.3 miles south on US 285. Turn right onto CR 18 (4 Mile Creek Road) and drive for 12.2 miles or until you need to park your vehicle. Reach the 4WD trailhead at a total of 13.4 miles. GPS: N39° 12.43'/W106° 09.94'

The Hike

At 14,036 feet Mount Sherman is far from the tallest peak in Colorado. The mountain has a long history of mining, as anyone can see from the remains of mines and buildings that cover the peak. The mountain was named in honor of William Tecumseh Sherman, a Union general in the Civil War.

Miners were likely the first Europeans to summit Sherman, in the mid- to late 1800s. The biggest mine, the Sherman Mine, is a silver–lead–zinc deposit on the western side, in the upper Iowa Gulch. The mine was launched in 1968 and ran on and off until 1982. During its active time, it produced more than 10 million ounces of silver.

The mountain also has a unique claim to fame. In January 1967 a charter plane landed on the summit during a violent storm. Jimmy Williamson safely landed the Cessna 310 on the mountain, and rescue crews were able to evacuate the pilot and

Mount Sherman in the background, just right of center

crew 20 hours after landing. It's the first and only time that has happened on a Colorado fourteener.

If you have a 2WD vehicle with low clearance or if parking near the trailhead is full, you may have to park lower and hike up. The 4WD trailhead is at 12,065 feet, and the trail follows the good dirt road. Pass the dilapidated Dauntless Mine at 12,330 feet and 0.3 mile, and continue on the main road. At 12,530 feet and 0.5 mile, take a right at the junction to stay on the main road. Follow the main road as it switches back at just under 1.0 mile and 12,800 feet. At the next turn, heading north, pass more mining remains close to the road.

The road curls back around to head south until it reaches a road spur at 12,940 feet and 1.2 miles. Take the first right at the spur, heading west up a scree slope that crosses over old roads. At 1.4 miles and 13,080 feet, the trail horseshoes back, heading north toward Sherman's ridge. From here on out it's a decent 900-foot ascent in just under a mile to gain the peak. Stay just left of the ridge as you head northeast toward the top, gaining the peak at 2.3 miles. Return via the same route.

Mount Sherman

0   Kilometer   0.3

0   Mile   0.3

N

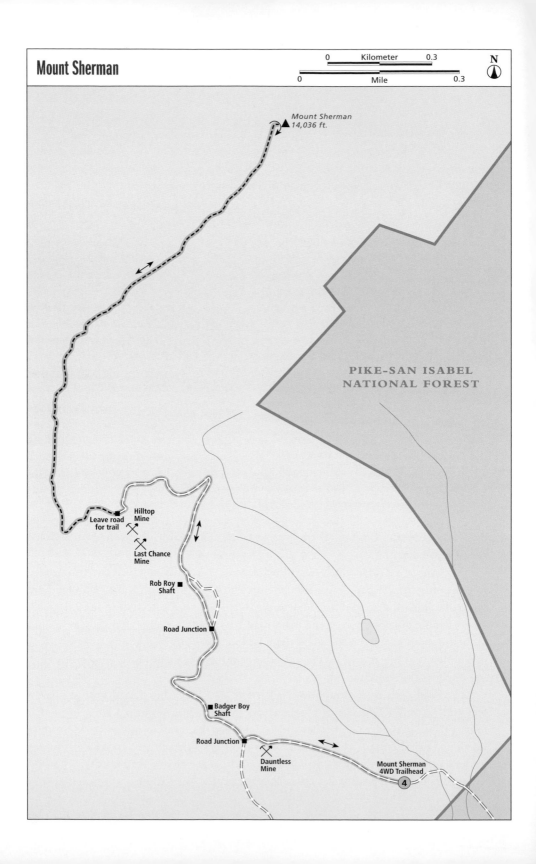

Mount Sherman
14,036 ft.

PIKE-SAN ISABEL
NATIONAL FOREST

Hilltop
Mine

Leave road
for trail

Last Chance
Mine

Rob Roy
Shaft

Road Junction

Badger Boy
Shaft

Road Junction

Dauntless
Mine

Mount Sherman
4WD Trailhead

4

Miles and Directions

0.0 Start at the trailhead gate and head up the dirt road.

0.3 Pass the Dauntless Mine remains.

0.5 Turn right at a junction and stay on the main road.

0.8 The road heads right (north).

1.0 The road switches back to the left then meanders.

1.2 At a road junction take hard right and start hiking up a scree slope.

1.3 The trail does a 180, from heading south to north, and then heads toward the ridge.

1.5 Gain the ridge and hike the remaining 0.8 mile to the peak.

2.3 Gain the peak. Return via the same path.

4.6 Arrive back at the trailhead.

Hiking Information

Closest Outfitters

Melanzana, 716 Harrison Ave., Leadville; (719) 486-3245; melanzana.com

Check out this company. They make outdoor clothes in Leadville and can do some customizations on-site.

Leadville Outdoors, 225 Harrison Ave., Leadville; (719) 486-7392; leadvilleoutdoors .com

Great Pre- or Post-Mountain Spots

As of 2015, two breweries are under construction in Leadville, Two Mile Brewing and Periodic Brewing. The town had a distillery, but it was closed as of this writing—emblematic of this boom-and-bust town.

Silver Dollar Saloon, 315 Harrison Ave., Leadville; (719) 486-9914; silverdollarsaloon .com. An authentic saloon, established in 1879!

Golden Burro Cafe & Lounge, 710 Harrison Ave., Leadville; (719) 486-1239; golden burro.com

Tennessee Pass Cafe, 222 Harrison Ave., Leadville; (719) 486-8101

5 Grays Peak

14,270' (NGVD29), 14,279' (NAVD88), 9th highest

Grays Peak and its sister, Torreys Peak, are among the closest and easiest fourteeners to Denver. Both relatively easy climbs, they're extensively hiked. Grays Peak is the highest point along the Continental Divide in North America. While there are higher peaks in Colorado, they aren't on the divide itself. Charles Parry ascended the mountains in 1861 and named them for Asa Gray and John Torrey, botanists who published *Flora of North America* in 1838. Gray and his wife climbed his peak in July 1872. Native Americans called the peaks the Ant Hills; miners called them the Twin Peaks.

Start: Grays Peak Trailhead (also called Stevens Gulch Trailhead)
Distance: 8.0 miles
Hiking time: 6 to 8 hours
Elevation gain: 3,000 feet
Difficulty: Class 1
Trail surface: Dirt trail leading to talus
Trailhead elevation: 11,270 feet
Camping: Some campsites near the parking area
Fees: None

Best seasons: Summer and fall
Maps: USGS: Grays Peak, Loveland Pass, Montezuma; National Geographic Trails Illustrated #104: Idaho Springs, Georgetown, Loveland Pass
Nearest town: Georgetown
Trail contacts: Arapaho National Forest, (970) 295-6600; USDA Forest Service, Clear Creek District, (303) 567-3000; Clear Creek County Sheriff's Office, (303) 679-2376

Finding the trailhead: Take the Bakerville exit (exit 221) off I-70. Cross to the south-facing side of the interstate to find a sign for Grays Peak. This is FR 189, a rough road best suited for 4WD and high-clearance vehicles. (***Note:*** This is also the winter trailhead, as the road is closed in winter.) In summer follow this road for 1 mile until you reach a junction. At the junction go left toward Stevens Gulch; continue for another 2 miles to reach the trailhead. There are restrooms near the parking area. GPS: N39° 39.65' / W105° 47.08'

The Hike

Grays Peak is the highest point in Clear Creek and Summit Counties (the counties are divided by the Continental Divide). The mountain is the highest point along Colorado's Front Range and the highest peak visible from the Great Plains, but it's still only the ninth-tallest fourteener in Colorado.

Grays' apex offers a spectacular view. Looking east from the peak, you can see the Rockies slough off to lower, greener mountains and even as far as the Great Plains. On a clear day you might see Pikes Peak (14,110 feet) to the south. Closer by you'll see the San Luis Valley, with the highest concentration of fourteeners. To the northeast

Grays Peak from Stevens Gulch

climbers will see first Torreys (14,267 feet) then Longs Peak (14,255 feet) and Rocky Mountain National Park.

A road for horses and pack trains was built for miners and visitors over one hundred years ago. Because of this the peak has a long history of climbers and is an easy trail to hike.

While it's an easy trail, ranked as a Class 1 climb, the lower parts of the trail face north. Depending on the weather, these sections can be covered with snow into early July.

From the parking lot, cross the pedestrian bridge and follow the trail (also part of the Continental Divide Trail). Encounter the first easy switchbacks at about 11,700 feet along the eastern side of Kelso Mountain (13,164 feet) at about 0.75 mile into the hike. At 11,870 feet the trail climbs southwest, along the east ridge of Kelso. At about 1.75 miles and 12,100 feet, a trail branches off to the left. Stay to the right and enter a small basin, heading in a westerly direction. The trail turns south and at about 2.75 miles, 12,700 feet, begins a slightly more strenuous ascent. Come to a junction at about 13,240 feet—a little over 3.0 miles; stay to the left. (The right takes you to Torreys Peak.) At 13,440 feet the trail begins switchbacking and you pass a small rock pinnacle called The Rascal. Just east of that is Lost Rat Couloir. Looking north, you can see the remainder of the trail switchbacking up the northeastern face of Grays Peak. Gain the peak and then return on the same path or head northeast to take on Torreys.

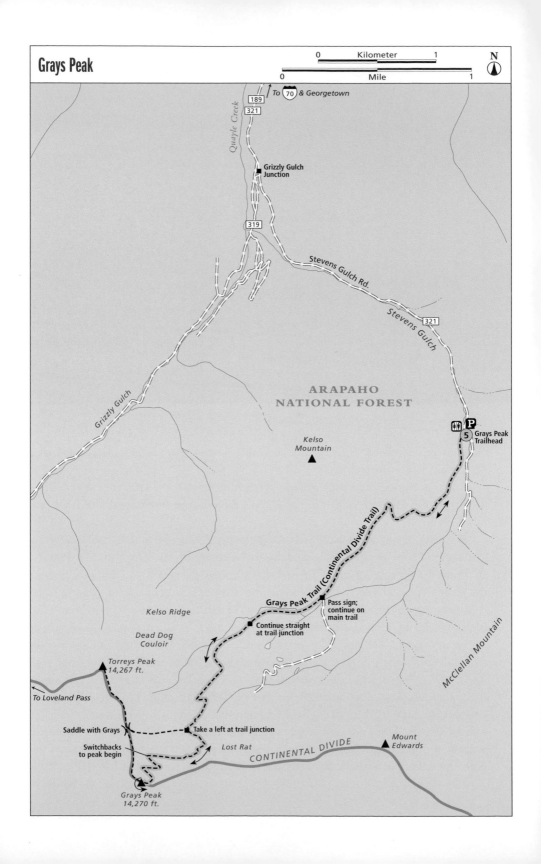

Grays Peak

0   Kilometer   1

0   Mile   1

N

To 70 & Georgetown

189
321

Quayle Creek

Grizzly Gulch Junction

319

Stevens Gulch Rd.

Stevens Gulch

321

Grizzly Gulch

ARAPAHO NATIONAL FOREST

Kelso Mountain ▲

P
5
Grays Peak Trailhead

Grays Peak Trail (Continental Divide Trail)

Pass sign; continue on main trail

Kelso Ridge

Grays Peak Trail (Continental Divide Trail)

Continue straight at trail junction

Dead Dog Couloir

McClellan Mountain

Torreys Peak 14,267 ft. ▲

To Loveland Pass

Saddle with Grays

Take a left at trail junction

Switchbacks to peak begin

Lost Rat

CONTINENTAL DIVIDE

Mount Edwards ▲

Grays Peak 14,270 ft. ▲

Looking across at Torreys Peak from Grays

Miles and Directions

0.0 Start at the parking lot and cross a wide footbridge to the Grays Peak Trail (FT 54, a National Recreation Trail).

1.5 Reach an information sign. Continue on the well-defined trail.

3.4 At about 13,200 feet take trail to the left toward Grays Peak.

4.0 Gain the summit. Return down same path. (***Option:*** Descend roughly 600 feet north to hike toward Torreys Peak.)

8.0 Arrive back at the parking lot.

Hiking Information

Closest Outfitters

Clear Creek Outdoors, 1524 Miner St., Idaho Springs; (303) 567-1500; clearcreek outdoors.com

Great Pre- or Post-Mountain Spots

Tommyknocker Brewery & Pub, 1401 Miner St., Idaho Springs; (303) 567-4419; tommy knocker.com

Dillon Dam Brewery, 100 Little Dam St., Dillon; (970) 262-7777; dambrewery.com

Pug Ryan's, 104 Village Place, Dillon; (970) 468-2145; pugryans.com

The Alpine Restaurant and Bar, 1106 Rose St., Georgetown; (303) 569-0200; alpine restaurantgeorgetown.com

6 Quandary Peak

14,265' (NGVD29), 14,270' (NAVD88), 13th highest

Quandary Peak is among the easiest of Colorado's fourteeners, partly because of its proximity to Breckenridge and Denver. The highest and most singular mountain in the Tenmile-Mosquito Range, its easy access makes it a popular mountain year-round. In winter skiers, mountaineers, snowboarders, and snowshoers take various approaches to this peak. Hikers take to its slopes in spring and summer. The standard route on Quandary (featured here) is a 3.1-mile (one-way), Class 1 hike with a 3,300-foot incline up its east slopes.

Start: Quandary Trailhead
Distance: 6.2 miles
Hiking time: 5 to 6 hours
Elevation gain: 3,345 feet
Difficulty: Class 1
Trail surface: Dirt, scree
Trailhead elevation: 10,920 feet
Camping: Backcountry camping
Fees: None

Best seasons: Year-round (winter snow sports)
Maps: USGS Breckenridge, Copper Mountain; National Geographic Trails Illustrated #109: Breckenridge, Tennessee Pass
Nearest town: Breckenridge
Trail contacts: White River National Forest, Dillon Ranger District, (970) 468-5400; Summit County Sheriff's Office, (970) 453-2232

Finding the trailhead: From the junction of CO 9 and CR 850, just 8 miles south of Breckenridge, turn west onto CR 850. Go 0.1 mile and turn right onto CR 851 (McCullough Gulch Road). Continue to 0.25 mile to a dirt lot on the side of the road with good trail and information signage. Park here. If there's no parking available, drive a little farther ahead to an overflow parking lot or return to CR 850 to find more overflow parking near CO 9. Do not park along the road; nearby residents have complained about people parking in front of their homes. GPS: N39° 23.1' / W106° 03.71'

The Hike

Quandary Peak is in an interesting position. Located in the White River National Forest, it's the only fourteener in the Tenmile-Mosquito Range that's north and west of the Continental Divide. The fourteeners in the Democrat Group, in the same mountain range, are directly south of Quandary yet on the both the south and east side of the Continental Divide because it takes an interesting jag through this part of Colorado. This peak is the largest in the range and offers some technical routes, but the standard route from the Quandary Trailhead is a long but easy trail to this spectacular, rocky peak.

The mountain itself has had many names, including Ute Peak, McCullough's Peak, and Hoosier Peak. You might think that confusion was the origin of the ultimately

The lesser hiked west ridge of Quandary Peak

agreed-upon name—Quandary—but actually the name came about because miners in the region couldn't decide on what a mined mineral from the mountain was. Hence it became Quandary Peak. Since miners frequented this area, there's no record of an official first ascent.

The main challenges of this Class 1 trail are length and elevation gain. It's popular with people new to climbing fourteeners and also pretty crowded, especially on weekends. It's best to climb this mountain during the week, particularly in summer. Along with people, climbers are likely to share the trail with mountain goats. Moose and elk are often found in the valleys below.

The trailhead is in the dirt parking lot. The trail begins just northeast of the parking lot across CR 851 and immediately enters forest. Follow the well-worn dirt trail as it winds through the forest, heading northwest as it gains altitude. Follow signs to stay on the trail—old mining roads cross the trail here. Look for a boulder at a little over 0.1 mile and 11,050 feet; stay to its right side. Continue hiking through the coniferous forest. It thins at a little bit over 0.5 mile and 11,340 feet.

Climbers enjoy a snack atop Quandary Peak

At just over 1.1 miles and 11,700 feet, the trail exits the forest, allowing views of the trail as it courses up the southern side of the peak; the peak itself looms ahead. At about 1.4 miles and 11,990 feet, the trail becomes talus and continues upward on the south-facing side of Quandary's east slope, passing through a short section of smaller brush and trees. The trail comes closer to the ridgeline at 1.7 miles (12,470 feet). Cairns can guide climbers back to the trail to minimize damage in the summer. At 1.9 miles (12,807 feet) the trail gains the ridge of Quandary.

The trail continues up the ridge as it narrows at 13,100 feet and 2.25 miles. From here climbers can see the remainder of the trek.

After a brief respite the trail resumes its upwards climb at 2.4 miles and 13,180 feet. This is a good place to stop for a break before the final summit push or to allow people to pass on the way down.

At 2.75 miles the trail starts snaking across the ridge, making it a little easier to climb and reducing the impact of human-caused erosion. Please stay on the trail! Continue hiking to gain the summit ridge, and peak out at 14,265 feet and 3.1 miles. The path becomes rockier toward the top but still only requires Class 1 hiking.

From the peak of Quandary, hikers get great views of many mountains. The most visible are the closest—the Democrat group, directly south. Large and lumpy Bross (14,172 feet) is on the left side of the range. Mount Lincoln's peak (14,286 feet) rises like an anthill to Bross's right. That's followed by Cameron (14,238 feet). Between

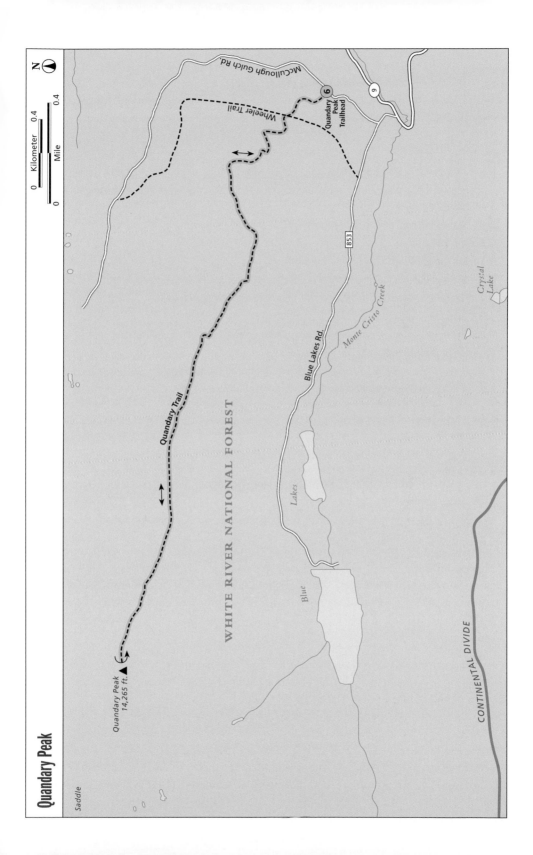

Quandary Peak

Saddle

Quandary Peak ▲
14,265 ft.

Quandary Trail

WHITE RIVER NATIONAL FOREST

Blue

Lakes

Crystal
Lake

Blue Lakes Rd.

Monte Cristo Creek

853

CONTINENTAL DIVIDE

Wheeler Trail

McCullough Gulch Rd.

6

Quandary
Peak
Trailhead

9

N

0   Kilometer   0.4

0   Mile   0.4

Cameron and Democrat (14,148 feet), Mount Sherman (14,036 feet), Mount Harvard (14,420 feet), and Mount Oxford (14,153 feet) are often visible in the distance. Mount of the Holy Cross (14,005 feet) is almost directly west. To the northeast Torreys Peak (14,267 feet) and Grays Peak (14,270 feet) nestle next to each other.

Miles and Directions

0.0 Start at the trailhead in the parking lot. Follow the dirt road, heading northeast to a well-marked trail just across the street. The trail snakes through the forest, largely heading west toward the peak.

0.1 Stay to the right around a large boulder.

0.5 The forest thins.

1.1 Exit the forest.

1.4 The trail becomes talus and stays under the ridgeline on the slope's south face.

1.7 The trail comes closer to the ridgeline. Look for cairns to stay on-trail.

1.9 Gain the ridge.

2.25 The ridge narrows as drop-offs steepen. Shortly thereafter, reach a relatively flat spot.

2.4 Resume steeper climbing.

3.1 Reach the summit at 14,265 feet. Rejoice! Return via the same path.

6.2 Arrive back at the trailhead.

Hiking Information

Closest Outfitters

Clear Creek Outdoors, 1524 Miner St., Idaho Springs; (303) 567-1500; clearcreek outdoors.com

Great Pre- or Post-Mountain Spots

Tommyknocker Brewery & Pub, 1401 Miner St., Idaho Springs; (303) 567-4419; tommy knocker.com

Dillon Dam Brewery, 100 Little Dam St., Dillon; (970) 262-7777; dambrewery.com

Pug Ryan's, 104 Village Place, Dillon; (970) 468-2145; pugryans.com

The Alpine Restaurant and Bar, 1106 Rose St., Georgetown; (303) 569-0200; alpine restaurantgeorgetown.com

7 Mount Bierstadt

14,060' (NGVD29), 14,065' (NAVD88), 38th highest

Bierstadt is one of the most popular fourteeners. It's close to Denver and easy to access on a paved road. Most of the hike is on a good Class 1 trail, with some Class 2 scrambling near the top. The Colorado Fourteeners Initiative finished improvements to the trail in 2002. Thanks to the improvements, there's now a boardwalk through a previously frustrating section of willows near its base. Between that and the improved road, this mountain is now packed in summer.

Start: West slope from Guanella Pass Trailhead
Distance: 7.1 miles
Hiking time: About 6 hours
Elevation gain: 2,850 feet
Difficulty: Class 1, some Class 2
Trail surface: Dirt, scree
Trailhead elevation: 11,210 feet
Camping: Camping spots along Guanella Pass
Fees: None
Best seasons: Mid-May to October; also a popular winter fourteener
Maps: USGS Mount Evans; National Geographic Trails Illustrated #104: Idaho Springs, Georgetown, Loveland Pass

Nearest towns: Georgetown, Idaho Springs
Trail contacts: Arapaho National Forest, (970) 295-6600; USDA Forest Service, Clear Creek Ranger Station, (303) 567-3000
Trail tips: This is an easy fourteener compared to more-technical mountains, and it's close to Denver. For a more rewarding summertime experience, and the likelihood of seeing more wildlife and fewer people, hike this trail during the week or early in the season. It's also great for training hikes in winter.

Finding the trailhead: From I-70 take exit 228 to Georgetown. From US 6 and Argentine Street, head south on Argentine for 0.6 mile. Turn left onto 6th Street and right in 2 blocks onto Rose Street. Head south on Rose Street for 4 blocks and then turn right onto 2nd Street. At 1 mile the road becomes Guanella Pass Road. Follow this for 10 miles to reach the pass at 11 miles. The trailhead is on the left in a paved parking lot. An overfill parking lot is on the right. GPS: N39° 35.79'/W105° 42.62'

The Hike

Mount Bierstadt is easy to get to, and it's a relatively easy hike. That makes it one of the most-climbed fourteeners in the state—year-round. During the summer months it's popular with novice peak baggers; in winter it's popular with those who want to complete winter ascents and those who want to practice mountaineering skills.

The mountain was named for landscape painter Albert Bierstadt, who, along with William Byers, may have made one of the first ascents of the mountain in the 1860s.

Facing east, clouds reflect the sunset on Bierstadt in winter

His famous 12 x 7-foot landscape painting *Storm in the Mountains* was based on sketches he made in the region. Bierstadt originally named Mount Evans "Mount Rosa" in honor of both Monte Rosa in Switzerland and his future wife, Rosalie Ludlow. Denver high school botany teacher Ellsworth Bethel was the first to suggest the name Mount Bierstadt.

The most popular route up Mount Bierstadt is the West Slope Route, which is accessed via Guanella Pass Road. The paved road is open most of the year, but when snow builds up in winter, it is plowed (as of 2015) only to the Silver Dollar Lake parking lot, about 1.5 miles from the Guanella Pass parking areas.

The biggest obstacle to climbing up the West Slope route was an area known as The Willows, essentially a quagmire of willows and wetland that left no hiker's boots, pants, or legs dry and without marks from whipping willow branches. Thankfully the Colorado Fourteeners Initiative and its army of volunteers completed a boardwalk across the marshy land in 2002, making it easier for hikers to make it through and offering the willows protection from hikers as well. However, since the land is in the Mount Evans Wilderness Area, there is some concern that the boardwalk is against regulations.

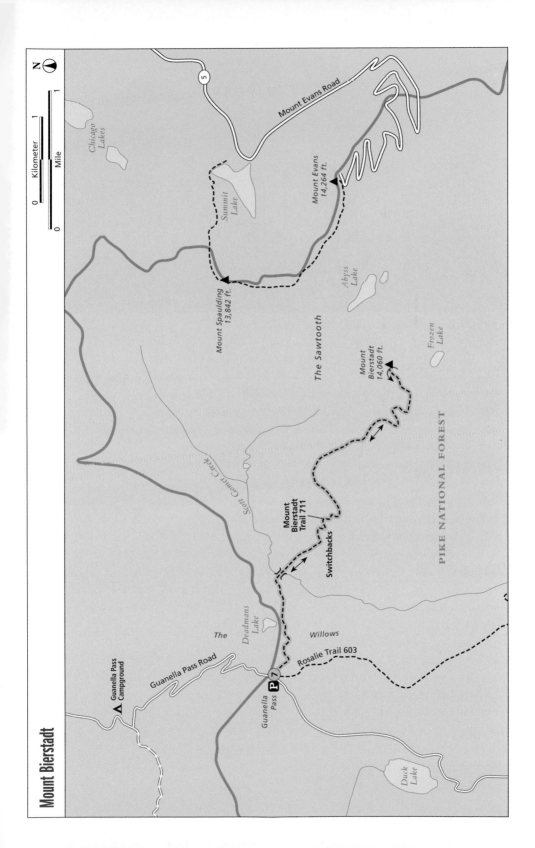

Mount Bierstadt

N

0 Kilometer 1
0 Mile 1

Guanella Pass Campground

Guanella Pass Road

The

Deadmans Lake

Willows

Guanella Pass

P 7

Rosalie Trail 603

Mount Bierstadt Trail 711

Switchbacks

Scott Gomer Creek

The Sawtooth

Mount Spaulding
13,842 ft.

Summit Lake

Chicago Lakes

Mount Evans Road

5

Mount Evans
14,264 ft.

Abyss Lake

Mount Bierstadt
14,060 ft.

Frozen Lake

PIKE NATIONAL FOREST

Duck Lake

Bierstadt's summit block. People are dots on the peak.

Miles and Directions

0.0 Start at the Guanella Pass Trailhead and head east on a great trail.

0.2 The trail becomes a series of boardwalks as it goes through The Willows.

0.3 Cross over the last of the boardwalks and continue hiking on the excellent dirt path as it comes close to and passes Deadmans Lake on the left (north).

1.1 The trail begins a gradual incline and begins a series of switchbacks.

2.2 Exit tree line and begin hiking southeast.

2.9 The trail turns left, heading east up and up to Bierstadt's peak.

3.55 Reach Bierstadt's peak. Return via same route.

7.1 Arrive back at the trailhead.

Hiking Information

Closest Outfitters

Clear Creek Outdoors, 1524 Miner St., Idaho Springs; (303) 567-1500; clearcreek outdoors.com

Great Pre- or Post-Mountain Spots

Tommyknocker Brewery & Pub, 1401 Miner St., Idaho Springs; (303) 567-4419; tommy knocker.com

Dillon Dam Brewery, 100 Little Dam St., Dillon; (970) 262-7777; dambrewery.com

Pug Ryan's, 104 Village Place, Dillon; (970) 468-2145; pugryans.com

The Alpine Restaurant and Bar, 1106 Rose St., Georgetown; (303) 569-0200; alpine restaurantgeorgetown.com

8 Mount Elbert

14,433' (NGVD29), 14,440' (NAVD88), 1st

Ahhh, Mount Elbert, Colorado's surprisingly tallest peak—many think it's shorter than nearby Mount Massive upon first glance. Once on top you'll know it's the highest point and can imagine seeing the oceans from this 14,433-foot-tall beast. But it's not really a beast to climb. It's one of the easier fourteeners in Colorado, with a Class 1, albeit long, hike to the top. The trail is straightforward and though steep—ascending more than 4,000 feet over 4.5 miles—easy to follow and trod.

Start: North Mount Elbert Trailhead
Distance: 9.0 miles
Hiking time: 6 to 9 hours
Elevation gain: 4,700 feet
Difficulty: Class 1
Trail surface: Solid stone trail to the top
Trailhead elevation: 10,040 feet
Camping: Halfmoon Creek and Elbert Creek Campgrounds (fee)
Fees: None
Best seasons: Year-round; summer for hiking
Maps: USGS Mount Elbert, Mount Massive, Granite, Independence Pass; National

Geographic Trails Illustrated #127: Aspen, Independence Pass; #110: Leadville, Fairplay
Nearest towns: Twin Lakes, Leadville
Trail contacts: San Isabel National Forest, Leadville Ranger District, (719) 486-0749; Lake County Sheriff's Office, (719) 486-1249
Trail tips: This is a long trail and can be windy and cold. Be prepared for temperatures in the 50s in summer. Bring lots of water, at least 2 liters per person; there's little if any available on the trail, especially if you don't have water treatment.

Finding the trailhead: Traveling from Leadville take US 24 south. From 3rd Street and US 24 (Harrison Avenue in Leadville), travel roughly 3.6 miles. Turn right (west) onto CO 300, crossing a set of railroad tracks. In 0.7 mile you'll see a brown sign for Halfmoon Creek; turn left here onto CR 11 (Halfmoon Creek Road). In 1.3 miles take a right to stay on Halfmoon Creek Road, which becomes a good dirt road. Follow the road for about 5.2 miles, passing signs for San Isabel National Forest, Half Moon Campground, and Half Moon West Campground to reach the North Mount Elbert Trailhead on the left (south) side. GPS: N39° 09.10' / W106° 24.72'

The Hike

In a story that echoes that of "The Englishman Who Went Up a Hill but Came Down a Mountain," in the 1930s fans of 14,421-foot Mount Massive—the closest fourteener to Elbert and second-highest in Colorado—tried to pile enough stones on Massive's peak to make it higher than Elbert. It didn't work. Fans of Elbert trekked to Massive and knocked the giant piles down.

In the Sawatch Range, and indeed throughout Colorado, Mount Elbert remained king. It's the tallest in Colorado and the second-tallest peak—behind California's

Looking north to Mount Elbert from the Colorado Trail in fall

14,505-foot Mount Whitney—in the contiguous United States. Yet it's not the most impressive or dramatic mountain. Longs Peak and the Maroon Bells offer more grandeur, drama—and danger. Mount Elbert is a kind grandparent of a mountain by comparison. Easy to access and full of wisdom—if wisdom means unparalleled views of the spine of the continent.

The mountain takes its moniker from Samuel Hitt Elbert. Elbert, who arrived in then Colorado Territory, was secretary to Gov. John Evans, second governor of the territory. Elbert married Evans's daughter Josephine. Elbert was appointed territorial governor of Colorado by President Ulysses S. Grant. By then miners had already started calling it Mount Elbert. Elbert later served on the Colorado Supreme Court for twenty years. The first documented climb of Elbert was completed by H. W. Stuckle in 1874. He was part of the Hayden Survey.

Like many mountains in the Sawatch Range, Mount Elbert essentially makes its own weather. Clouds scrape against its splintered quartzite and metamorphic basement rock peak, causing hazardous snow and lightning storms sometimes called thundersnow—even in the summer months. So it's best to get up Elbert early and get down quickly.

Mount Elbert from its northeast ridge

There are two trails up Mount Elbert. The main trail starts at the North Mount Elbert Trailhead, which is generally accessible only in summer. The South Half Moon Creek Trailhead is accessible year-round and is good for winter climbs.

The trail to Elbert starts at 10,040 feet in a spruce-and-conifer forest then joins up with the Colorado Trail within about 0.5 mile of the parking lot. Take a left onto the Colorado Trail, heading southwest. At just over 1.0 mile (at about 10,560 feet), find a junction to Mount Elbert. Go right, leaving the Colorado Trail, and hike slightly downward before resuming the uphill trek. The trail begins to go through a series of switchbacks as the trail steepens. At about 2.4 miles in and 11,600 feet, you'll find yourself in a small clearing that affords some glimpses of Elbert in the distance. At 2.7 miles (11,920 feet) you'll reach tree line and get a good look at one of Elbert's false summits as well as the trail leading to the top. At 3.25 miles and 12,720 feet you'll start climbing along Elbert's north side, looking into Box Creek Cirque. At 4.0 miles and 13,700 feet the trail skirts around the hill you've been on. At 4.1 miles (13,900 feet) reach a false summit and get your first look at the next false summit—and very likely a good taste of the winds that swirl around this peak. At 4.4 miles and 14,300 feet reach a small flat spot. Now you can see Elbert's true majesty—and it's only an easy 0.1 mile and 133 feet up! Hike to the peak at 14,433 feet and look down at the

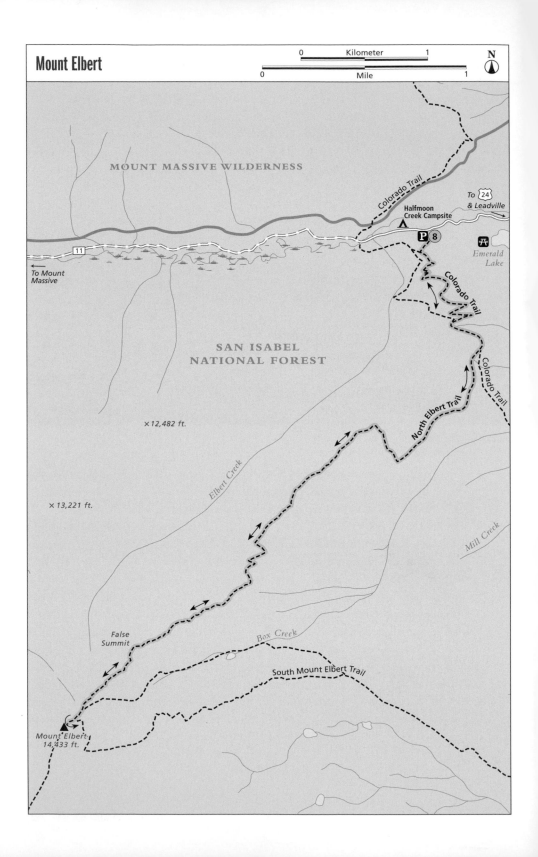

world below you. Nothing within 660 miles in any direction is higher than you at this moment!

Take a break and take in the mountains around you, like Mount Massive to your immediate north and Mount of the Holy Cross beyond that. To the west you can make out 14,092-foot Snowmass Mountain, the Maroon Bells, and 14,265-foot Castle Peak. To the south, La Plata Peak (14,336 feet) is closest; then you see a great panorama of the Sawatch Range and Collegiate Peaks in the not-too-far distance as you pan toward the east. On a clear day you can make out lonely Pikes Peak (14,110 feet) to the southeast beyond the Twin Lakes.

Miles and Directions

0.0 Start at the parking lot.
0.5 Turn left onto the Colorado Trail.
1.0 Go right at the junction, leaving the Colorado Trail.
2.7 Enter tundra.
3.3 Start climbing a ridge on Elbert's north side.
4.1 Reach the first false summit.
4.4 Reach last false summit to see Elbert's peak.
4.5 Reach Elbert's summit. Return the same way.
9.0 Arrive back at the parking lot.

Hiking Information

Closest Outfitters

Melanzana, 716 Harrison Ave., Leadville; (719) 486-3245; melanzana.com. Check out this company. They make outdoor clothes in Leadville and can do some customizations on-site!

Leadville Outdoors, 225 Harrison Ave., Leadville; (719) 486-7392; leadvilleoutdoors.com

Great Pre- or Post-Mountain Spots

As of 2015 two breweries are under construction in Leadville, Two Mile Brewing and Periodic Brewing. The town had a distillery, but it was closed as of this writing—emblematic of this boom-and-bust town.

Silver Dollar Saloon, 315 Harrison Ave., Leadville; (719) 486-9914; silverdollarsaloon.com. An authentic saloon, established in 1879!

Golden Burro Cafe & Lounge, 710 Harrison Ave., Leadville; (719) 486-1239; goldenburro.com

Tennessee Pass Cafe, 222 Harrison Ave., Leadville; (719) 486-8101; tennesseepasscafe.com

9 San Luis Peak

14,014' (NGVD29), 14,019' (NAVD88), 50th highest

Though San Luis Peak likes to hide, it's the easiest fourteener in the San Juan Range to climb. The trail to the top is easy to follow, and it's a solid walkable route. The trick to San Luis Peak is getting there. The dirt roads to San Luis are good, and most passenger vehicles should be able to make it—if driven carefully. But you still must travel on more than 20 miles of them to get to the Stewart Creek Trailhead. Once on the trail, you won't see the peak for a good while; but it's there, hiding behind 13,801-foot Organ Mountain and 13,689-foot Baldy Alto.

Start: Stewart Creek Trailhead
Distance: 12.7 miles
Hiking time: 6.5 to 8 hours
Elevation gain: 3,543 feet
Difficulty: Class 1
Trail surface: Dirt and small rock; larger rock near the peak
Trailhead elevation: 10,482 feet
Camping: Backcountry camping
Fees: None
Best seasons: Spring through fall

Maps: USGS San Luis Peak, Stewart Peak, Elk Park, Half Moon Pass; National Geographic Trails Illustrated #139: La Gartia, Cochetopa Hills
Nearest towns: Creede, Lake City, Gunnison
Trail contacts: Gunnison National Forest, (970) 874-6600; Gunnison Ranger District, (970) 641-0741; Saguache County Sheriff's Office, (719) 655-2544
Trail tips: You won't see San Luis Peak until well into the hike, but the path is easy to follow.

Finding the trailhead: This may be the most difficult part of the trip. The trail is more than 20 miles from paved road on a series of good but sometimes bumpy dirt roads. From the north and east of Gunnison, take CO 114 south. After 20.2 miles turn right onto CR NN 14. Follow this for 7 miles then turn right onto CR 15 GG (also known as FR 794 on national forestland). Stay on the main road for 4.1 miles; it will become CR 14 DD. Take this for roughly 16.4 miles, following signs to the Stewart Creek Trailhead. The trailhead used to have parking spaces, but the road was widened in 2014, allowing cars to park on the road. GPS: N38° 01.49' / W106° 50.49'

The Hike

San Luis Peak is part of the volcanic La Garita Range. The nearby La Garita Caldera is 10 miles across. The caldera was formed between 40 and 25 million years ago and saw massive eruptions between 26 and 28 million years ago—depositing more than 1,200 cubic miles of ash, cinder, and lava. Thankfully it's not active anymore.

No one's sure where San Luis Peak got its name, though it's assumed it comes from the valley at its feet, which was named by an early Spanish explorer. The name first appeared in Hayden's 1877 *Atlas of Colorado*. It's believed that the Utes were the first to ascend the mountain, but there is no recorded first ascent of San Luis.

Shy San Luis Peak finally appears from the trail

The path to San Luis Peak via the Stewart Creek Trailhead begins with an easy stroll through a lovely mountain meadow on a very solid dirt trail with a babbling creek to the left. As you walk you'll pass through tall grasses and wildflowers, including asters, shrubby cinquefoil, cow parsnip, trumpet flowers, and larkspur.

At about 1.0 mile, move away from the stream and start a slight ascent. Just before 3.0 miles, cross over to the south side of Stewart Creek, crossing it again shortly thereafter. At 3.7 miles reach the first switchback on the trail as the path starts to move out of the valley. At 4.0 miles enter a willow thicket, passing through a series of small streams, which may be dry in summer. Reach a good stream at 4.8 miles—this is the last opportunity to treat water for drinking on the way up.

At 5.3 miles and 13,100 feet, gain the saddle between Organ Mountain and San Luis. This is the first glimpse hikers will have of San Luis Peak. Hike west over the saddle to gain the south flank of San Luis on a good path, beginning the gradual yet straightforward ascent to the peak. At roughly 13,300 feet and 5.5 miles, the trail becomes broken rock that's easy to walk across. Closer to the summit the trail becomes dirt before returning to solid rock. At 6.35 miles gain the summit block. Return the same way.

Miles and Directions

0.0 Start at the roadside near the Stewart Creek Trailhead.

1.4 Pass a decrepit wooden fence.

2.9 Cross Stewart Creek on a log bridge.

San Luis Peak

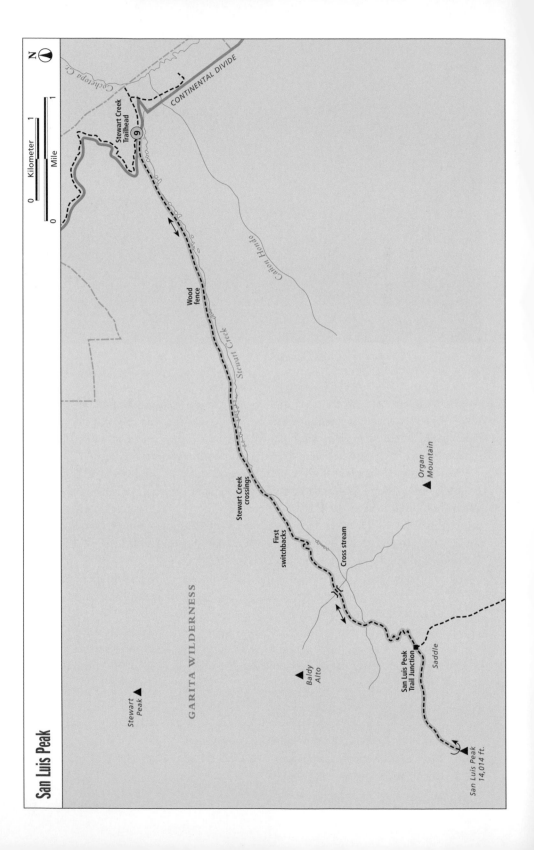

Stewart Peak ▲

GARITA WILDERNESS

Cochetopa Cr.

Stewart Creek Trailhead

9

CONTINENTAL DIVIDE

Cañon Hondo

Wood fence

Stewart Creek

Stewart Creek crossings

First switchbacks

Cross stream

Baldy Alto ▲

Organ Mountain ▲

San Luis Peak Trail Junction ■

Saddle

San Luis Peak 14,014 ft. ▲

N

Kilometer
0   1   1
Mile
0   1

A cirque near San Luis Peak

3.1 Cross Stewart Creek again.

3.7 Reach the first switchbacks.

4.0 Enter into a willow thicket.

4.4 Cross a series of smaller streams.

4.7 Cross a good, small stream. Leave the willows and start the ascent toward the saddle between Organ Mountain and San Luis Peak.

5.5 The trail becomes broken rock as it skirts Organ Mountain.

6.35 Reach San Luis Peak's apex. Return the same way.

12.7 Arrive back at the trailhead.

Hiking Information

Closest Outfitters

San Juan Sports, 102 S Main St., Creede; (719) 658-2359; sanjuansports.com

Gene Taylors Sporting Goods, 201 W Tomichi Ave., Gunnison; (970) 641-1845; gene taylors.com

Great Pre- or Post-Mountain Spots

Kip's Grill, E 5th and Main Streets, Creede; (719) 658-0220; kipsgrill.com

Freemon's Guest Ranch & General Store, 39284 Hwy. 149, Creede; (719) 658-2454

Mario's Pizza & Pasta, 213 W Tomichi Ave., Gunnison; (970) 641-1374; marios gunnison.com

Blue Table, The Inn at Tomichi Village, 41883 US 50 East, Gunnison; (970) 642-8005; theinntv.com

10 Huron Peak

14,003' (NGVD29), 14,012' (NAVD88), 52nd highest

Huron Peak is the littlest big guy in the Sawatch Range. At 14,003 feet it's much shorter than its nearby peers, which include the tallest mountain in Colorado, 14,433-foot Mount Elbert. In fact, at 14,001 feet, only Sunshine Peak in the San Juans is shorter. Located in San Isabel National Forest and the Collegiate Peaks Wilderness, Huron is the most isolated fourteener in the range, which means it offers some amazing views. The standard trail, the South Winfield Trail, also called the Clear Creek Trail, begins on a 4WD road near the abandoned mining town of Winfield.

Start: South Winfield Trailhead
Distance: 4WD trailhead: 5.8 miles (*Option:* 2WD trailhead: 9.9 miles)
Hiking time: 4 to 9 hours, depending on start location
Elevation gain: 4WD trailhead: 3,200 feet (*Option:* 2WD trailhead: 3,700 feet)
Difficulty: Class 1
Trail surface: Dirt road to scree
Trailhead elevation: 4WD trailhead: 10,570 feet (*Option:* 2WD trailhead: 10,240 feet)

Camping: Backcountry
Fees: None
Best seasons: Spring through fall
Maps: USGS Winfield; National Geographic Trails Illustrated #129: Buena Vista, Collegiate Peaks
Nearest towns: Granite, Buena Vista
Trail contacts: San Isabel National Forest Leadville Ranger District, (719) 486-0749; Chaffee County Sheriff's Office, (719) 539-2596

Finding the trailhead: Head west from the junction of US 24 and CR 390 in Granite. Drive west on CR 390, a good dirt road, for 11.8 miles, passing the Missouri Gulch Trailhead and the ghost towns of Vicksburg, Winfield, and Rockdale. At the end of Winfield take a left, continuing on FR 390.2 B and crossing Clear Creek on a bridge. (*Option:* About 100 yards up there are parking spots along the road, at the 2WD, official trailhead, GPS: N38° 58.94'/W106° 26.60'.) Assuming you're driving a 4WD vehicle, travel another 2.1 miles along the road, also called Loop Trail, to reach the 4WD trailhead at 10,570 feet. GPS: 4WD trailhead: N38° 57.62'/W106° 27.65'

The Hike

Huron was named either for the Huron (Wyandot) Native Americans or for a nearby mine that shared the same name; the origin isn't clear. Huron is in one sense among the youngest fourteeners. It wasn't recognized as a fourteener until 1956, when the US Geological Survey recorded its height.

Leave the 4WD trailhead, heading south. Hike to a forest service closure and take the trail to the left. Continue hiking through a largely coniferous forest. The trail crosses a small stream at 0.4 mile. Shortly thereafter it starts switching back as it climbs a hillside. At 1.4 miles and 11,800 feet the Three Apostles come into view to

Russ approaches Huron Peak

the south. At 1.5 miles and 11,900 feet the trail exits the forest and heads east as it climbs a small ridge into a moraine basin where the trail levels out. At 1.9 miles and 12,300 feet the trail heads up and east out of the basin to start climbing southeast toward Huron's peak.

The trail maintains a mainly southern trajectory to the top. At roughly 12,900 feet it starts a series of long, lazy switchbacks to 13,500 feet at 2.7 miles, when it reaches a ridge just below the summit. From here the remainder of the trail zigzags across steep scree and summits at 14,003 feet and 2.9 miles. Return via the same route.

Miles and Directions

0.0 Start at the 4WD trailhead and walk to the forest service closure, about 100 yards away. Take the trail to the left before the gate. (**Option:** If you're driving a two-wheel-drive vehicle, park at the easier-to-reach, official trailhead located about 2.1 miles north of the 4WD trailhead. The out and back total for the hike starting at the 2WD trailhead is 9.9 miles.)

0.4 Come to and cross a small stream. Shortly thereafter the trail begins a series of switchbacks.

1.5 Exit the forest and start climbing toward an alpine basin.

1.9 Begin ascending out of the basin, following a ridge that leads up Huron's broad north-western face.

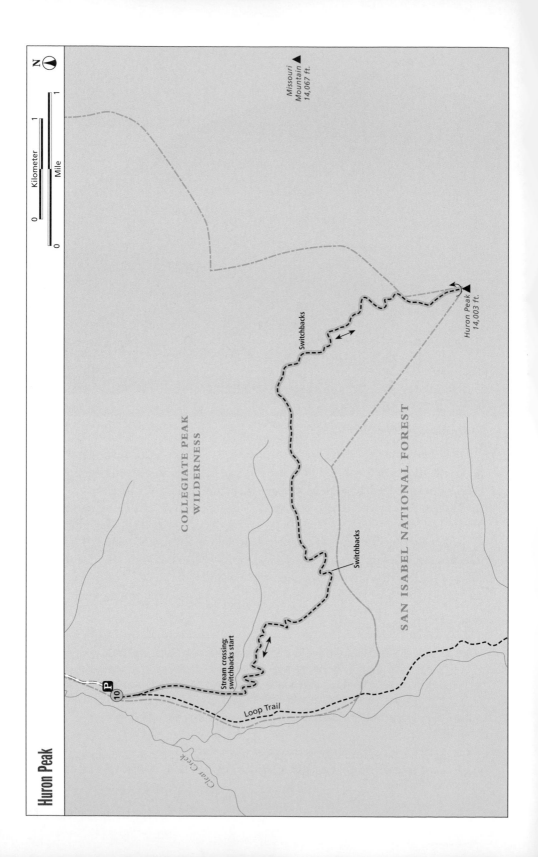

Huron Peak

Clear Creek

Stream crossing;
switchbacks start

Loop Trail

P
10

COLLEGIATE PEAK
WILDERNESS

Switchbacks

Switchbacks

SAN ISABEL NATIONAL FOREST

Huron Peak
14,003 ft.

Missouri
Mountain
14,067 ft.

N

Kilometer
0   1

Mile
0   1

Huron Peak from Missouri Mountain

2.7 Reach a ridge just below the summit. The trail surface becomes scree as the summit is approached.

2.9 Reach the summit at 14,003 feet. Return via same route.

5.8 Arrive back at the trailhead.

Hiking Information

Closest Outfitters

The Trailhead, 707 US 24 North, Buena Vista; (719) 395-8001; thetrailheadco.com

Salida Mountain Sports, 110 North F St., Salida; (719) 539-4400; salidamountain sports.com

Great Pre- or Post-Mountain Eats and Drinks

Eddyline Brewing Restaurant, 926 S Main St., Buena Vista; (719) 966-6017; eddyline brewing.com

Deerhammer Distilling Company, 321 E Main St., Buena Vista; (719) 395-9464; deer hammer.com

Moonlight Pizza & Brewpub, 242 F St., Salida; (719) 539-4277; moonlightpizza.biz

Here's the Scoop, 215 F St., Salida; (719) 539-9727

11 Torreys Peak

14,267' (NGVD29), 14,272' (NAVD88), 11th highest

Torreys Peak is the second-highest point along the Continental Divide—that amazing apex where almost all streams and rivers flow either east or west from the peaks of North America. There are higher peaks in Colorado but none on the divide itself. Torreys Peak is easy to see from I-70 as you pull off exit 221. Many fourteeners are obscured by shorter, closer peaks. Heck, Torreys obscures the view of its taller sibling, Grays, which is only about 0.5 mile away.

Start: Grays Peak Trailhead (also called Stevens Gulch Trailhead)
Distance: 8.0 miles
Elevation gain: 3,000 feet
Hiking time: 6 to 9 hours
Difficulty: Class 1, Class 2
Trail surface: Dirt trail leading to talus, some slab
Trailhead elevation: 11,270 feet
Camping: Some campsites near the parking area

Fees: None
Best seasons: Summer and fall
Maps: USGS Grays Peak, Loveland Pass, Montezuma; National Geographic Trails Illustrated #104: Idaho Springs, Georgetown, Loveland Pass
Nearest town: Georgetown
Trail contacts: Arapaho National Forest, (970) 295-6600; USDA Forest Service Clear Creek District, (303) 567-3000; Clear Creek County Sheriff's Office, (303) 679-2376

Finding the trailhead: Take the Bakerville exit (exit 221) off I-70. Cross to the south-facing side of the interstate to find a sign for Grays Peak. This is FR 189, a rough road best suited for 4WD and high-clearance vehicles. (**Note:** This is also the winter trailhead, as the road is closed in winter.) In summer follow this road for 1 mile until you reach a junction. At the junction go left toward Stevens Gulch; continue for another 2 miles to reach the trailhead. There are restrooms near the parking area. GPS: N39° 39.645'/W105° 47.082'

The Hike

The first recorded ascent of Torreys Peak was by Charles Parry in 1861. Parry, a botanist, named the peaks in honor of fellow botanists Asa Gray and John Torrey, who published *Flora of North America* in 1838. Native Americans called the peaks the Ant Hills; some miners called them the Twin Peaks.

Early prospectors also called Torreys Peak Irwin's Peak in honor of Richard Irwin, a prospector who constructed the first horse trail on the mountain. The current trail to the top of Grays Peak was built more than one hundred years ago to accommodate pack trains and horses. The trail that branches off to Torreys wasn't built for horses.

The trail to Torreys mainly follows the Grays trail and requires a little talus hiking in the summer months. In winter and into summer, the saddle that separates the

Torreys Peak from Stevens Gulch

two is usually snow covered and windswept, forming a cornice. It's easier—and a lot safer—to stay on the cornice's south side, below its top. The cornice could fail underfoot, particularly in summer, turning an easy hike into a nasty fall.

Lower parts of the trail face north. Depending on the weather, these sections can be covered with snow into early July.

From the parking lot, cross the pedestrian bridge and follow the trail (also part of the Continental Divide Trail). Encounter the first easy switchbacks at about 11,700 feet along the eastern side of Kelso Mountain (13,164 feet) at about 0.75 mile into the hike. At 11,870 feet the trail climbs southwest, along the east ridge of Kelso. At about 1.75 miles and 12,100 feet a trail branches off to the left. Stay to the right and enter a small basin, heading in a westerly direction. The trail turns south and at about 2.75 miles and 12,700 feet begins a slightly more strenuous ascent. Come to a junction at about 13,240 feet and veer to the right. The left-hand trail continues on to Grays. Follow the cairns for a little more than 0.25 mile over a talus trail to the saddle at roughly 13,700 feet. After reaching the saddle, it's an easy talus traverse across the

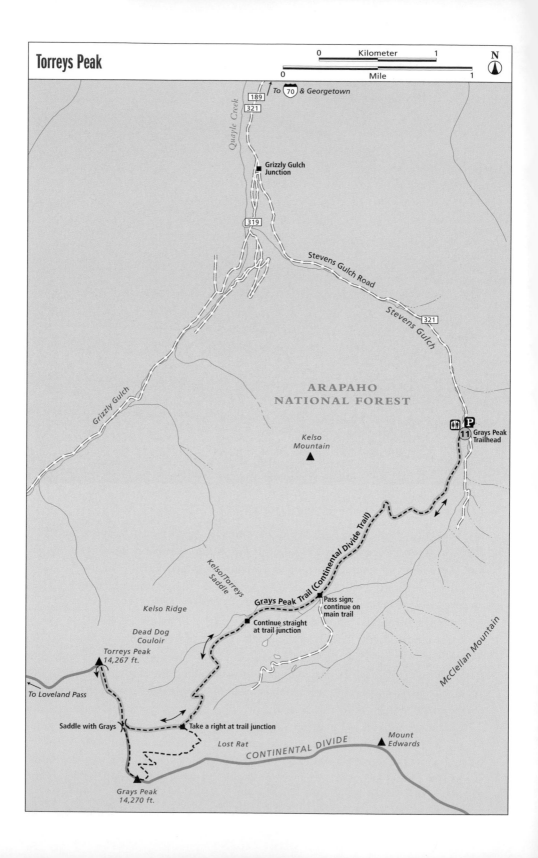

Torreys Peak

0   Kilometer   1

0   Mile   1

Quayle Creek

189
321

To 70 & *Georgetown*

Grizzly Gulch
Junction

319

Stevens Gulch Road

Stevens Gulch

321

Grizzly Gulch

ARAPAHO
NATIONAL FOREST

*Kelso
Mountain*

11

Grays Peak
Trailhead

Grays Peak Trail (Continental Divide Trail)

*Kelso/Torreys
Saddle*

Kelso Ridge

Grays Peak Trail (Continental Divide Trail)

Pass sign;
continue on
main trail

*Dead Dog
Couloir*

Continue straight
at trail junction

McClellan Mountain

*Torreys Peak
14,267 ft.*

To Loveland Pass

Saddle with Grays

Take a right at trail junction

Lost Rat

CONTINENTAL DIVIDE

*Mount
Edwards*

*Grays Peak
14,270 ft.*

saddle and to the peak, less than 0.5 mile away. Return by the same route, or cross the saddle to ascend Grays.

The view from Torreys' top is spectacular, and the surrounding mountains look different than from the top of Grays, even though it's just 0.75 mile away. The ridges to the east drift off into the plains, which you can see on the clearest of days. To the north the highest peak you'll see on a clear day is Longs Peak (14,255 feet), which is flanked by Mount Meeker (13,911 feet). Those are surrounded by the rightfully ballyhooed Rocky Mountain National Park.

Looking west you'll see the Gore Range in the distance. As you turn toward the south from the west, you'll see more fourteeners—first Mount of the Holy Cross (14,005 feet) then Mount Massive (14,421 feet).

Miles and Directions

0.0 Start at the trailhead and cross a wide footbridge to the Grays Peak Trail (FT 54, a National Recreation Trail).

1.5 Reach an information sign. Continue on the well-defined trail.

3.4 At about 13,240 feet, take the trail to the right toward Torreys Peak.

3.6 Gain the saddle between Grays and Torreys; follow the saddle to the visible trail climbing up Torreys.

4.0 Reach the peak of Torreys. Return down the same path.

8.0 Arrive back at the trailhead.

Hiking Information

Closest Outfitters

Clear Creek Outdoors, 1524 Miner St., Idaho Springs; (303) 567-1500; clearcreek outdoors.com

Great Pre- or Post-Mountain Spots

Tommyknocker Brewery & Pub, 1401 Miner St., Idaho Springs; (303) 567-4419; tommy knocker.com

Dillon Dam Brewery, 100 Little Dam St., Dillon; (970) 262-7777; dambrewery.com

Pug Ryan's, 104 Village Place, Dillon; (970) 468-2145; pugryans.com

The Alpine Restaurant and Bar, 1106 Rose St., Georgetown; (303) 569-0200; alpine restaurantgeorgetown.com

12 Mount Lincoln and Mount Cameron

14,286' (NGVD29), 14,291' (NAVD88), 8th highest

Mount Lincoln is the tallest fourteener in the Democrat Group, in the Tenmile-Mosquito Range, and in Park County. It's the eighth-tallest mountain in Colorado. An easy Class 2 hike compared to many of Colorado's mountains, it's also the longest single hike in this group of fourteeners.

Start: Kite Lake Trailhead
Distance: 5.4 miles
Elevation gain: 2,600 feet
Hiking time: 3 to 5 hours
Difficulty: Class 2
Trail surface: Mostly talus
Trailhead elevation: 12,000 feet
Camping: Campsites available (fee)
Fees: Parking fee.
Best seasons: Summer and fall (snowshoeing in winter)

Maps: USGS Alma, Climax; National Geographic Trails Illustrated #109: Breckenridge, Tennessee Pass
Nearest towns: Alma, Fairplay
Trail contacts: Pike National Forest, (719) 553-1400; USDA Forest Service South Park Ranger District, (719) 836-2031; Park County Sheriff's Office, (719) 836-2494
Trail tips: This is a well-used trail. It's best to hike early in the day and during the week, when there's less traffic.

Finding the trailhead: From CO 9 in Alma, go west on Kite Lake Road (CO 8), a poorly marked dirt road in the middle of Alma. It's by the Alma Fire House and Mining Museum, housed in an old log cabin. Follow the road for 6 miles along Buckskin Gulch to reach Kite Lake. The last mile is rougher, but most 2WD vehicles should be able to navigate the road in summer. The road closes at Paris Mill in winter, which is 3 miles from Kite Lake. There are two parking areas. The upper area has some campsites and requires users to pay a fee; the lower area doesn't. GPS: N39° 19.67'/W106° 07.76'.

The Hike

In 1861 Wilbur Stone, who later helped draft Colorado's constitution, named Mount Lincoln—not surprisingly—in honor of then President Abraham Lincoln, the first Republican president. In retaliation, Southern miners who had come to the mountains to seek their fortune started calling the other dramatic peak in this cluster of fourteeners Mount Democrat.

Though miners were known to have climbed the mountain as early as 1861, it's not clear who first summited the mountain. Like other mountains in the range, Mount Lincoln is pockmarked with old mines from prospectors who hoped to strike it rich in Colorado's high country. And the mineral riches of these peaks are significant.

One of the amazing things about these mountains, and particularly on an ascent of Mount Lincoln, is how different they are because the rock is so different. While

Hiking toward Mount Lincoln just beyond Mount Cameron

hiking the saddle between Mount Democrat and Mount Lincoln, you're hiking mainly on well-broken, dark gray granite. After you gain the ridge and head toward Mount Lincoln, the color of the rock lightens to almost-white granite interspersed with clay-color shale. It's almost like walking on Mars.

Lincoln, the tallest mountain in the range, is the northernmost mountain in the group and offers breathtaking views of its brethren as well as other mountains in the region. A hike up Mount Lincoln also nets a bonus—14,238-foot Mount Cameron. Mount Cameron is not considered a fourteener because it doesn't rise 300 feet from the saddle it shares with Mount Lincoln. Depending on the measuring system used, Mount Cameron only rises about 130 to 150 feet.

The hike up Mount Lincoln is pretty straightforward. The well-established trail ascends gradually from Kite Lake until you reach the remnants of the Kentucky Belle Mine at 12,398 feet. The former gold and silver mine was established in 1900. At just over 0.5 mile the trail makes a sharp, short dogleg to the right (west) before resuming its northward progress to the ridge between it and Mount Democrat. At about 12,720 feet and 0.75 mile, the trail takes a sharp left (east) toward Mount Democrat. That's followed by a series of switchbacks. At just under 1.0 mile, about 12,975 feet, the trail stops switchbacking and ascends to the saddle between the mountains. Gain the ridge at 1.3 miles and 13,415 feet and take the trail to the right. Follow the easy-to-see trail across the spectacular ridge to Mount Cameron at 2.2 miles. Mount Lincoln is just

Mount Lincoln and Mount Cameron

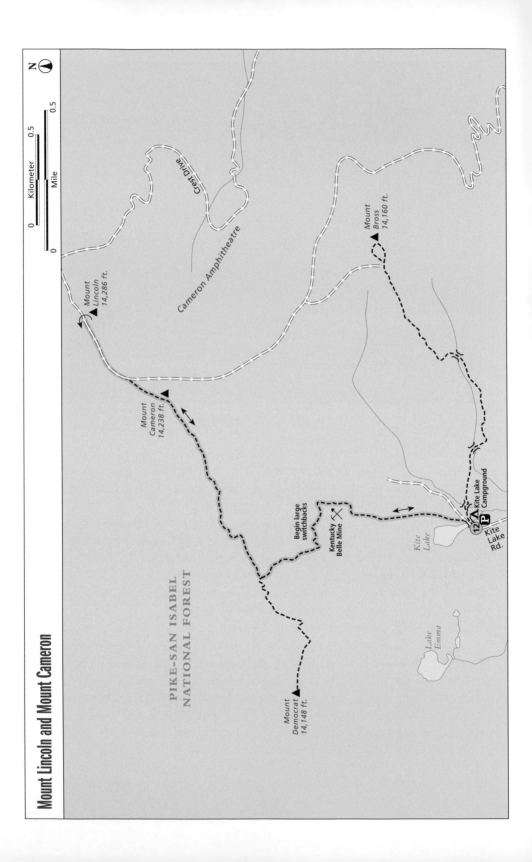

over 0.5 mile northwest of Mount Cameron along an easy trail. Return via the same route, or continue on to conquer Mount Bross.

Miles and Directions

0.0 From the Kite Lake Trailhead, follow the well-established but blocked dirt road past the lake in a northerly direction to the ruins of the Kentucky Belle Mine.

0.5 The trail takes a sharp right turn for a short dogleg then turns left and resumes its trajectory up the mountain.

0.75 The trail goes right toward Mount Cameron and begins a relatively gentle ascent with switchbacks.

1.3 Gain the saddle between Mount Democrat and Mount Cameron and hike a well-worn talus trail.

2.2 Ascend Mount Cameron's peak and continue on the trail.

2.7 Reach the peak of Mount Lincoln. Return down the same path.

5.4 Arrive back at the trailhead.

Hiking Information

Closest Outfitters

High Alpine Sports, 525 Main St., Fairplay; (719) 836-0201; highalpinesports.com

Mountain Outfitters, 112 S Ridge St., Breckenridge; (970) 453-2201; mtnoutfitters .com

Great Pre- or Post-Mountain Spots

South Park Brewing, 297½ US 285, Fairplay; (719) 836-1932; southparkbrewing co.com

Mason's High Country BBQ, 450 US 285, Fairplay; (719) 836-3465; masonshigh countrybbq.com

Broken Compass Brewing, 68 Continental Ct., Breckenridge; (970) 368-2772; broken compassbrewing.com

Breckenridge Brewery & Pub, 600 S Main St., Breckenridge; (970) 453-1550; breck brew.com

Breckenridge Distillery, 1925 Airport Rd., Breckenridge; (970) 547-9759; brecken ridgedistillery.com

Downstairs at Eric's, 111 S Main St, Breckenridge; (970) 453-1401; downstairsaterics .com/new

13 Mount Evans

14,264' (NGVD29), 14,270' (NAVD88), 14th highest

Mount Evans is the closest fourteener to Denver. It's one of two fourteeners in Colorado with a paved road to the top and has the highest paved road in the United States. The peak of this fourteener is actually reachable without a hike—ho-hum. So why bother? This mountain can be summited a number of ways, and trekking through forest and across rock face is a lot more exciting than driving up a toll road. The standard route up allows for some good Class 2 climbing pretty quickly after you park. Since it's the highest paved road in the United States, the upper part of the road generally closes in September—it's like The Shining up there in winter.

Start: Summit Lake Trailhead
Distance: 5.0 miles
Hiking time: 4 to 5 hours
Elevation gain: 1,414 feet
Difficulty: Class 2
Trail surface: Dirt, scree
Trailhead elevation: 12,850 feet
Camping: Camping near Echo Lake
Fees: Entrance fee
Best seasons: Mid-May to October; also a popular winter fourteener

Maps: USGS Mount Evans; National Geographic Trails Illustrated Map #104: Idaho Springs, Georgetown, Loveland Pass
Nearest towns: Georgetown, Idaho Springs
Trail contacts: Arapaho National Forest, (970) 295-6600; USDA Forest Service, Clear Creek Ranger Station, (303) 567-3000
Trail tips: Hike this trail during the week or early in the season.

Finding the trailhead: From exit 240 on I-70, head south on CO 103 and continue for 13.2 miles. Just beyond Echo Lake turn right onto CO 5 South (Mount Evans Road) and pay the entrance fee at the forest service kiosk. Follow the windy mountain road 9.1 miles to the parking lot at Summit Lake, on the west side of the road. GPS: N39° 35.98'/W105° 38.45'

The Hike

Mount Evans is a mere 36 miles from Denver. It's a constant reminder to Denver's Front Range residents that the mountains are calling. It's also a popular destination for visitors looking to enjoy the Rockies.

The mountain was named Mount Rosalie by Albert Bierstadt, who had neighboring Mount Bierstadt (14,060 feet) named for him. The painter, famous for his western landscapes, immortalized his wife, Rosalie, in the painting *A Storm in the Rocky Mountains, Mount Rosalie*. The painting may actually have portrayed Mount Spalding (13,842 feet) instead of Mount Evans. It is based on sketches he made during his 1863 trip with guide William Byers.

Approaching Mount Evans's summit. LEE MAUNEY

Unfortunately love lost out to politics or history in 1895, when legislators voted to rename the peak for John Evans, Colorado's second territorial governor and a businessman who helped establish the state and the railroads that allowed Denver and Colorado to flourish.

The standard route to Mount Evans takes climbers around the northern edge of Summit Lake then quickly starts gaining elevation as it arcs west and then south toward Mount Spalding. The trail begins easy enough at an old stone building. The trail echoes the shoreline of Summit Lake's east side, heading north on a good dirt trail. The trail cuts to the left across a small saddle between Mount Spalding and Mount Warren. Follow the trail that goes up the ridge of Spalding rather than the one that stays close to the lake.

Here's where the fun begins. The initial scramble up to the ridge is tough and courses up a couple of switchbacks to make the initial elevation gain easier. From there the trail largely follows the ridge crest at 13,000 feet. The trail becomes easier but continues to gain elevation rapidly—within 1.0 mile it gains nearly 1,000 feet, peaking out on Mount Spalding before continuing on to Evans.

The trail dips under the ridge crest at 0.4 mile (13,200 feet) then regains the crest at 0.6 mile and 13,470 feet. It continues to follow the ridgeline to the peak of

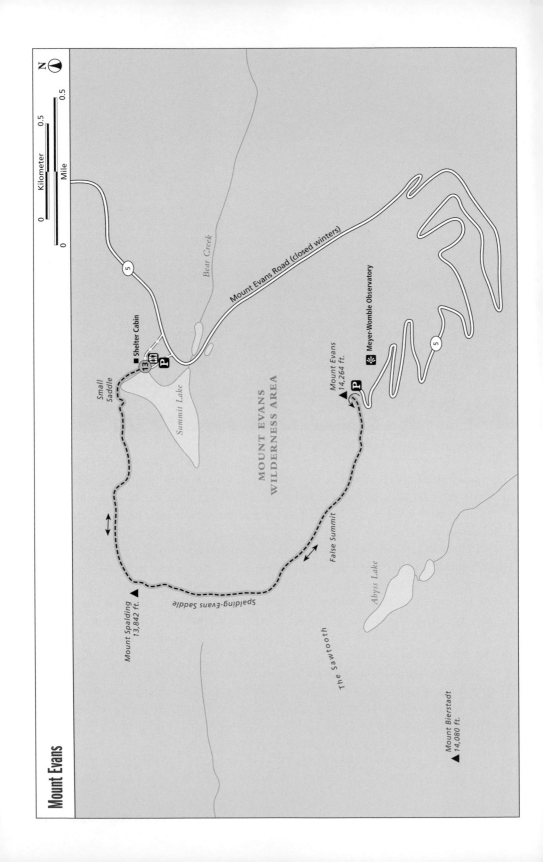

Mount Evans

Spalding, climbing over some small false summits along the way and heading south near the peak. From the top of Spalding, climbers get a spectacular view of Mount Evans's west ridge and summit—from the side people who drive to the top will never see. The summit also offers a dizzying view 1,000 feet down to Summit Lake.

Continue on, following the trail and cairns into the saddle between Spalding and Evans. The trail drops back down to 13,600 feet at 1.25 miles before it begins an ascent up Evans's west ridge. The trail climbs back up to a hump on Evans's west ridge to 13,900 feet at 1.7 miles. The trail skirts under the ridge until reaching 14,000 feet at 1.9 miles. Climbers who want a more-challenging experience can edge their way along the ridge. Continue on or near the ridgeline until you reach 14,130 feet at 2.25 miles, and tackle the final approach to the peak as the road and water station come into view. Reach the summit at 2.5 miles. Descend via the same route; or, for a steeper, quicker, more difficult descent, head down the northeast face of Evans.

Miles and Directions

0.0 Start at the old brick building just north of the parking lot.

0.1 Cross the saddle between Spalding and Warren heading west. Ascend Spalding's eastern ridge.

0.4 Dip under Spalding's crest.

0.6 Regain the crest.

1.0 Reach Spalding's peak at 13,842 feet. Head south.

1.25 Enter the saddle between Evans and Spalding.

1.7 Climb the false summit at 13,900 feet. Dip south under the ridge crest.

1.9 Regain the ridge.

2.25 Make the final approach.

2.5 Reach the peak. Return the same way. (***Option:*** Descend via Evans's northeastern ridge.)

5.0 Arrive back at the trailhead.

Hiking Information

Closest Outfitters

Clear Creek Outdoors, 1524 Miner St., Idaho Springs; (303) 567-1500; clearcreek outdoors.com

Great Pre- or Post-Mountain Spots

Tommyknocker Brewery & Pub, 1401 Miner St., Idaho Springs; (303) 567-4419; tommy knocker.com; (303) 567-4419

Dillon Dam Brewery, 100 Little Dam St., Dillon; (970) 262-7777; dambrewery.com

Pug Ryan's, 104 Village Place, Dillon; (970) 468-2145; pugryans.com

The Alpine Restaurant and Bar, 1106 Rose St., Georgetown; (303) 569-0200; alpine restaurantgeorgetown.com

Hard Fourteeners

Most of these fourteeners are Class 2 climbs with longer hikes and bigger ascension gains than the easier fourteeners. Most people should have no problem climbing these peaks; you just have to work a little harder to get to the top. None of these mountains require Class 3 or higher scrambling, meaning you shouldn't need to climb with your hands.

Lee climbs a rocky section below Mount Belford (hike 15)

14 Redcloud Peak

14,034' (NGVD29), 14,037' (NAVD88), 46th highest

It's not easy to get a glimpse of this magnificent yet gentle Colorado giant until you've wandered into the wilderness, but when you do, wow! Redcloud Peak is stunning and aptly named. Its peak is a celebration of the spectrum of red, thanks to the mineral richness of the volcanic rock. It's still a relatively easy mountain to climb, requiring some Class 2 hiking/scrambling across scree near the top.

Start: Silver Creek Trailhead
Distance: 8.6 miles
Hiking time: 6 to 8 hours
Elevation gain: 3,864 feet
Difficulty: Class 1, some Class 2 near top
Trail surface: Mostly dirt trail; turns into good scree near peak, with little to no scrambling
Trailhead elevation: 10,409 feet
Camping: Numerous campsites at trailhead
Fees: None
Best seasons: Year-round; access easier in late spring through fall
Maps: USGS Redcloud Peak, Handies Peak, Lake San Cristobal; National Geographic Trails Illustrated #141: Telluride, Silverton, Ouray, Lake City

Nearest town: Lake City
Trail contacts: Bureau of Land Management, Gunnison Field Office, (970) 642-4940; USDA Forest Service, Gunnison Ranger District, (970) 641-0471; Hinsdale County Sheriff's Office, (970) 944-2291
Trail tips: This is a good, stable trail with steady elevation gains.
Special considerations: Do not go directly down Sunshine's west face or the saddle between Redcloud and Sunshine. The scree is loose and rotten—it's a great way to fall and break a leg or ankle or worse. It's much easier and safer to find another route down; even if it's longer, it will be quicker.

Finding the trailhead: From the corner of 4th Street and Gunnison Avenue (CO 149) in Lake City, drive 2.5 miles on Gunnison Avenue. Turn right (south) onto Cinnamon Pass Road (CR 30) and drive 16.2 miles, following a ridgeline and eventually turning northwest and finally north to the Silver Creek/Grizzly Gulch Trailheads (**Note:** After passing Lake San Cristobal, the road becomes a good dirt road that's passable by most passenger vehicles. However, the road is narrow in some places and is used for dirt bikes, ATVs, and 4X4s, which may come whipping around blind corners, so drive carefully. GPS: N37° 56.23'/W107° 27.63'

The Hike

Overall, the trail to Redcloud resembles a giant fishhook, which will quickly hook climbers with verdant forests, wide-open meadows, and hidden peaks—both Redcloud and Sunshine are hidden behind 13,432-foot Sundog.

Redcloud Peak was first called Red Mountain or Jones Peak. When J. C. Spiller, topographer of the Wheeler US Government Survey, made the peak's first ascent in 1874, he gave it the more majestic name of Redcloud.

The summit of Redcloud Peak

The Silver Creek Trail that leads to Redcloud and Sunshine Peaks is on the northeast side of the parking area and campsites at Grizzly Gulch and Silver Creek—across from some abandoned cabins and privies. It starts out easily enough as a brisk ascent on a trail that two people can walk abreast on. The trail courses through a small meadow before quickly whisking climbers into a beautiful aspen and conifer-riddled forest. There's a sign-in box close to the beginning of the forest, a few hundred feet from the parking lot.

At 0.4 mile cross a small gully and stream. The trail's ascent mellows out here somewhat. At 1.1 miles cross a small stream at a gully and exit the forest as the trail more closely mirrors Silver Creek.

At just over 1.4 miles, reach another gully and stream crossing, as well as a very large cairn—about 5 feet high. Continue heading northeast on the main trail—the cairn marks the trail to Sunshine Peak. Also at this point the trail becomes somewhat rocky. Pass a small snowfield to the right that persists into August at just under 2.0 miles.

Redcloud Peak

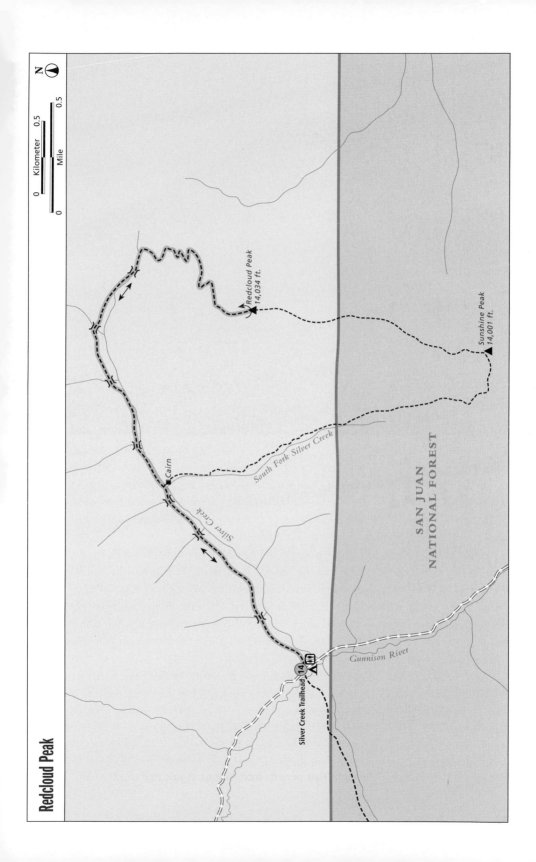

N

Kilometer
0   0.5

Mile
0   0.5

Redcloud Peak
14,034 ft.

Sunshine Peak
14,001 ft.

South Fork Silver Creek

Cairn

Silver Creek

SAN JUAN
NATIONAL FOREST

Gunnison River

Silver Creek Trailhead
14

The summit of Redcloud Peak

At 2.3 miles and 12,000 feet cross another small stream as you exit from brush into alpine meadows, heading slightly north but mostly east, and get your first glimpses of Redcloud's peak to the southeast. Views of craggy 13,000-foot peaks are directly ahead. At this point the trail becomes dirt again.

At 2.8 miles pass a small alpine pond as the glacially carved basin opens up. At 3.0 miles pass a sign directing hikers to the left for Redcloud Peak. Follow it and begin the ascent to Redcloud's ridgeline through some large, easy switchbacks.

Gain the saddle to Redcloud at 13,010 feet and 3.6 miles. Stay straight, passing a sign at 3.75 miles warning of hazardous conditions on a trail to the right. The path gets steeper here, and you'll encounter steeper, shorter switchbacks on some loose scree and pebbly trail.

At 4.3 miles reach the top of Redcloud. Directly south of the peak, you can see the russet flanks of a ridge that leads to Sunshine Peak (14,001 feet) and the easy path over to it. Just beyond that lies photogenic Handies Peak (14,048 feet). To the north you can see Wetterhorn (14,015 feet) and Uncompahgre (14,309 feet) Peaks; to the northwest you can see 14,150-foot Mount Sneffels.

Return via the same route or continue on to Sunshine Peak.

Miles and Directions

0.0 Start at the Silver Creek Trailhead. Check in at the sign-in box shortly after entering the forest.

0.23 Enter a forest.

0.5 Cross a small stream as the initial ascent lessens.

1.1 Cross another stream as you come into an opening.

1.45 Pass a large cairn, continuing on the main trail straight ahead (northeast).

1.9 Pass a small snowfield to the right as the trail remains rocky.

2.3 Pass another small stream.

2.8 Pass a small alpine lake just after crossing over into an alpine meadow, gaining sight of Redcloud's northern face. The trail becomes dirt again.

3.0 Come to a sign directing hikers to Redcloud Peak on the left. Follow that sign and begin a series of long switchbacks.

3.6 Gain Redcloud's saddle, heading southwest.

3.75 Continue heading straight beyond the trail sign. From here the trail starts switchbacking up steeper scree and pebbles to the peak.

4.3 Reach Redcloud's peak. Return via the same route.

8.6 Arrive back at the trailhead.

Hiking Information

Closest Outfitters

The Sportsman Outdoors & Fly Shop, 238 S Gunnison Ave., Lake City; (970) 944-2526; lakecitysportsman.com

San Juan Sports, 102 S Main St., Creede; (719) 658-2359; sanjuansports.com

Great Pre- or Post-Mountain Spots

Packer Saloon & Cannibal Grill, 310 N Silver St., Lake City; (970) 944-4144

Lake City Cafe, 310 Gunnison Ave., Lake City; (970) 944-0301; lakecityswitchbacks .com/restaurants.html

San Juan Soda Co., 227 N Silver St., Lake City; (970) 944-0500; sanjuansodacompany .com

15 Mount Belford

14,197' (NGVD29), 14,205' (NAVD88), 19th highest

Sandwiched between Mount Oxford (14,153 feet) and Missouri Mountain (14,067 feet), Belford is the tallest peak in the Missouri Gulch. Located in San Isabel National Forest and the Collegiate Peaks Wilderness, it's a strenuous Class 1 hike to the top, requiring more than 4,000 feet of elevation gain in a little over 3.6 miles. It is a popular hike in spring and summer, but people also ski or snowboard it in winter. Climbers often combine this peak with Mount Oxford, which is about 1.5 miles east of Belford.

Start: Missouri Gulch Trailhead
Distance: 7.2 miles
Hiking time: 6 to 8 hours
Elevation gain: 4,600 feet
Difficulty: Class 1
Trail surface: Dirt trail, some scree
Trailhead elevation: 9,640 feet
Camping: No camping at the trailhead; primitive campsites along CR 390 and along the trail

Fees: None
Best seasons: Spring through fall
Maps: USGS Winfield, Harvard, Harvard Lakes; National Geographic Trails Illustrated #129: Buena Vista, Collegiate Peaks
Nearest towns: Granite, Buena Vista
Trail contacts: San Isabel National Forest, Leadville Ranger District, (719) 486-0749; Chaffee County Sheriff's Office, (719) 539-2596

Finding the trailhead: From the junction of US 24 and CR 390, drive west on CR 390, a good dirt road, for 7.7 miles to Vicksburg. Stay left on CR 390 and turn left (south) into the parking lot. The trailhead is at the southwest corner of the lot. GPS: N38° 59.88' / W106° 22.50'

The Hike

Mount Belford was named for James Belford, the first US Representative from Colorado. Belford, known as "The Red-Headed Rooster of the Rockies," was renowned for his mop of red hair and beard. Miners named the mountain in his honor, perhaps also in reference to the red rock that tops this gentle giant.

Belford is an easy but long hike. Depending on the climbing party's fitness, it can consume a full day. The summit, at 14,197 feet, is more than 4,450 feet above the trailhead. That's 0.8 mile of elevation gain in 3.6 miles, and it requires hiking up a multitude of switchbacks—at a grade in excess of 25 degrees at some points. The main risk of exposure, however, is weather. Electric storms can roll into the Missouri Gulch quickly. If storm clouds come into the valley quickly in the afternoon, start hiking down immediately. Because of the elevation gain and the potential for storms, it's a good idea to start this mountain close to dawn if you're hiking from the parking lot.

Climbers gain a small ridge below Mount Belford.

The trail to the peak begins easily enough at the southwest end of the parking area. Cross over Clear Creek at about 150 feet and enter a coniferous forest of spruce and fir. Shortly thereafter, pass a child's gravestone behind a fence—the remains of an abandoned graveyard for miners and their families. At 0.3 mile reach the first switchbacks that wind through the forest on an easy-to-follow trail that gains elevation rapidly. At 0.6 mile (10,375 feet) the trail stops switching back as it enters the west side of Missouri Gulch. You can hear a stream babbling below. The trail etches the east side of the gulch until it crosses over the stream at 10,800 feet and 1.0 mile. The trail climbs up the west side of the gulch. It reenters thicker forest before turning southeasterly.

At 1.3 miles (11,280 feet) find the remains of an old cabin on the left. The trail immediately bursts into a fantastic alpine meadow. Belford comes into view on the left, and the hefty flanks of Missouri Mountain are to the right. Continue on the clear trail. (On many mountains the trail might've disappeared by now, but the Colorado Fourteeners Initiative and volunteers completed some excellent work on this trail in 1996).

Stay left at 1.8 miles (11,600 feet) at the trail junction to Missouri Mountain. The trail winds its way through the awesome alpine meadow filled with wildflowers, willows, and alpine conifers. At 2.0 miles (11,900 feet) the trail crosses a small

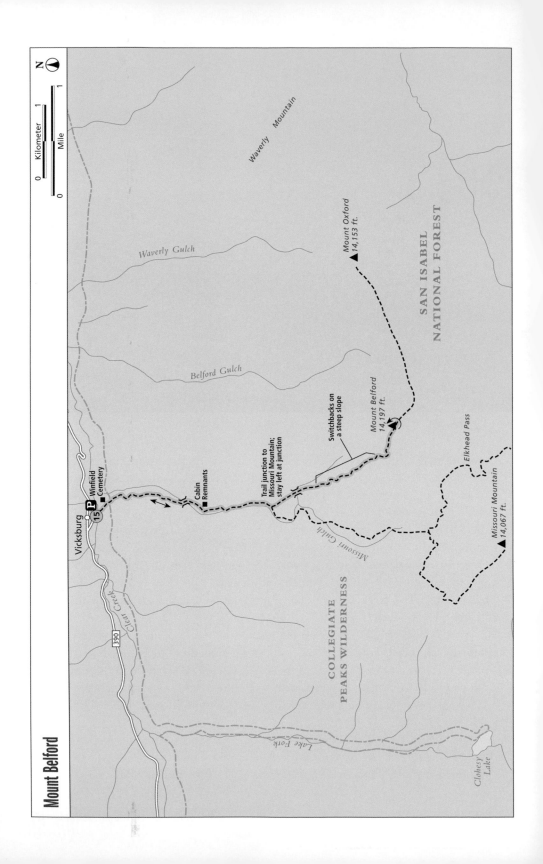

Mount Belford

N

0 1 Kilometer

0 1 Mile

Vicksburg

390

Clear Creek

15

P

Winfield
Cemetery

Waverly Gulch

Waverly Mountain

Belford Gulch

Cabin
Remnants

Trail junction to
Missouri Mountain;
stay left at junction

Switchbacks on
a steep slope

Mount Belford
14,197 ft.

Mount Oxford
14,153 ft.

SAN ISABEL
NATIONAL FOREST

Missouri Gulch

Elkhead Pass

Missouri Mountain
14,067 ft.

COLLEGIATE
PEAKS WILDERNESS

Lake Fork

Clohesy Lake

stream before it gains the bottom of Belford's northwest ridge. From here on up it's a ziggity-zaggity time as the trail switches back and forth up the ridge for more than a mile. The zigzags stop at 13,950 feet, 3.4 miles into the hike. Turn left to ascend the remaining 0.2 mile to the summit. There is a small false summit, but it's just a few hundred feet from the real summit of this tall peak.

To the south, the Missouri Basin is beautiful. The valley stretches out below 13,904-foot Emerald Peak and the deep blue alpine lake at its base. To the west is Mount Oxford.

Miles and Directions

0.0 Start at the trailhead on the southwest side of the lot. Go 150 feet and cross Clear Creak on a metal bridge.

0.3 Begin switchbacks in forest.

0.6 Exit switchbacks and enter the east side of Missouri Gulch.

1.0 Cross a stream.

1.3 Pass cabin remnants on the left and enter alpine meadow.

2.0 Cross a stream. Gain the northwest ridge of Belford and start a switchback ascent of the ridge.

3.4 Reach a flat spot below the summit push.

3.6 Peak out. (**Option:** Push on to Oxford or return via same route.)

7.2 Arrive back at the trailhead.

Hiking Information

Closest Outfitters

The Trailhead, 707 US 24 N, Buena Vista; (719) 395-8001; thetrailheadco.com

Salida Mountain Sports, 110 North F St., Salida; (719) 539-4400; salidamountain sports.com

Great Pre- or Post-Mountain Eats and Drinks

Eddyline Brewing Restaurant, 926 S Main St., Buena Vista; (719) 966-6017; eddyline brewing.com

Deerhammer Distilling Company, 321 E Main St., Buena Vista; (719) 395-9464; deer hammer.com

Moonlight Pizza & Brewpub, 242 F St., Salida; (719) 539-4277; moonlightpizza.biz

Here's the Scoop, 215 F St., Salida; (719) 539-9727

16 Culebra Peak

14,047' (NGVD29), 14,051' (NAVD88), 41st highest

This sinuous peak is Colorado's southernmost fourteener. Culebra is also the state's most expensive fourteener to climb, requiring a considerable sum per person to reserve the honor. However, be thankful this mountain can be climbed by the public at all. It is on the Cielo Vista Ranch, which improved the road allowing access to the mountain at its expense. The hike starts as a Class 1 trek, leading up to a fantastic Class 2 ridge walk and summit. The mountain is closed to hikers September to June.

Start: Cielo Vista Ranch 4WD trailhead (*Option:* 4-Way 2WD trailhead)
Distance: 4WD trailhead: 4.8 miles (*Option:* 2WD trailhead: 6.8 miles)
Hiking time: About 5 hours (*Option:* About 6 hours from 4-Way 2WD trailhead)
Elevation gain: 4WD trailhead: 2,580 feet (*Option:* 2WD trailhead: 3,060 feet)
Difficulty: Class 1 start, Class 2 finish
Trail surface: Meadow, dirt, scree
Trailhead elevation: 4WD trailhead: 11,660 feet (*Option:* 2WD trailhead: 11,250 feet)
Camping: Check with ranch owners.
Fees: Check with ranch owners.

Best seasons: Spring through early fall
Maps: USGS Culebra Peak, El Valle Creek, Cielo Vista Ranch (Taylor Ranch, historically); no National Geographic Trails Illustrated map for this location
Nearest towns: San Luis, Alamosa
Trail contacts: Cielo Vista Ranch, (254) 897-7872; cielovistaranchco.com/climbing/
Trail tips: If traveling in a group, do not follow one another; instead fan out and pick individual routes.
Special considerations: Caution: This is a rural area, watch for dogs crossing the road—wherever they want to!

Finding the trailhead: From the junction of CO 159 and 5th Street in San Luis, head south to 4th Street, which is also CO 152 and CR P.6. Drive 4 miles and turn left onto CR L.7 (Whiskey Pass Road). At 10.5 miles turn right onto CR 25.5; at 11 miles turn left onto CR M.5. At 12.1 miles reach the gates of Cielo Vista Ranch and wait for access. Continue on to the headquarters, 14.1 miles from San Luis, and check in. After checking in, continue on a good 4WD road. Turn right at a junction at 14.2 miles. At 17.6 miles reach the 4-Way junction. (*Option:* Park 2WD vehicles here. GPS: N37° 08.53'/W105° 13.93') Those with 4WD can continue another mile to the 4WD trailhead. GPS: N37° 08.35'/W105° 12.94'

The Hike

Culebra—Spanish for harmless snake, is an apt name for this mountain, though climbers could argue that the steep reservation fee is not harmless. But considering that the peak is on private land—and has been since Spaniards settled the land in the early 1800s—the public is lucky to have access to this "private mountain" at all. That the mountain is on private rather than public land also has some advantages.

Culebra Peak at sunset. CHRIS SEAVER

For instance, the ranch owners limit how many people can summit the mountain in a day. The peak doesn't have a defined trail to the peak; hence it feels wilder and has a greater air of discovery than climbing some of the more trekked and—some might say—trashed mountains.

Though the mountain was visited by Europeans in the late 1600s, when Diego de Vargas named the region Culebra, it's a sure bet that Ute, Comanche, Apache, and other Native Americans visited this peak first. Culebra would have made an ideal location for scouting to hunt buffalo and antelope in the region. The name Culebra Peak appeared as early as 1810 on Zebulon Pike's map of the region.

Part of the 80,000-plus-acre Cielo Vista Ranch, Culebra is one of the least-visited fourteeners. The owners want to preserve the land and allow reasonable access to the mountain June to September. They close the mountain for hunting season and for most of the winter.

To hike this last southern sentinel of Colorado's Rockies, visit the Cielo Vista Ranch website (see "Trail contacts"), sign a waiver, and reserve a date on the calendar. Plan ahead, because the mountain can fill up quickly. If interested in camping on the property, discuss it with ranch personnel first. Failure to comply with the ranch's regulations can result in fines and even getting kicked out. The nearest public camping spots are likely at the Como Lake trailhead. Otherwise find a hotel in nearby Alamosa or San Luis.

(**Option:** Some opt to start at the 2WD parking lot called 4-Way, where the trail technically starts, 11,250 feet, because of the steepness of the next mile of road. From there, hike the road for 1.0 mile to the 4WD trailhead at 11,660 feet.) A vehicle with good clearance should be able to reach the 4WD trailhead, from which it's a 2.4-mile hike to the peak.) From either trailhead, there's only one way to hike Culebra: Head southeast.

Hike up and across a small stream in an easterly direction. Then, particularly in a group, practice dispersed hiking. The landowners prefer this method because it does

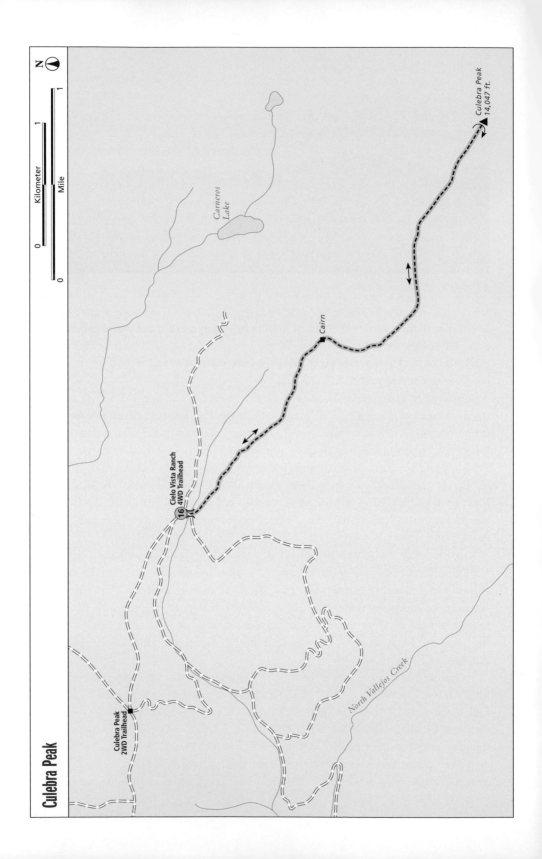

Culebra Peak

N

0 ___ 1 Kilometer
0 ___ 1 Mile

Culebra Peak
14,047 ft.

Carneros Lake

Cairn

Cielo Vista Ranch
4WD Trailhead
16

Culebra Peak
2WD Trailhead

North Vallejos Creek

less permanent harm to the land. Continue hiking up this slope for about 1.1 miles then angle right (south) to reach the ridge, passing a giant cairn just before gaining the 13,310-foot ridge.

Follow the ridge, avoiding large rocks and other hazards. It starts dropping at 1.25 miles and dips to 13,190 feet from 13,330 feet. The trail curves up and around the bowl to the next small peak, at 13,549 feet. At this point the trail turns left (east) and crosses over a short saddle at 13,550 feet and 1.6 miles. At 1.8 miles the saddle ends and the push for the peak begins at 13,750 feet. From here the summit is only 0.5 mile. Before getting to it, though, pass a false summit at 13,900 feet. After that it's a short jaunt to the top at 2.4 miles and 14,047 feet. Return via roughly the same route. The landowners don't want people traveling up and down by exactly the same route—again to minimize damage to the land.

Miles and Directions

0.0 Start at the 4WD trailhead and head southeast up a broad face, practicing dispersed hiking. (**Option:** Start at the 2WD trailhead; hike southeast to the 4Wd trailhead and add 2 miles to your total hike.)

1.1 Reach a large cairn and ridge at 13,310 feet; turn right and follow the ridge.

1.6 Cross over a short saddle, heading east.

1.8 Begin the final ascent to the peak.

2.0 Reach a false summit.

2.4 Peak out on "the snake." Return via a similar route.

4.8 Arrive back at the 4WD trailhead.

Hiking Information

Closest Outfitters

Kristi Mountain Sports, 3223 Main St., Alamosa; (719) 589-9759; kristimountain sports.com

Great Pre- or Post-Mountain Spots

San Luis Valley Brewing Co., 631 Main St., Alamosa; (719) 587-2337; slvbrewco.com

Calvillo's Mexican Restaurant, 400 Main St., Alamosa; (719) 587-5500; calvillos .qwestoffice.net

The Rubi Slipper, 506 State Ave., Alamosa; (719) 589-2641

17 Sunshine Peak

14,001' (NGVD29), 14,006' (NAVD88), 53rd highest

Sunshine is the biggest little mountain you'll encounter in Colorado—or the rest of the country for that matter! At 14,001 feet, it's the shortest fourteener in the United States. However, short doesn't necessarily mean easiest. Sunshine is most often climbed with Redcloud Peak, which adds 2 easy miles to that trek. Climbed on its own, it's a more-challenging mountain because the trails up it are less solid than those that go up Redcloud. The easiest route from Silver Creek is up its northwest face, but it still requires a fair amount of Class 2 hiking.

Start: Silver Creek Trailhead
Distance: 8.0 miles
Hiking time: 6 to 8 hours
Elevation gain: 3,657 feet
Difficulty: Class 1; some Class 2 and higher near top
Trail surface: Dirt trail at lower elevations; scree after leaving Silver Creek Trail
Trailhead elevation: 10,409 feet
Camping: Numerous campsites at trailhead
Fees: None
Best seasons: Year-round; access easier in late spring through fall
Maps: USGS Redcloud Peak, Handies Peak, Lake San Cristobal; National Geographic Trails Illustrated #141: Telluride, Silverton, Ouray, Lake City

Nearest town: Lake City
Trail contacts: Bureau of Land Management, Gunnison Field Office, (970) 642-4940; USDA Forest Service, Gunnison Ranger District, (970) 641-0471; Hinsdale County Sheriff's Office, (970) 944-2291
Trail tips: This is a good, stable trail with steady elevation gains.
Special considerations: Do not go directly down Sunshine's west face or the saddle between Redcloud and Sunshine. The scree is loose and rotten—it's a great way to fall and break a leg or ankle or worse. It's much easier and safer to find another route down; even if it's longer, it will be quicker.

Finding the trailhead: From the junction of 4th Street and Gunnison Avenue (CO 149) in Lake City, drive 2.5 miles on Gunnison Avenue. Turn right (south) onto Cinnamon Pass Road (CR 30) and drive 16.2 miles, following a ridgeline and eventually turning northwest and finally north to the Silver Creek/Grizzly Gulch Trailheads. (**Note:** After passing Lake San Cristobal, the road becomes a good dirt road that's passable by most passenger vehicles. However, the road is narrow in some places and is used for dirt bikes, ATVs and 4X4s, which may come whipping around blind corners, so drive carefully.) GPS: N37° 56.23'/W107° 27.63'

The Hike

Also once called Niagara Peak and Sherman Mountain, this fourteener gained the more winsome name of Sunshine Peak in 1904. Sunshine Peak was first climbed by A. D. Wilson and Franklin Rhoda of the Hayden US Government Survey in 1874.

Hiking toward Sunshine Peak from Redcloud Peak

They gave this rocky peak the lovely name of Station 12, since it was used as a triangulation station during the survey. They were run off the peak by static electricity, lightning, and an incoming storm.

The hike up Sunshine starts on the same path as the hike to Redcloud Peak. Traditionally the two peaks are climbed together by climbing Redcloud first then hiking the 1.0 mile to Sunshine. The easiest way to complete the two requires re-ascending Redcloud on the way back down, making it a more than 11-mile hike. However, climbers can ascend or descend Sunshine by its northeast ridge—creating a loop out of both mountains.

The best, and safest, way up Sunshine by this route passes through a beautiful forest along the gully from South Fork Spring.

The Silver Creek Trail to Sunshine Peak and Redcloud starts on the northeast side of the parking area and campsites at Grizzly Gulch and Silver Creek—across the dirt road from some abandoned cabins and privies. The trek starts as an ascent on a trail that was likely an old miner's road, and two people can walk abreast on parts of it. The trail courses through a small meadow before entering a beautiful aspen and conifer-riddled forest. There's a sign-in box close to the beginning of the forest, a few hundred feet from the parking lot.

The trail starts out on a decent but manageable ascent. Cross a small stream in a small gully at 0.4 mile. Beyond that, the ascent mellows as Silver Creek comes into view for the first time. At 1.1 miles cross another small stream at a gully and exit the forest as the trail more closely mirrors Silver Creek.

At about 1.5 miles come to a large cairn, as the trail comes closer to Silver Creek, walk down to the stream and look for a decent place to cross near the scrubby brush. Here the trail leaves the main branch of Silver Creek and follows its south fork. The Sunshine Trail is on the left side of the fork and parallels South Fork Silver Creek until you reach 1.9 miles. There it climbs a short slope before reentering forest. At just about 2.0 miles and 11,800 feet, pass the remains of an old shed.

At around 2.25 miles and 11,900 feet, reach tree line. From here most of the remaining route, which travels south before hooking back around to Sunshine's peak, is visible. At 2.9 miles and 12,400 feet ascend a small rock glacier. At this point the trail becomes primarily talus. Continue south toward a craggy ridge, finding an opening between two imposing gendarmes; cairns provide some guidance through this rocky trek.

Reach the base of the gendarmes at 3.4 miles and start ascending. While a scree trail goes through the middle of the route, a much easier climb is to stay to the left on the rocks, using them as a sort of railing to help you climb the route. Exit the gendarmes at about 13,150 feet and resume hiking on a talus slope.

At about 3.5 miles and 13,300 feet, the trail levels off a bit and the braided trail branches off in different directions. The safest and best option is to the right, hiking across the bowl and up to Sunshine's western ridge. Following this route, at 3.7 miles (about 13,700 feet) turn left to gain the talus ridge up to Sunshine's summit; scramble up the remainder to the peak, gaining the 14,001-foot summit at 4.0 miles.

Return via the same route, reaching the trailhead at 8.0 miles. Or continue down the ridgeline of the saddle between Sunshine and Redcloud to make a loop out of the two.

Miles and Directions

0.0   Start at Silver Creek Trailhead. Check in at the sign-in box shortly after entering the forest.

0.2   Enter a forest.

0.5   Cross a small stream as the initial ascent lessens.

1.1   Cross another stream as you come into an opening.

1.5   Come to a large cairn and cross Silver Creek to the South Fork Silver Creek.

1.9   Climb a short slope, moving away from South Fork and into forest again.

2.0   Pass the remains of an old shed.

2.25 Reach tree line.

2.9   Ascend a small rock glacier.

3.4   Reach base of gendarmes.

3.5   Hike across the bowl on a braided, rocky trail below Sunshine's face to its western ridge.

Sunshine Peak

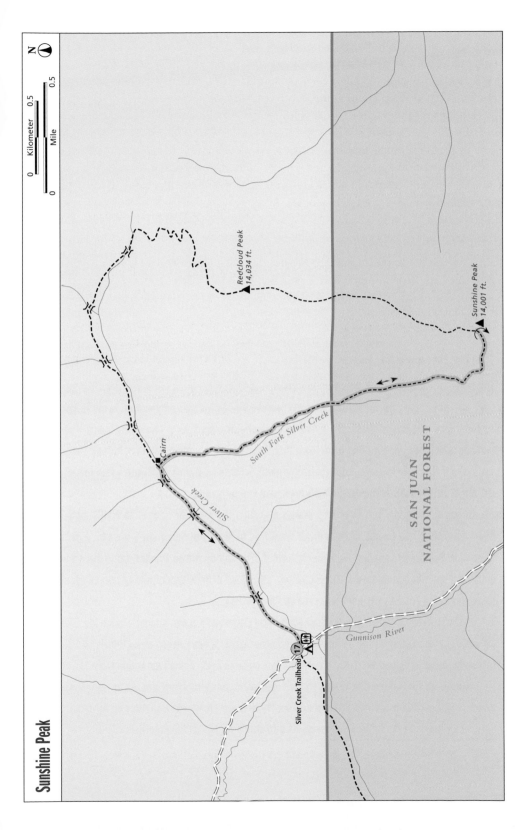

N

0   Kilometer   0.5

0   Mile   0.5

Redcloud Peak
14,034 ft.

Sunshine Peak
14,001 ft.

South Fork Silver Creek

Silver Creek

Cairn

SAN JUAN
NATIONAL FOREST

Gunnison River

Silver Creek Trailhead   17

3.7 Gain the ridge, and climb toward Sunshine's Peak.

4.0 Reach the peak. Return via the same route.

8.0 Arrive back at the trailhead.

Hiking Information

Closest Outfitters

The Sportsman Outdoors & Fly Shop, 238 S Gunnison Ave., Lake City; (970) 944-2526; lakecitysportsman.com

San Juan Sports, 102 S Main St., Creede; (719) 658-2359; sanjuansports.com

Great Pre- or Post-Mountain Spots

Packer Saloon & Cannibal Grill, 310 N Silver St., Lake City; (970) 944-4144

Lake City Cafe, 310 Gunnison Ave., Lake City; (970) 944-0301

San Juan Soda Co., 227 N Silver St., Lake City; (970) 944-0500; sanjuansodacompany
.com

LAKE CITY, A PEAK EXPERIENCE

There are a couple a towns or cities in Colorado that can serve as ideal locations for peak bagging—going out and summiting as many fourteeners in an area as you can. In areas such as Lake City and Buena Vista, it's great to have these places as a launching point and a fallback. Lake City is a beautiful little town that lives up to its motto: Lake City, A Peak Experience. From this town you've got—relatively—quick access to five of Colorado's fourteeners: Redcloud and Sunshine, Handies, Wetterhorn, and Uncompahgre.

If you're camping out, Lake City makes a great rally point or access to civilization—a place to grab a bite to eat, a well-earned shake or malt at the San Juan Soda Co., a drink at Packer Saloon & Cannibal Grill (named for the infamous Alfred Packer, Colorado's only convicted cannibal), and even a shower, which, after four or five days of hiking and climbing, feels almost as good as the best massage you'll ever have.

If you're tired of camping out or just want to do day trips, you can stay at a place like G&M Cabins, a series of quaint little cabins with kitchens, showers, beds, even—ugh—televisions. The rates are reasonable, and there are plenty of other options in this small mountain town.

A base of operations like Lake City can also offer you important access to your emergency contacts. While cell reception is still spotty in many smaller towns, they do have cafes, bars, and libraries with Internet access—oh, and these things called landlines.

18 Mount Oxford

14,153' (NGVD29) 14,160' (NAVD88), 26th highest

Mount Oxford is the northernmost of the collegiate peaks in the Sawatch Range. Its brethren, 14,197-foot Mount Belford and 14,067-foot Missouri Mountain, are west of it. It offers spectacular views across the Arkansas River Basin. This mountain is almost always climbed with Belford, which is 1.2 miles away as the crow flies. The standard, Class 1 route requires reaching more than 14,000 feet three times in one day (climbers have to summit Belford twice to hike to Oxford), making it a long day with an overall elevation gain of nearly 6,000 feet.

Start: Missouri Gulch Trailhead
Distance: 10 miles
Hiking time: About 10 hours
Elevation gain: 6,000 feet
Difficulty: Class 1
Trail surface: Dirt trail; some scree
Trailhead elevation: 9,640 feet
Camping: No camping at the trailhead; primitive campsites along CR 390 and along the trail

Fees: None
Best seasons: Spring through fall
Maps: USGS Winfield, Harvard, Harvard Lakes; National Geographic Trails Illustrated #129: Buena Vista, Collegiate Peaks
Nearest town: Granite
Trail contacts: San Isabel National Forest, Leadville Ranger District, (719) 486-0749; Chaffee County Sheriff's Office, (719) 539-2596

Finding the trailhead: From the junction of US 24 and CR 390, drive west on CR 390, a good dirt road, for 7.7 miles to Vicksburg. Stay left on CR 390 and turn left (south) into the parking lot. The trailhead is at the southwest corner of the lot. GPS: N38° 59.88'/W106° 22.50'

The Hike

Like all the prestigious schools named in the range, it takes some work to get to the top. At least with this Oxford U.S.-based climbers don't have to board a plane or ship and travel to England!

Ironically Mount Oxford was the last named collegiate peak in Colorado seeing as it was undoubtedly the first university founded among the Collegiates. The peak was named after Stephen Hart, and Albert Ellingwood surveyed the mountain from Harvard and Columbia, confirming its pedigree. Stephen's brother John L. Jerome Hart found the peak had no name. He named it after his and his brother's alma mater in his 1925 book *Fourteen Thousand Feet: A History of the Naming and Early Ascents of the High Colorado Peaks*, which was published by the then fledgling Colorado Mountain Club.

The trail begins easily enough at the southwest end of the parking area. Cross over Clear Creek at about 150 feet and enter a coniferous forest of spruce and fir. Shortly

The short, but tiring jaunt to Mount Oxford from Mount Belford

thereafter, pass a child's gravestone behind a fence—the remains of an abandoned graveyard for miners and their families. At 0.3 mile reach the first switchbacks that wind through the forest on an easy-to-follow trail that gains elevation rapidly. At 0.6 mile (10,375 feet) the trail stops switching back as it enters the west side of Missouri Gulch. You can hear a stream babbling below. The trail etches the east side of the gulch until it crosses over the stream at 10,800 feet and 1.0 mile. The trail climbs up the west side of the gulch. T reenters thicker forest before turning southeasterly.

At 1.3 miles (11,280 feet) find the remains of an old cabin on the left. The trail immediately bursts into a fantastic alpine meadow. Belford comes into view on the left, and the hefty flanks of Missouri Mountain are to the right. Continue on the clear trail. (On many mountains the trail might've disappeared by now, but the Colorado Fourteeners Initiative and volunteers completed some excellent work on this trail in 1996.)

Stay left at 1.8 miles (11,600 feet) at the trail junction to Missouri Mountain. The trail winds its way through the awesome alpine meadow filled with wildflowers, willows, and alpine conifers. At 2.0 miles (11,900 feet) the trail crosses a small stream before it gains the bottom of Belford's northwest ridge. From here on up it's a ziggity-zaggity time as the trail switches back and forth up the ridge for more than a mile. The zigzags stop at 13,950 feet, 3.4 miles into the hike. Turn left to ascend the remaining 0.2 mile to the summit. There is a small false summit, but it's just a few hundred feet from Belford's real summit.

After summiting Belford—hopefully early enough in the day—step off the peak and head southeast on the Mount Oxford Trail toward the saddle that separates Oxford and Belford. At 3.8 miles (14,075 feet) turn left, abandoning a ridge that would lead to a difficult ascent of Missouri Mountain. Instead, head east and down

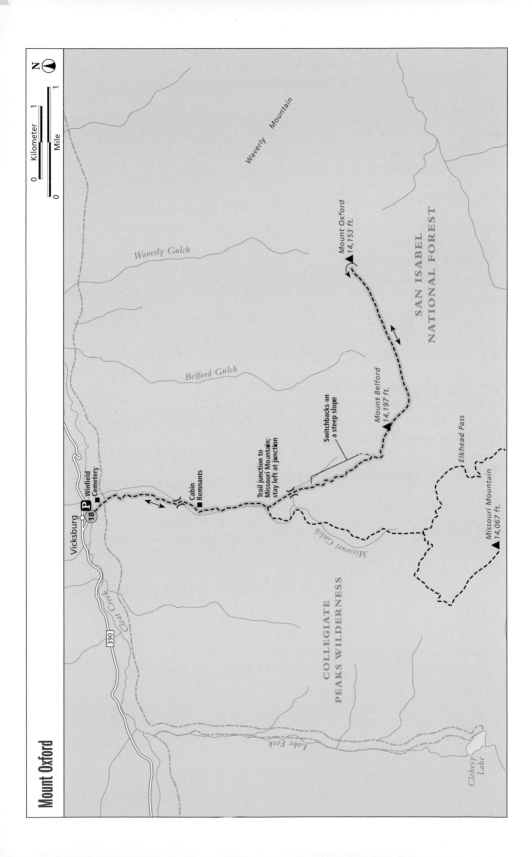

Mount Oxford

N

0 Kilometer 1

0 Mile 1

Vicksburg

390

Cheat Creek

18

P Winfield Cemetery

Cabin Remnants

Trail junction to Missouri Mountain; stay left at junction

Switchbacks on a steep slope

Waverly Gulch

Belford Gulch

Waverly Mountain

Mount Oxford 14,153 ft.

Mount Belford 14,197 ft.

SAN ISABEL NATIONAL FOREST

Elkhead Pass

Missouri Gulch

COLLEGIATE PEAKS WILDERNESS

Lake Fork

Missouri Mountain 14,067 ft.

Clohesy Lake

to a 13,490-foot saddle at 4.25 miles then start climbing up an easy-to-hike ridge. At just over 14,000 feet and 4.8 miles, pass a small false summit and hike the remaining 0.1 mile to the 14,153-foot summit.

Celebrate by looking in every direction—except back, where Belford pops up like a mosquito bite out of an impressive landscape of cirques and ridges. Oxford is a mountain that reveals the breadth and scope of the Rockies as mountain peaks leap out of the north—south spine of the Continental Divide.

Miles and Directions

0.0 Start at the trailhead at the southwest side of the lot. Go 150 feet and cross Clear Creek on a metal bridge.

0.3 Begin switchbacks in a forest.

0.6 Exit switchbacks and enter the east side of Missouri Gulch.

1.0 Cross a stream.

1.3 Pass cabin remnants on the left and enter into alpine meadow.

1.8 Stay left at a trail split, heading toward Belford's northwestern spine.

2.0 Cross a stream. Gain the northwest ridge of Belford and start a switchback ascent of the ridge.

3.4 Reach a flat spot below the summit push.

3.6 Peak out. Head southeast.

3.8 Turn left toward the saddle between Oxford and Belford.

4.25 Reach bottom of the saddle. Start climbing.

4.8 Pass a false summit.

5.0 Reach Mount Oxford's summit at 14,153 feet. Return via same route.

10.0 Arrive back at the trailhead.

Hiking Information

Closest Outfitters

The Trailhead, 707 US 24 North, Buena Vista; (719) 395-8001; thetrailheadco.com

Salida Mountain Sports, 110 North F St., Salida; (719) 539-4400; salidamountain sports.com

Great Pre- or Post-Mountain Eats and Drinks

Eddyline Brewing Restaurant, 926 S Main St., Buena Vista; (719) 966-6017; eddyline brewing.com

Deerhammer Distilling Company, 321 E Main St., Buena Vista; (719) 395-9464; deer hammer.com

Moonlight Pizza & Brewpub, 242 F St., Salida; (719) 539-4277; moonlightpizza.biz

Here's the Scoop, 215 F St., Salida; (719) 539-9727

19 Mount Shavano

14,229' (NGVD29), 14,236' (NAVD88), 17th highest

Mount Shavano is one of the most visible fourteeners in the Arkansas River Basin. It's also one of the most divine, given that its eastern face is graced with an angel. The mountain is on the harder side of easy and has a lot to enjoy. It starts in a beautiful forest filled with aspen and conifers. This peak gets into some Class 2 scampering near the top and shares some trail space with the Colorado Trail. The standard route to Tabeguache Peak (14,155 feet) is also over Shavano, but it makes for a long day with a lot of elevation gain.

Start: Blank Gulch Trailhead
Distance: 8.6 miles
Hiking time: 7 to 9 hours
Elevation gain: 4,480 feet
Difficulty: Class 1, Class 2
Trail surface: Dirt, scree
Trailhead elevation: 9,740 feet
Camping: Backcountry
Fees: None

Best seasons: Spring through fall; winter sports via Angel of Shavano route
Maps: USGS Mount Antero, St. Elmo, Garfield; National Geographic Trails Illustrated #130: Salida, St. Elmo, Shavano Peak
Nearest towns: Poncha Springs, Salida
Trail contacts: San Isabel National Forest, (719) 553-1400; USDA Forest Service, Salida Ranger District, (719) 539-3591; Chaffee County Sheriff's Office, (719) 539-2596

Finding the trailhead: From the intersection of US 50 and US 285 near Poncha Springs, head north on US 285. Turn left (west) onto CR 140. At 2.9 miles make a right onto FR 250, heading north-northwest for 4 miles. Veer left onto FR 252 and drive for another 3.2 miles to a dirt parking lot. The trail begins at the northeast end of the parking lot. GPS: N38° 35.83' / W106° 11.81'

The Hike

Mount Shavano is the southernmost fourteener in the Sawatch Range. It's also one of two divine fourteeners in Colorado, thanks to the prominent Angel of Shavano that graces its eastern flanks. The other is the Mount of the Holy Cross, which is the northern end cap to the same range. It fits, because this whole range is blessed by nature.

Shavano's angel spreads her wings each spring as the snow melts. One legend attributed to Native Americans but of unsure origin is that a chief's daughter pleaded for rain during a drought. A deity, hearing her pleas, transformed her into the angel that feeds the region water as the snow melts.

Shavano is one of three fourteeners in the Indian Group, along with Tabeguache and Mount Antero (14,269 feet). It's also one of four or five fourteeners named for Native Americans. Uncompahgre (14,309 feet) is the fourth. Huron (14,003

Hiking toward Mount Shavano on the Colorado Trail

feet) also was likely named for a Native American nation, but its naming origins are unknown. Ironically none of them are in Rocky Mountain National Park Indian Peaks Wilderness.

Shavano was named for Chief Shavano, who led the Tabeguache band of Utes in the 1850s to the 1870s. He worked as peacemaker with European settlers. The mountain was named Shavano on a map by 1875, and the US Board of Geographical Names made it official in 1907, despite the Wheeler survey calling it Usher Peak.

The hike starts just northwest of the parking lot and the restrooms. At 0.1 mile take a right at the junction with the Colorado Trail and hike north along the fence. At 0.25 mile come to a trail junction and turn left, following the sign to Shavano. Continue heading northwest on a wide dirt trail as the trail begins a pretty steady ascent that will continue for most of the climb. Heading farther into the forest, the trail becomes narrower and a little harder to see, but many trees are marked, and the wear of foot traffic is evident on roots and rocks. In some places streams may course across the trail in spring.

At 1.4 miles (10,800 feet) cross Squaw Creek. Cross the creek two more times and head northwest, reaching 11,000 feet at 1.8 miles. At 11,240 feet come to the first sharp right at a talus field; continue heading northeast before curving back around.

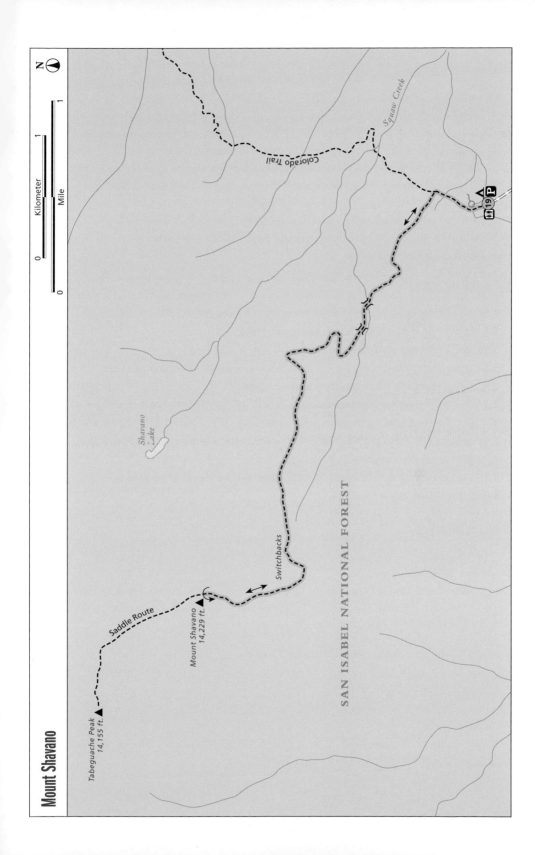

Mount Shavano

Tabeguache Peak
14,155 ft.

Saddle Route

Mount Shavano
14,229 ft.

Switchbacks

Shavano Lake

Squaw Creek

Colorado Trail

SAN ISABEL NATIONAL FOREST

N

Kilometer
0   1

Mile
0   1

At 1.9 miles reach one of the flatter parts of the hike, which might be a good place to camp.

Come close to Shavano's east ridge near a clearing at 2.3 miles and 11,800 feet then make a dramatic cut back to the left (south). Shortly afterward turn right (west) as the trees thin out. At 2.7 miles and 12,220 feet, exit the forest and start hiking across a good but rocky trail that heads toward Shavano's eastern slope. At 3.4 miles and 12,840 feet the trail starts switching back toward the south ridge of Shavano. Take a right and head north at 13,350 feet and 3.7 miles to gain the broad saddle that leads to the top; scramble the last 0.6 mile to the summit.

From the peak the closest mountains are to the north, Tabeguache is just 1 mile away. Antero is just a few miles away over the next major ridge; a dirt road can be seen going up its southern flanks.

Miles and Directions

0.0 Start at the northwest corner of the parking lot and follow the trail to the fence.
0.1 Take a right and join the Colorado Trail heading north.
0.25 Take a left heading northwest.
1.4 Cross Squaw Creek. In the next 0.1 mile the trail crosses the creek two more times.
1.8 Take a sharp right near a talus field heading northeast.
2.3 Take a sharp left heading south then turn back to the right and head west.
2.7 Exit forest and head to Shavano's eastern slope.
3.4 Gain the face of the eastern slope and follow switchbacks to the broad southern saddle.
3.7 Gain the saddle and scramble to the peak.
4.3 Gain the peak. Return via the same route. (***Option:*** Head over to Tabeguache.)
8.6 Arrive back at the trailhead.

Hiking Information

Closest Outfitters

The Trailhead, 707 US 24 North, Buena Vista; (719) 395-8001; thetrailheadco.com
Salida Mountain Sports, 110 North F St., Salida; (719) 539-4400; salidamountain
    sports.com

Great Pre- or Post-Mountain Eats and Drinks

Eddyline Brewing Restaurant, 926 S Main St., Buena Vista; (719) 966-6017; eddy
    linebrewing.com
Deerhammer Distilling Company, 321 E Main St., Buena Vista; (719) 395-9464; deer
    hammer.com
Moonlight Pizza & Brewpub, 242 F St., Salida; (719) 539-4277; moonlightpizza.biz
Here's the Scoop, 215 F St., Salida; (719) 539-9727

20 Mount Princeton

14,197' (NGVD29), 14,205' (NAVD88), 18th highest

Mount Princeton is a prominent peak easily visible from the Arkansas River Valley below. It's the southernmost collegiate peak and the only one not in the Collegiate Peak Wilderness. It's an impressive but relatively easy to climb Class 2 hike. Having a 4WD or high-clearance vehicle is an asset, as it can cut more than 7 miles off a round-trip hike. The mountain is famous for its chalk cliffs and has some nearby (very commercial) hot springs to soak in after a long day of trekking.

Start: Mount Princeton 4WD trailhead (*Option:* Mount Princeton Road 2WD trailhead)

Distance: 4WD trailhead: 6.4 miles (*Option:* Mount Princeton Road: 13.8 miles)

Hiking time: 4WD trailhead: 7 to 8 hours (*Option:* Mount Princeton Road: about 14 hours)

Elevation gain: 4WD trailhead: 3,180 feet (*Option:* Mount Princeton Road: 7,340 feet)

Difficulty: Class 2

Trail surface: Mostly talus

Trailhead elevation: 4WD trailhead: 11,020 feet (*Option:* Mount Princeton Road: 8,900 feet)

Camping: Backcountry camping

Fees: None

Best seasons: Spring through fall

Maps: USGS Mount Antero, St. Elmo, Buena Vista West, Mount Yale; National Geographic Trails Illustrated #129: Buena Vista, Collegiate Peaks; #130: Salida, St. Elmo, Mount Shavano

Nearest town: Buena Vista

Trail contacts: San Isabel National Forest, Leadville Ranger District, (719) 486-0749; Chaffee County Sheriff's Office, (719) 539-2596

Trail tips: After the 4WD trailhead, particularly in late summer or fall, there are no reliable water sources on this mountain, so bring plenty of water. Don't let the clouds roll in too quickly. This region of the Rockies scrapes the bottoms of clouds and attracts a lot of lighting.

Finding the trailhead: From CR 306 and CO 285, head southwest on CR 306 for 0.6 mile. Turn left onto CR 321. Go 6.7 miles and turn right onto CR 322 (Mount Princeton Road). Continue 0.9 mile and take a slight right, staying on CR 322 until you reach a parking lot. (*Option:* This is the 2WD trailhead for Mount Princeton, 8,900 feet. GPS: 2WD trailhead: N38° 44.40'/W106° 10.54)

Trucks, jeeps, and other 4WD vehicles can continue on this rugged road for up to another 3.6 miles. Continue up the main dirt road. There are some parking and camping spots close to the towers and just beyond them. The 4WD trailhead is at a fence at 11,020 feet. The road does continue, but there is little to no parking along the road until 0.5 mile after the trail branches off.

Note: On busy days many vehicles are sawing gears going up or down this steep, twisty, bumpy one-lane road, making traffic jams inevitable. What should be a 20- or 30-minute trip could turn into an hour or more of frustrating, creative vehicle shuffling. It goes by more quickly with patience, cooperation with other drivers, and a music player or good conversation. Do not park vehicles on the broad hairpin turns, which allow vehicles to pass each other. The 4WD road also is the trail. Please be considerate of climbers going up or down it. GPS: 4WD trailhead: N38° 44.71'/W11° 12.38'

The Hike

Though first called Chalk Mountain, Mount Princeton was likely named by, ironically, Harvard University graduate Henry Gannet, who was with the Wheeler Survey in 1873. The mountain was likely first climbed by Native Americans or grubby miners, as the Hortense Mine (12,000 feet) was discovered before Princeton geology professor William Libbey Jr. made the first recorded ascent of the peak on July 17, 1877.

Besides its dominance in the landscape, particularly when snowcapped, Mount Princeton's most impressive feature is the Chalk Cliffs, which are not chalk at all but rather a crumbling gray-white quartz monzonite that was formed roughly 65 million years ago during the Laramide orogeny as was the rest of this mountain.

Legend has it that Spaniards from New Mexico raided a Native American village in 1780, absconded with the booty to Colorado, and hid the treasure in the Chalk Cliffs. No treasure has been found there, and given the crumbling nature of the cliffs, it's not likely to be found, if it ever existed.

Starting at the 4WD trailhead, head northwest on the dirt road for 1.25 miles (11,820 feet). Shortly after exiting the forest, take a short set of stone stairs on the right (northwest) side of the road that lead to the remainder of the trail. The trail quickly cuts back to the northeast then zags back to the northwest.

From here the easy-to-follow trail sweeps across the top of four gullies that can contain snow into summer—particularly the fourth, northeast-facing gully. The second and most prominent gulley passes under 13,300-foot Tigger Peak. Princeton quickly comes into view. By about 12,100 feet and 1.6 miles, the trail is largely above alpine meadows, though still easy to see and follow, requires hiking across some patches of scree.

Ignoring an old trail that cuts across Princeton's face, at 2.25 miles and 12,700 feet follow the trail left (south) and up a series of switchbacks to reach Princeton's east slopes at 2.5 miles and 13,040 feet; turn right. From here the trail resumes heading northwest along Princeton's southeastern ridge. The prize is less than 1 mile away on a relatively easy traverse with little exposure. At roughly 1,3230 feet and 2.75 miles there's a short flat spot that could be ideal for a quick break before taking on the last 0.5 mile and 900 feet of elevation gain, which requires Class 2 scrambling. At 3.2 miles and 14,197 feet reach the peak on this, the backbone of the continent.

The summit isn't giant, but there is ample space for numerous parties to hang out before afternoon storms roll in. Return by the same route.

Miles and Directions

0.0 Start at the 4WD trailhead. (***Option:*** Start at the 2WD trailhead, adding maybe 7 miles to the overall distance.)

1.25 Climb the stone stairs on the right side of road.

2.25 Turn left and take the trail up switchbacks to Princeton's ridge.

2.5 Reach Princeton's ridge at 13,040 feet.

Mount Princeton

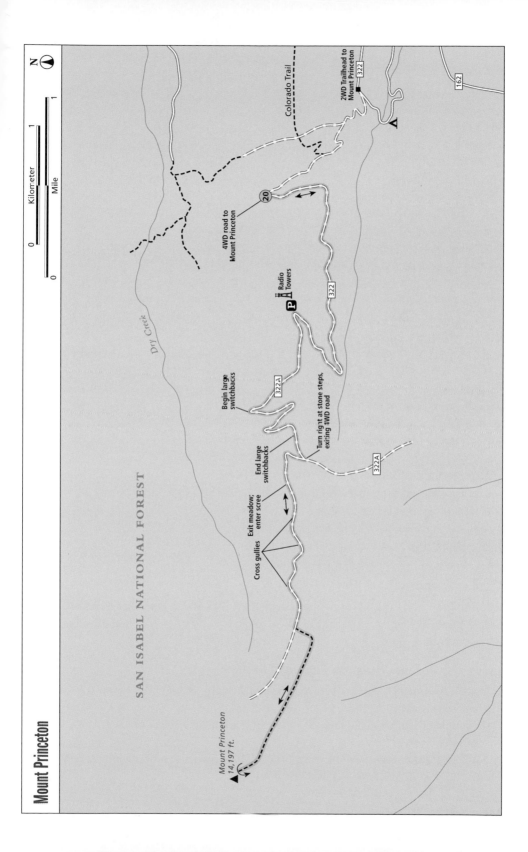

SAN ISABEL NATIONAL FOREST

Dry Creek

Mount Princeton
14,197 ft.

Cross gullies

Exit meadow;
enter scree

End large
switchbacks

Begin large
switchbacks

322A

Turn right at stone steps,
exiting 4WD road

322A

Radio
Towers

P

322

4WD road to
Mount Princeton

20

Colorado Trail

2WD Trailhead to
Mount Princeton

322

162

N

Kilometer
0   1

Mile
0   1

Mount Princeton and its famous Chalk Cliffs from the Colorado Trail

2.75 Reach a short flat spot before the final hump of Princeton.

3.2 Summit. Retrace the route back down.

6.4 Arrive back at the 4WD trailhead.

Hiking Information

Closest Outfitters

The Trailhead, 707 US 24 North, Buena Vista; (719) 395-8001; thetrailheadco.com

Salida Mountain Sports, 110 North F St., Salida; (719) 539-4400; salidamountain sports.com

Great Pre- or Post-Mountain Eats and Drinks

Eddyline Brewing Restaurant, 926 S Main St., Buena Vista; (719) 966-6017; eddy linebrewing.com

Deerhammer Distilling Company, 321 E Main St., Buena Vista; (719) 395-9464; deer hammer.com

Moonlight Pizza & Brewpub, 242 F St., Salida; (719) 539-4277; moonlightpizza.biz

Here's the Scoop, 215 F St., Salida; (719) 539-9727

21 Mount Massive

14,421' (NGVD29), 14,428' (NAVD88), 2nd highest

Located in its eponymous wilderness area, Mount Massive is aptly named. At 14,421 feet it falls short of 14,431-foot Mount Elbert, which is its closest neighbor. Still, the mountain is unique. No other fourteener in Colorado, or the United States, has more acreage at or above 14,000 feet. In fact, Massive has five distinct summits over 14,000 feet along a 3-mile summit ridge. Climbing the standard, Class 2 route up Massive's east slope takes trekkers only to the main peak, but ambitious climbers can summit all five of the 14,000-foot summits in one day with only a little Class 3 climbing.

Start: Mount Massive Trailhead
Distance: 13.4 miles
Hiking time: 8 to 10 hours
Elevation gain: 4,350 feet
Difficulty: Class 2
Trail surface: Dirt, scree
Trailhead elevation: 10,070 feet
Camping: Campsites near the trailhead; backcountry
Fees: None
Best seasons: Spring through fall

Maps: USGS Mount Massive, Mount Champion, Leadville South; National Geographic Trails Illustrated #127: Aspen, Independence Pass
Nearest town: Leadville
Trail contacts: San Isabel National Forest, Leadville Ranger District, (719) 486-0749; Lake County Sheriff's Office, (719) 486-1249
Trail tips: This is a long trail and can be windy and cold. Be prepared for temperatures in the 50s in summer. Bring lots of water, at least 2 liters; there's little if any available on the trail, especially if you don't have water treatment.

Finding the trailhead: From the intersection of US 24 and CO 300 south of Leadville, head west on CO 300. In 0.8 mile turn left onto CR 11. Go 1.3 miles and turn right onto the dirt road toward Halfmoon Creek, which is still CR 11. Pass the Elbert Creek Campground at 4.8 miles. Reach the destination at 5.5 miles. GPS: N39° 09.11'/W106° 25.15'

The Hike

This giant peak—by some measures the largest damned fourteener out there—has more land over 14,000 feet than any mountain in the continental United States, but to some locals' chagrin, Elbert still has it beat in height. In the 1930s locals rallied to pile enough rocks on its peak to make it taller than Elbert, but Elbert's fans retaliated by trekking to Massive and knocking their rock dreams down.

Massive is the only mountain in Colorado to have five summits above 14,000 feet. In addition to Massive's peak, they are North Massive (14,340 feet), Massive Green (14,300 feet), Point (14,169 feet), and South Massive (14,132 feet).

The mountain was named by Henry Gannett of the Hayden Survey in 1873, who also made the first documented climb of the behemoth. The name stuck despite

Mount Massive's peaks basking in morning sun, taken from Mount Elbert

numerous attempts to change it. Other proposed names were McKinley, Churchill, and Gannett.

Roughly half of the hiking on this epic trail across this 1.75-billion-year-old beast is in a forest rife with lodgepole pine. Higher up, Engelmann spruce and subalpine fir flaunt their branches before climbers reach tree line at nearly 12,000 feet.

The Colorado Trail joins the trail to Massive as it begins on the northeast side of the parking lot near Half-moon Creek. The good dirt trail heads northeast through a relatively flat patch of forest and quickly moves away from the creek. Shortly after 0.7 mile and 10,450 feet the trail turns left and begins heading on a northern trajectory.

Cross a stream at 1.25 miles and 10,770 feet as the trail turns right. Shortly afterward it turns back to the left as the initial climb eases. At 1.9 miles cross another stream, and at 2.3 miles and 10,830 feet cross South Willow Creek. Cross Willow Creek at 2.9 miles and 11,000 feet.

The trail flattens out after the Willow Creek Crossing for about 0.25 mile. Then, at 3.3 miles and 11,260 feet, turn left (west) at the junction on the Mount Massive Trail. From here on out the trail goes up. At 11,630 feet and 3.75 miles the forest starts thinning, entering flowery alpine meadows dotted with willow thickets and revealing Massive's large, humped ridge.

At 4.2 miles and 11,850 feet enter a series of switchbacks. Exit the switchbacks at 4.6 miles and 12,160 feet. Continue up the hill to roughly 12,400 feet at 4.8 miles,

Mount Massive

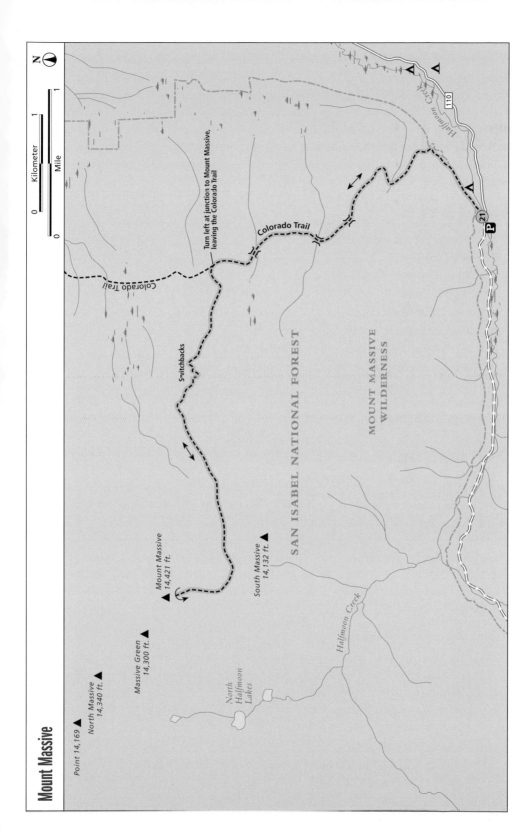

Point 14,169 ▲

North Massive ▲
14,340 ft.

Massive Green ▲
14,300 ft.

Mount Massive ▲
14,421 ft.

South Massive ▲
14,132 ft.

North
Halfmoon
Lakes

Halfmoon Creek

SAN ISABEL NATIONAL FOREST

MOUNT MASSIVE
WILDERNESS

Switchbacks

Turn left at junction to Mount Massive,
leaving the Colorado Trail

Colorado Trail

Colorado Trail

Halfmoon Creek

110

21

P

N

0   1   Kilometer

0   Mile   1

when most of the summit comes into view. It is still nearly 2 miles away across a long, lovely basin. At 6.25 miles and 14,000 feet, gain the saddle between South Massive to the southeast and Massive to the north. The peak is now less than 0.5 mile away. Turn right and head up Massive's south ridge, scrambling up a rocky path. At 6.5 miles reach the top of a small false summit at 14,398 feet; continue on the trail and start ascending to the actual 14,421-foot summit at 6.7 miles. Enjoy the conquest—and don't think about the long trek down. Enjoy the vast panorama of fourteeners to the south, west, and north.

Miles and Directions

0.0 Start at Mount Massive Trailhead.

0.7 Head north.

1.25 Cross a stream as trail heads right.

1.9 Cross a stream.

2.3 Cross South Willow Creek.

2.9 Cross Willow Creek.

3.3 Turn left (west) at the junction on the Mount Massive Trail.

3.75 Enter flowery alpine meadows and willow thickets.

4.2 Reach switchbacks.

4.6 Exit switchbacks.

4.8 Most of the summit is in view.

6.25 Gain the saddle between South Massive and Massive.

6.5 Reach the top of a small false summit.

6.7 Reach the summit. Retrace your route.

13.4 Arrive back at the trailhead.

Hiking Information

Closest Outfitters

Leadville Outdoors, 225 Harrison Ave., Leadville; (719) 486-7392; leadvilleoutdoors
.com

Great Pre- or Post-Mountain Spots

As of 2015 two breweries are under construction in Leadville, Two Mile Brewing and
Periodic Brewing. The town had a distillery, but it was closed as of this writing—
emblematic of this boom-and-bust town.

Silver Dollar Saloon, 315 Harrison Ave., Leadville; (719) 486-9914; silverdollarsaloon
.com. An authentic saloon, established in 1879!

Golden Burro Cafe & Lounge, 710 Harrison Ave., Leadville; (719) 486-1239; golden
burro.com

Tennessee Pass Cafe, 222 Harrison Ave., Leadville; (719) 486-8101; tennesseepasscafe.com

22 Pikes Peak

14,110' (NGVD29), 14,115' (NAVD88), 30th highest

Pikes Peak has gained the name "America's Peak." It's one of the most prominent peaks in Colorado and the easternmost fourteener in the state. Rising 7,800 feet from base to peak, Pikes has the biggest altitude gain of all the Colorado fourteeners. It's a peak of contradictions—geographically farthest from any other fourteener and simultaneously the closest to civilization. A road climbs to the top, yet the standard route up the peak is a more than 20-mile marathon of a Class 1 trek. But climbers can eat at a fancy restaurant up top and might be able to catch a train ride down.

Start: Barr Trailhead (Forest Service Trail 620)
Distance: 24 miles
Hiking time: 14 to 16 hours
Elevation gain: 7,430 feet
Difficulty: Class 1
Trail surface: Dirt, scree
Trailhead elevation: 6,680 feet
Camping: Backcountry camping, shelter at 9 miles into hike, or a stay (fee) at the Barr Camp
Fees: None

Best seasons: Late June through late fall
Maps: USGS Pikes Peak, Manitou Springs, Woodland Park, Cascade; National Geographic Trails Illustrated #137: Pikes Peak, Cañon City
Nearest towns: Manitou Springs, Colorado Springs
Trail contacts: USDA Forest Service, Pikes Peak District, (719) 636-1602; El Paso County Sheriff's Office, (719) 390-5555; Barr Camp (barrcamp.com)

Finding the trailhead: The trailhead is off Ruxton Avenue, in Manitou Springs, above the Pikes Peak Cog Railroad Depot. Some visitors ride to the summit by auto, bus, or cog railroad and hike down the trail. GPS: N38° 51.34'/W104° 56.03'

The Hike

Pikes Peak is an ultra-prominent peak (a summit with more than 4,921 feet of vertical prominence from any other peak on the same mountain), one of three in Colorado, along with Mount Elbert (14,431 feet) and Blanca Peak (14,345 feet). The mountain has a long and storied history. Pikes was first described by Zebulon Pike in 1806; he called it Grand Peak. He attempted to climb the peak but failed. The first documented summit of the mountain was by a party led by botanist Edwin James of the Stephen H. Long Expedition in 1820.

The mountain, made up of 1-billion-year-old granite, is among the most popular in Colorado. The USDA Forest Service estimates that more than 150,000 people attempt to climb Pikes Peak via the Barr Trail every year. Fully 500,000 people visit the mountain annually. People run it, bike it, drive it, climb it, motorcycle it—pretty much get to the top just about any ol' way they can.

Pikes Peak ascent finish line. Lee Mauney

The Barr Trail was built and completed in 1921 by Fred Barr, following his Christmas ascent of the mountain via the East Slope route in 1918. Given its popularity, the trail now needs annual attention and it gets it thanks to the Friends of the Peak, which does annual trail maintenance, and, more recently, the AdAmAn Club. There are a number of old metal signs along the trail with mileage figures—don't rely on them for an accurate count.

The trail to the peak is difficult mainly because of its length. It's strenuous and has difficult parts, yes, but this is still a Class 1 hike. The trail is often thought of as having four segments. Each segment has one difficult and one easier part.

From the Barr Trailhead head northwest. Immediately encounter a series of switchbacks called the "Ws" that will last for the first 1.8 miles to 7,960 feet. The trail levels out for a bit and the switchbacks ease up. At 2.7 miles and 8,575 feet the trail passes under a natural rock arch formed by two giant boulders leaning up against each other. Shortly after, the trail hits two switchbacks then passes a junction that leads to the old Mount Manitou incline railway. Stay straight at the junction.

Cross No Name Creek at 8,720 feet and 3.0 miles in a gully in the forest, passing a sign that reads "Pikes Peak Summit 9.5, Barr Camp 3.5." This creek is often dry by August.

From here the wide trail starts an ascent and goes through a couple of switchbacks then mellows out, at some points descending a little through the picturesque forest. This is the mellowest part of the climb. Continue on and at 4.6 miles and 9,450 feet reach a sign that says "Pikes Peak 7.8, Top of Incline 2.5." At 5.5 miles cross a small stream. In another 0.25 mile continue straight past a sign that reads "Barr Trail Elev. 9,800', Barr Camp 0.5, Pikes Peak Summit 6.5, Manitou Springs 6.5."

At 6.25 miles and 10,160 feet reach Barr Camp on the right (north) side of the trail. This is halfway up Pikes Peak. The camp is staffed year-round, and climbers can stay here if they've reserved a spot. It has two cabins, two lean-to shelters, and an A-frame for weary climbers. The camp has some amenities, including propane stoves, some bottled water for sale, and water that can be filtered. Climbers can also arrange to have a meal prepared.

After passing Barr Camp the incline increases and there are no more pleasant flat spots. Continue straight on the trail, passing a junction to Elk Park Trail.

The trail comes close to Cabin Creek at 6.6 miles and 10,360 feet; it then heads right in a northerly direction and starts to climb at a steeper incline.

Cross a couple of switchbacks and at 7.3 miles and 10,840 feet reach a sign on the northwest side of a switchback that says, "Pikes Peak Summit 4.8, Bottomless Pitt 2.4." Turn back to the left (southwest) and continue climbing. This is a nearly mile-long zag on a series of fifteen switchbacks that lead above tree line and to the A-frame shelter at 11,900 feet. Continue up the switchbacks of varying sizes until reaching the fifteenth at 8.8 miles and 11,900 feet. Find a sign that reads "Timberline Shelter, Pike National Forest" and a short trail on the left that leads to the shelter—one last resting spot before the remaining slog above tree line. This also is near the so-called Dismal Forest—named for the remains of trees that burned in a forest fire in 1910.

After passing the sign for the A-frame, continue hiking on a couple more switch-backs and reach an incorrect sign that reads "Barr Trail Elev 11,500', Pikes Peak Summit 3." Don't worry, the elevation is wrong. It's closer to 12,000 feet at this point.

The trail begins crisscrossing the rocky southern face of Pikes Peaks as it gains more than 700 feet of elevation in just over 1 mile.

At 9.2 miles, at a point just below the southern ridge, is a sign that says, "Barr Trail Elev 12,700', Pikes Peak 2." The trail then cuts back to the southwest and begins crossing the broad eastern cirque of Pikes. Reach the southern ridge of the cirque at 10.7 miles and 13,275 feet; take a short switchback up and reach a sign that says "Peak 1 MI, Elevation 13,300'." The route sews up this ridge on seven switchbacks then crosses back over the upper part of the cirque twice before reaching one of Colorado's and Pikes' most infamous challenges: the "16 Golden Stairs" as the sign proclaims at 13,770 feet and 11.4 miles. From here the trail zigs and zags back and forth under the summit block a stunning and exhausting thirty-two times. Near the top is a plaque honoring Barr. Then you reenter humanity and tourists and everything you just spent the day forgetting. The highpoint is west of the summit house

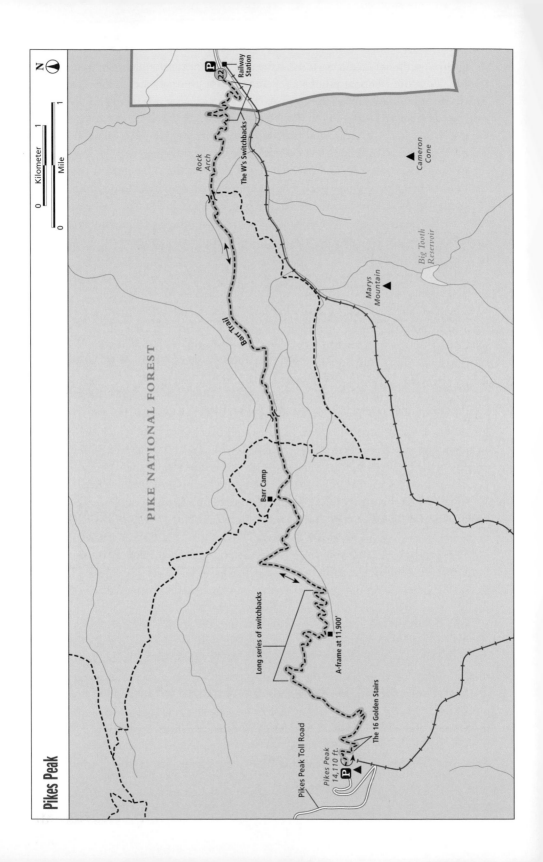

Pikes Peak

N

0 Kilometer 1
0 Mile 1

PIKE NATIONAL FOREST

Rock Arch

The W's Switchbacks

Railway Station

Barr Trail

Barr Camp

Long series of switchbacks

A-frame at 11,900'

The 16 Golden Stairs

Pikes Peak Toll Road

Pikes Peak 14,110 ft.

Cameron Cone

Marys Mountain

Big Tooth Reservoir

and is marked with a sign atop a rock monument. Return via the same route, or try to catch a ride back down on the train. Go ahead; no one's looking.

Miles and Directions

0.0 Begin at the Barr Trailhead.

1.8 Reach the end of the "W's."

2.75 Pass under a rock arch.

3.0 Cross No Name Creek and pass a sign for "Pikes Peak Summit 9.5, Barr Camp 3.5."

5.5 Cross stream.

6.25 Reach Barr Camp.

7.3 Cut back to the left at sign that reads, "Pikes Peak Summit 4.8, Bottomless Pitt 2.4"; begin switchbacks.

8.8 Reach sign for "Timberline Shelter, Pike National Forest" and a short trail on the left that leads to the shelter.

9.2 Reach sign that says "Barr Trail Elev 12,700', Pikes Peak 2" and begin crossing the eastern cirque of Pikes.

10.7 Begin the next series of switchbacks.

11.4 Reach the "16 Golden Stairs," a series of thirty-two switchbacks.

12.0 Summit Pikes Peak. Return via same route, or take one of the other methods of transportation back down.

24.0 Arrive back at the trailhead.

Hiking Information

Closest Outfitters

Mountain Chalet, 226 N Tejon St., Colorado Springs; (719) 633-0732; mtnchalet .com

Gearonimo Sports, 2727 Palmer Park Blvd., Colorado Springs; (719) 465-2450; gearonimo sports.com

Great Pre- or Post-Mountain Spots

Phantom Canyon Brewing Co., 2 E Pikes Peak Ave., Colorado Springs; (719) 635-2800; phantomcanyon.com

Manitou Brewing Co., 725 Manitou Ave., Manitou Springs; (719) 282-7709; manitou -brewing.com

Trinity Brewing Co., 1466 Garden of the Gods Rd. #184, Colorado Springs; (719) 634- 0029; trinitybrew.com

23 Mount Columbia

14,073' (NGVD29), 14,079' (NAVD88), 35th highest

Mount Columbia is one of the five collegiate peaks in the San Isabel National Forest's Collegiate Peak Wilderness. It's commonly climbed with its closest neighbor and bigger brother, Mount Harvard (14,420 feet). When climbed alone, the standard route up Columbia is up its west slopes via the North Cottonwood Trailhead. However, the western slopes of Columbia are badly eroded, and there is no definite path up the scree field, making it a Class 2 scramble to the top. To help keep erosion to a minimum, it's recommended that hikers not follow the exact same path.

Start: North Cottonwood Trailhead
Distance: 10.5 miles
Hiking time: 8.5 to 10 hours
Elevation gain: 4,190 feet
Difficulty: Class 2
Trail surface: Dirt, scree
Trailhead elevation: 9,880 feet
Camping: Backcountry camping
Fees: None
Best seasons: Spring through fall

Maps: USGS Mount Harvard, Mount Yale, Harvard Lakes, Buena Vista West; National Geographic Trails Illustrated #129: Buena Vista, Collegiate Peaks
Nearest town: Buena Vista
Trail contacts: San Isabel National Forest, Leadville Ranger District, (719) 486-0749; Chaffee County Sheriff's Office, (719) 539-2596

Finding the trailhead: From the intersection of US 24 and CR 356 in Buena Vista, just north of Buena Vista, go west on CR 356 for 1.6 miles. Turn left onto CR 361 and drive for 3.6 miles. Turn right onto CR 365 and drive 2.3 miles to the end of the road. The trailhead is on the right; the trail takes off from the northwest side of the dirt lot. The road to the trailhead is a dirt road and gets rough, but driven carefully, many 2WD vehicles can make it. GPS: N38° 52.25'/W106° 15.96'

The Hike

Mount Columbia is probably the least climbed of the five collegiate fourteeners in Colorado—at least on its own anyhow. It's commonly climbed with Harvard because it's possible to avoid the eroded western slopes of the mountain, which are still considered the standard route. Making a solo climb out of it ensures some exposure and a lot of scree.

Roger Toll made the first recorded ascent of the mountain in 1916 and got to name it when he installed a bronze summit register at the time. In naming it for his alma matter, Columbia University, Toll followed a tradition set by J. D. Whitney, who named Yale and Harvard for schools he attended and taught at, respectively.

The standard route, at more than 10 miles long, warrants consideration of an overnight stay. Thankfully there are opportunities to camp out pretty high up in the

Hello, mountain goat! Looking across to Mount Columbia from Mount Harvard with Bear Lake on the right. LEE MAUNEY

backcountry, making it easier to get a night's rest before summiting this and perhaps Harvard in one day. There are plenty of flat spots as the trail meanders through the beautiful Horn Fork Basin.

From the parking lot the North Cottonwood Creek Trail (FT 1449) heads west, quickly crossing to the south side of North Cottonwood Creek. Follow this fantastic trail through conifers and the occasional aspen grove for 1.5 miles until coming across a trail junction at 10,320 feet. Stay right at the junction toward Horn Fork Basin and Bear Lake. From here the trail crosses to the north side of the creek then begins heading northwest on the Horn Fork Trail, still FT 1449, which leads to Horn Fork Basin and Bear Lake. At 3.4 miles and 11,330 feet take a right at the junction to Bear Lake. Stay on the trail until roughly 11,400 feet and 3.5 miles—near tree line. Take the trail that branches off to Columbia on the right. There are some good places to camp here; Horn Creek is west of the trail for filtering water.

Follow the trail as it begins to turn easterly and, at 3.7 miles, crosses a small gully and starts ascending rapidly above tree line. At 3.8 miles and 11,650 feet, exit tree line near a large rock formation. The path to Columbia's peak is relatively straight ahead, unfortunately across a mountain of rotten scree. Head up the slope, keeping close to a rock feature at 4.1 miles and 12,120 feet. Stay just north of the feature. When above

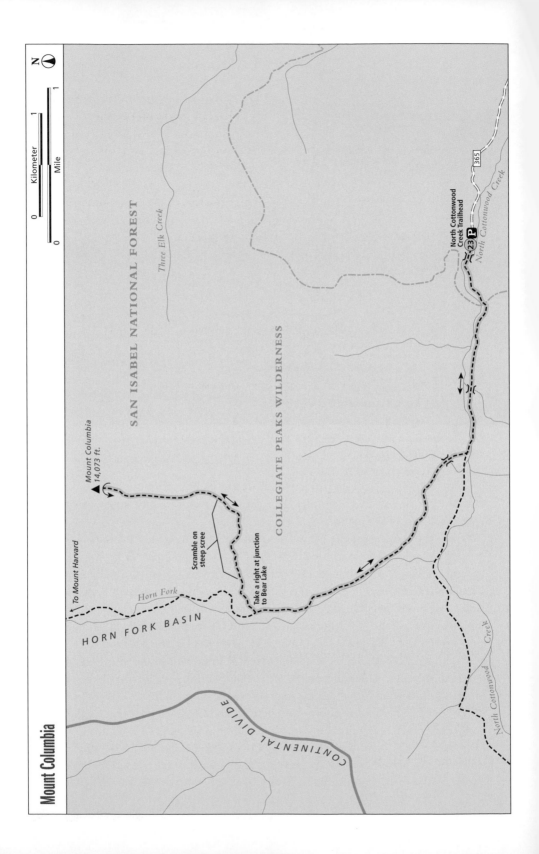

Mount Columbia

N

Kilometer
0   1

Mile
0   1

SAN ISABEL NATIONAL FOREST

Three Elk Creek

Mount Columbia
14,073 ft.

To Mount Harvard

Horn Fork

HORN FORK BASIN

Scramble on
steep scree

Take a right at junction
to Bear Lake

COLLEGIATE PEAKS WILDERNESS

CONTINENTAL DIVIDE

*North Cottonwood
Creek*

North Cottonwood
Creek Trailhead

P

23

365

North Cottonwood Creek

it, follow the trail remnants to the right (east). Switchback as needed, looking for the most stable ground.

After passing the rock formation, continue going northeast, following bits of trail as they become evident. The target is the 13,650-foot southeastern ridge of Columbia. To get there, hike over the rock formation and just over the lip of the next gully then turn left in a more northerly direction. Reach the ridge at 4.5 miles and turn left toward the peak. The summit is a 0.5-mile ridge walk from the southern ridge. Though scrambling up Columbia requires traversing some tough patches of scree, parts of the summit seem completely divorced from the challenges below. Just east of the crest, wildflowers grow on the eastern slope of the mountain and the ascent isn't too difficult. But returning down the same route gets pretty perilous on some of the scree sections. Try not to kick too many rocks loose—it causes erosion and can make it dangerous for others below.

Miles and Directions

0.0   Start at the trailhead and head west on the North Cottonwood Creek Trail (FT 1449).

1.5   Stay right at the junction toward Horn Fork Basin and Bear Lake.

3.4   Take a right at the junction to Bear Lake.

3.5   Take the trail to the right that branches off to Columbia.

3.7   Cross a small gully and ascend above tree line.

3.8   Exit tree line near a large rock formation.

4.1   Staying north of a large rock feature, get above it by following bits of trail.

4.5   Turn left toward the peak. The summit is a 0.5-mile ridge walk from the southern ridge.

5.25 Reach the summit. Return via the same route.

10.5 Arrive back at the trailhead.

Hiking Information

Closest Outfitters

The Trailhead, 707 US 24 North, Buena Vista; (719) 395-8001; thetrailheadco.com

Salida Mountain Sports, 110 North F St., Salida; (719) 539-4400; salidamountain sports.com

Great Pre- or Post-Mountain Eats and Drinks

Eddyline Brewing Restaurant, 926 S Main St., Buena Vista; (719) 966-6017; eddyline brewing.com

Deerhammer Distilling Company, 321 E Main St., Buena Vista; (719) 395-9464; deer hammer.com

Moonlight Pizza & Brewpub, 242 F St., Salida; (719) 539-4277; moonlightpizza.biz

Here's the Scoop, 215 F St., Salida; (719) 539-9727

24 Missouri Mountain

14,067' (NGVD29), 14,073' (NAVD88), 36th highest

In San Isabel National Forest and the Collegiate Peaks Wilderness, Missouri Mountain is the westernmost fourteener in the Missouri Gulch and is shorter than its peers, Mount Oxford (14,153 feet) and Mount Belford (14,197 feet). The mountain requires a long, 4.9-mile climb and some Class 2 scrambling. The basin below Missouri all the way up to the Elkhead Pass saddle is magnificent. It is a popular hike in spring and summer, and winter climbers may ski or board the mountain. Climbers can make a circuit of the whole group in one day, but most camp to climb all three.

Start: Missouri Gulch Trailhead
Distance: 9.9 miles
Hiking time: 8 to 9 hours
Elevation gain: 4,490 feet
Difficulty: Class 2
Trail surface: Dirt trail leading to scree
Trailhead elevation: 9,640 feet
Camping: No camping at the trailhead; primitive campsites along CR 390 and along the trail

Fees: None
Best seasons: Spring through fall
Maps: USGS Winfield, Harvard, Harvard Lakes; National Geographic Trails Illustrated #129: Buena Vista, Collegiate Peaks
Nearest town: Granite
Trail contacts: San Isabel National Forest, Leadville Ranger District, (719) 486-0749; Chaffee County Sheriff's Office, (719) 539-2596

Finding the trailhead: Head west from the junction of US 24 and CR 390, drive west on CR 390, a good dirt road, for 7.7 miles to Vicksburg. Stay left on CR 390 and turn left (south) into the parking lot. The trailhead is at the southwest corner of the lot. GPS: N38° 59.88'/W106° 22.50'

The Hike

Missouri Mountain was most likely first climbed by silver miners from Missouri, who arrived in the 1880s. Apparently they were fans of their homeland and named the gulch, the basin, and the mountain for their state because—let's be honest—the state and the mountain look nothing alike. Missouri's peak is a triangle of ridges that fan out like a throwing star.

Missouri Mountain is a slog; it's a long climb and a popular climb. Be prepared to see other people at the summit—especially in summer. The summit, at 14,067 feet, is more than 4,425 feet above the trailhead. That's a lot of altitude in a relatively short climb, and some of the switchbacks near the top and the final ridge offer more exposure than nearby Oxford and Belford, despite this being the shortest mountain in the group.

Missouri Mountain from Missouri Gulch

The main risk of exposure on Missouri Mountain is weather. Electric storms can roll into the Missouri Gulch quickly—and lightning bounds off the lower part of Missouri Mountain's northern ridge. If storm clouds come into the valley quickly in the afternoon, start hiking down. Because of the elevation gain and the potential for storms, it's a good idea to start this mountain close to dawn if hiking from the parking lot. If planning to do all three in the basin over a couple of days, there are plenty of areas to camp in the basin; follow Leave No Trace principles.

The trail to the peak begins easily enough at the southwest end of the parking area. Cross over Clear Creek at about 150 feet and enter into a coniferous forest of spruce and fir. Shortly thereafter pass a child's gravestone behind a fence—the remains of an abandoned graveyard for miners and their families. At 0.3 mile reach the first switchbacks, which wind through the forest on an easy-to-follow trail that gains elevation rapidly. At 0.6 mile and 10,375 feet the trail stops switching back as it enters the west side of Missouri Gulch. You can hear a stream babbling below. The trail etches the east side of the gulch until it crosses over the stream at 10,800 feet and 1.0 mile. The trail climbs up the west side of the gulch and reenters thicker forest before turning southeasterly.

Hiking toward Missouri Mountain from Mount Belford

At 1.3 miles and 11,280 feet find the remains of an old cabin on the left. The trail immediately opens onto a fantastic alpine meadow. Belford comes into view on the left; the hefty flanks of Missouri Mountain are to the right. Continue on the clear trail. (On many mountains the trail might've disappeared by now, but the Colorado Fourteeners Initiative and volunteers completed some excellent trail work on it in 1996.)

At 1.8 miles and 11,600 feet veer right at the trail junction to Missouri Mountain. From here the trail continues to follow the stream it's been chasing since leaving the first switchbacks. It begins crossing the shallow stream at 2.0 miles before ascending a small hill. Continue hiking south on the excellent trail into the upper basin of Missouri Gulch, with Missouri Mountain dead ahead. At 3.4 miles and 12,600 feet stay right (west) at the Elkhead Pass trail junction. Follow the trail up Missouri's western face, following a series of switchbacks. At 3.6 miles and 12,820 feet the trail turns right, heading northeast at an easier incline. At 3.9 miles it cuts back to the left, heading south, and at 4.1 miles zags back shortly before reaching the ridge crest at 13,700 feet and 4.2 miles. From here the trail becomes more rugged and requires some Class

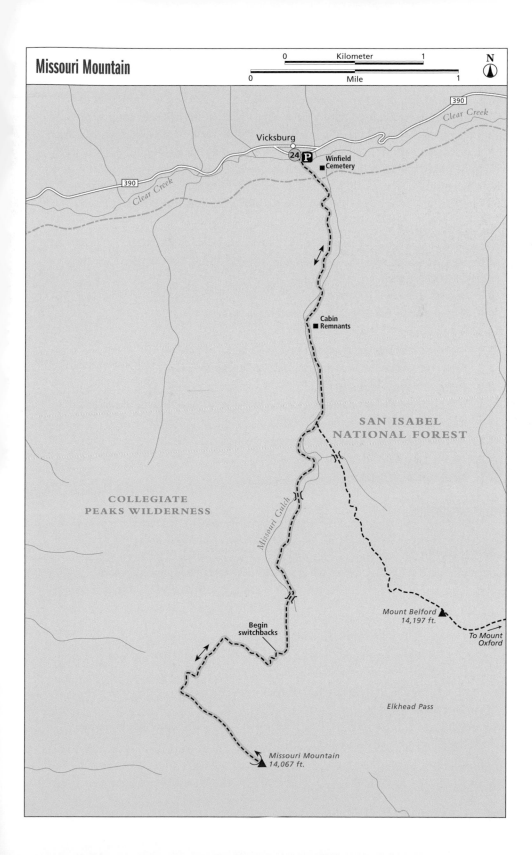

Missouri Mountain

0 Kilometer 1

0 Mile 1

N

390

Clear Creek

Vicksburg

24 P

Winfield Cemetery

Clear Creek

390

Clear Creek

Cabin Remnants

SAN ISABEL NATIONAL FOREST

COLLEGIATE PEAKS WILDERNESS

Missouri Gulch

Begin switchbacks

Mount Belford
14,197 ft.

To Mount Oxford

Elkhead Pass

Missouri Mountain
14,067 ft.

2 scrambling. Follow the trail up the ridge then skirt east of the point at 4.3 miles and 13,930 feet. Turn left to regain the ridge, heading southeast, and tackle the summit block. The trail abandons the ridgeline near some towers to make the ascent easier.

This is a peak awash in a sea of fourteeners. From Missouri's peak, mountains and other fourteeners stretch out in every direction. The closest are Belford and Oxford to the northeast, but Mount Elbert (14,433 feet) and La Plata (14,336 feet) are easily visible to the north. Huron (14,003 feet) is clearly visible to the west. Emerald Peak (13,904 feet) is directly south. Mount Yale (14,196 feet) and Mount Harvard (14,420 feet) are the most visible fourteeners in the southeast across the Missouri Basin.

Miles and Directions

0.0 Start at the trailhead on the southwest side of the lot. Go 150 feet and cross Clear Creek on a metal bridge.

0.3 Begin switchbacks in a forest.

0.6 Exit switchbacks and enter the east side of Missouri Gulch.

1.0 Cross a stream.

1.3 Pass cabin remnants on the left and enter into alpine meadow.

1.8 Head right, southwest, toward the broad face of Missouri Mountain.

2.0 Begin crossing a shallow stream.

3.4 Take the trail to the right and head up Missouri's western flank on a series of switchbacks.

4.2 Reach a ridge.

4.3 Skirt east of point at 13,930 feet then regain the ridge and climb to the summit block.

4.95 Arrive at the summit. Return via the same route.

9.9 Arrive back at the trailhead.

Hiking Information

Closest Outfitters

The Trailhead, 707 US 24 N, Buena Vista; (719) 395-8001; thetrailheadco.com

Salida Mountain Sports, 110 North F St., Salida; (719) 539-4400; salidamountain sports.com

Great Pre- or Post-Mountain Eats and Drinks

Eddyline Brewing Restaurant, 926 S Main St., Buena Vista; (719) 966-6017; eddyline brewing.com

Deerhammer Distilling Company, 321 E Main St., Buena Vista; (719) 395-9464; deer hammer.com

Moonlight Pizza & Brewpub, 242 F St., Salida; (719) 539-4277; moonlightpizza.biz

Here's the Scoop, 215 F St., Salida; (719) 539-9727

25 Mount Yale

14,196' (NGVD29), 14,204' (NAVD88), 21st highest

Mount Yale is the southernmost fourteener in the Collegiate Peak Wilderness (14,197-foot Mount Princeton is farther south but is not in the wilderness area). It doesn't have Princeton's prominence, but it does have the 4,000-foot-plus elevation gain that almost all Sawatch Range fourteeners do. The standard route from the Denny Creek Trailhead becomes a Class 2 hike and requires some scrambling after leaving tree line at roughly 12,000 feet. From the eastern edges of the Sawatch Range, the summit of Yale offers a spectacular panorama of fourteeners to the south, west, and north.

Start: Denny Creek Trailhead
Distance: 8.8 miles
Hiking time: 8 to 8.5 hours
Elevation gain: 4,286 feet
Difficulty: Class 2
Trail surface: Dirt, scree
Trailhead elevation: 9,910 feet
Camping: Backcountry camping
Fees: None
Best seasons: Spring through fall

Maps: USGS Mount Yale, Buena Vista West; National Geographic Trails Illustrated #129: Buena Vista, Collegiate Peaks
Nearest town: Buena Vista
Trail contacts: San Isabel National Forest, Leadville Ranger District, (719) 486-0749; Chaffee County Sheriff's Office, (719) 539-2596
Trail tips: Get down early. This mountain has a lot of electrical activity on summer afternoons.

Finding the trailhead: From US 24 and CR 360 head west on CR 360. Pass signs for Denny Gulch and at 12 miles find the well-marked Denny Creek Trailhead and parking area on the right. The trailhead is on the north side of the lot. GPS: N38° 48.9'/W106° 20.08'

The Hike

Giving Sawatch Range peaks the names of prestigious colleges began with Mount Yale. The first recorded climb of the peak was on August 18, 1869. The climb was led by Harvard University professor and Yale University alum J. D. Whitney, who was head of the Harvard School of Mining. A day later, members of the group, S. F. Sharpless and William M. Davis, summited Mount Harvard (14,420 feet). They named the higher of the two for their current university and the other for Whitney's alma mater. Hence a tradition was started.

Yale alumni who summit this peak used to pile rocks on the peak in attempt to make it higher than Mount Princeton's summit, which—at 14,187 feet—is a foot higher. Princeton's alumni did the same on their neighboring summit.

Mount Yale from Princeton

The standard route up Mount Yale from Denny Creek was completed by the Colorado Fourteeners Initiative and the USDA Forest Service in 2011. Prior to that, climbers used the Denny Gulch route, which was much steeper and prone to erosion. Now the Denny Creek Trail offers a good Class 1 hike through aspen, fir, and spruce before climbing across and up a Class 2 trail on Yale's broad western face on a scree-covered slope.

Hike north from the trailhead on a broad trail in a thick forest. The trail almost immediately passes through a number of switchbacks, gaining moderate altitude. The first part of the trail, except during the switchbacks, parallels Denny Creek.

At 1.1 miles and 10,550 feet cross Denny Creek on a log bridge. Shortly after that, at 1.25 miles, stay right at a junction on the trail to Yale. The trail begins to curve to the right over some relatively flat forestland in Denny Gulch. As it comes close to Delaney Gulch Stream, the trail takes a left, heading northeast at 1.6 miles and 10,950 feet.

Continue up the gulch, gaining elevation as the gulch narrows. Cross the stream on a log bridge at 11,220 feet and 2.1 miles. In 0.1 mile cross a tributary to the stream. Enjoy zigzagging through some small meadows, heading east. Reenter a swath of conifers, and at 11,630 feet and 2.5 miles cross over the streambed once again as the trail comes close to tree line.

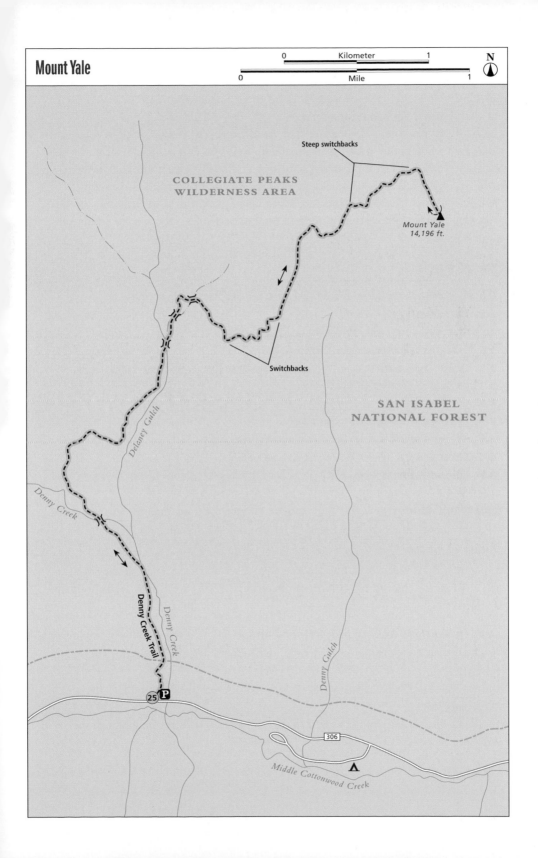

Mount Yale

0 ___ Kilometer ___ 1

0 ___ Mile ___ 1

N

Steep switchbacks

COLLEGIATE PEAKS
WILDERNESS AREA

Mount Yale
14,196 ft.

Switchbacks

SAN ISABEL
NATIONAL FOREST

Delany Gulch

Denny Creek

Denny Creek

Denny Creek Trail

Denny Gulch

25   P

306

Middle Cottonwood Creek

Reach tree line at 12,175 feet and 2.9 miles and get a great view of most of the arduous climb ahead. It's just 1.5 more miles and 2,000 feet to the top across a good trail. Climb up to the left (northeast) on Yale's broad southwest shoulder on an excellent trail—thanks, CFI and forest service!

At 13,200 feet and 3.7 miles the trail starts a series of switchbacks, first across a moderate incline then a much steeper one, the steps of which start at about 13,400 feet and 3.8 miles—feel the burn, if you haven't already. Reach Yale's northwestern saddle at 13,960 feet and 4.1 miles and head to the right toward the summit.

The trail disappears near the top, but cairns guide the way. Scramble up the remaining ridge to the peak, gaining just 236 feet over 0.25 mile, and reach the summit at 4.4 miles.

Miles and Directions

0.0 Start at the Denny Creek Trailhead parking lot and find the trail heading north.

1.1 Cross Denny Creek

1.25 Stay right at trail junction, taking the trail to Mount Yale.

1.6 Take a left near Delaney Gulch Stream.

2.1 Cross Delaney Gulch Stream. (Depending on the time of year, there could be two more crossings of the stream's tributary.)

2.9 Reach tree line.

3.7 Enter switchbacks that rise to the saddle.

4.1 Reach the saddle and head southeast toward the summit.

4.4 Celebrate at the summit. Return via the same route.

8.8 Arrive back at the parking lot.

Hiking Information

Closest Outfitters

The Trailhead, 707 US 24 N, Buena Vista; (719) 395-8001; thetrailheadco.com

Salida Mountain Sports, 110 North F St., Salida; (719) 539-4400; salidamountain sports.com

Great Pre- or Post-Mountain Eats and Drinks

Eddyline Brewing Restaurant, 926 S Main St., Buena Vista; (719) 966-6017; eddyline brewing.com

Deerhammer Distilling Company, 321 E Main St., Buena Vista; (719) 395-9464; deer-hammer.com

Moonlight Pizza & Brewpub, 242 F St., Salida; (719) 539-4277; moonlightpizza.biz

Here's the Scoop, 215 F St., Salida; (719) 539-9727

26 La Plata Peak

14,336', (NGVD29) 14,343' (NAVD88), 5th highest

La Plata Peak, in the San Isabel National Forest and the Collegiate Peak Wilderness, is one of the highest mountains in Colorado. That doesn't mean too much in the Sawatch Range; three of its neighbors are taller. However, the mountain is more isolated than other fourteeners in the range, which lets this giant stand out a little more. The standard route up La Plata starts at the Lake Creek Trailhead. It's mostly a Class 1 route but has some Class 2 scrambling at higher elevations.

Start: Lake Creek Trailhead
Distance: 9.0 miles
Hiking time: 9 hours
Elevation gain: 4,198 feet
Difficulty: Class 1, Class 2
Trail surface: Dirt, scree
Trailhead elevation: 10,140 feet
Camping: Backcountry camping
Fees: None
Best seasons: Year-round access
Maps: USGS Mount Elbert, Winfield, Independence Pass; National Geographic Trails

Illustrated #127: Aspen, Independence Pass; #129: Buena Vista, Collegiate Peaks
Nearest town: Buena Vista
Trail contacts: South Park Ranger District, (719) 836-2031
Trail tips: The first 0.25 mile on South Fork is on private land, so don't park on the side of the road near the trailhead. Roughly the first 1 mile of the trail also is on or very close to private land. There are some spots to pull off farther down the road, however. Please respect all property signs.

Finding the trailhead: From US 24 and CO 82, drive west toward Twin Lakes. At 14.5 miles find the parking area for Lake Creek Trail at the junction of CO 82 and South Fork Lake Creek Road (FR 399). GPS: N39° 03.85' / W106° 30.24'

The Hike

La Plata translates from Spanish as "the silver." That doesn't refer to the mountain's spectacular gray ramparts but the mineral richness and mines in the region. While the towns that supported the region's mines, like Winfield and Hamilton, are long gone, the mining legacy endures. *Note:* Some maps, sites, and other references show La Plata as 13,361 feet. It's not. An error in 1979 led to the USGS stating the wrong height for this mountain. Oddly that figure is still used in some places more than three decades later, even though it's been corrected.

Given that La Plata is in a mine-rich region, prospectors were likely the first to ascend its peaks on their quest to strike it rich. However, the first recorded ascent of the peak was on July 26, 1873, by the Hayden Survey team. The first recorded summit of La Plata via the impressive and jagged Ellingwood Ridge occurred in 1974.

La Plata Peak's summit

Nearly the first full mile of this trail is on private land. There's no camping and no parking available along CO 82—even though the trailhead is at the junction of CO 82 and South Fork Lake Creek Road.

From the parking lot walk 0.3 mile on South Fork Dirt Road. Find the trailhead on the left side of the road and head east into the forest. The next 0.5 mile of the trail is on private property, so follow all the No Trespassing signs. Shortly after entering the forest, cross a steel-and-wood bridge at 0.4 mile over the oddly olive-colored water of South Fork Lake Creek. As the trail turns right (south), it crosses La Plata Gulch Creek and enters US Forest Service land at roughly 0.8 mile. Let the climbing begin!

Close to the trailhead, the damage caused by pine and spruce beetles is clearly evident; but as the broad trail climbs south into La Plata Gulch on its eastern side and gains altitude, the forest appears healthier. Thanks to trail restoration work from Volunteers for Outdoor Colorado in 1999 and further work from the Colorado Fourteeners Initiative in 2005, the trail is in good condition, as evidenced by the steps, log and stone, placed on the trail to help climbers and reduce erosion between 1.1 miles and 1.3 miles, 10,340 feet and 10,700 feet, respectively. At 11,000 feet and 1.75 miles the trail levels out; at 11,052 feet and 2.1 miles it starts an epic elevation gain over the next 2.5 miles. At 2.4 miles and 11,528 feet the trail turns left and heads up a small gully across a series of switchbacks. The trail exits the gully at 2.6 miles and 11,830 feet, heading southeast for 0.25 mile.

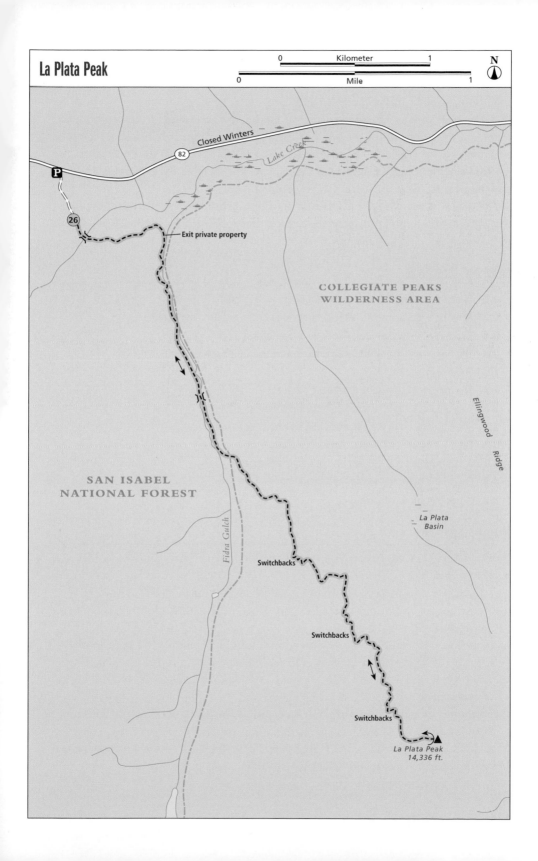

La Plata Peak

0   Kilometer   1
0   Mile   1

N

Closed Winters

82

P

Lake Creek

26

Exit private property

COLLEGIATE PEAKS
WILDERNESS AREA

Ellingwood Ridge

SAN ISABEL
NATIONAL FOREST

Fidra Gulch

La Plata
Basin

Switchbacks

Switchbacks

Switchbacks

La Plata Peak
14,336 ft.

The trail reaches the northern ridge of La Plata at 12,330 feet and 3.3 miles. Head right, basically due south, toward the peak. At 3.4 miles and 12,870 feet the trail moves to the right of the ridge and starts switchbacking up the west slope of La Plata. From here it's a little over 1 mile of hiking and scrambling to the top, but the trail is pretty visible all the way. At 3.9 miles and 13,550 feet reach a short flat spot and scramble over stable rock and the remaining switchbacks to the top. Reach the summit block at 14,200 feet and 4.3 miles. Head left and trek the remaining 130 feet and 0.2 mile to the peak. Return via the same route.

The view is stunning in all directions, but Ellingwood Ridge, the northeast ridge, is a particularly stunning masterpiece of rock that some strong climbers may choose to hike up.

Miles and Directions

0.0 From the parking lot, walk on the dirt South Fork Road.

0.3 Find the trailhead on the left side of the road and head east into the forest.

0.4 Cross over South Fork Lake Creek on a steel bridge.

0.8 The trail crosses La Plata Gulch Creek and enters forest service land.

1.75 The trail levels out.

2.1 The trail begins elevation gain to the peak.

2.4 Turn left, heading up a small gully on switchbacks.

2.9 The trail cuts up to the left over some switchbacks.

3.3 Start hiking up the northern ridge of La Plata.

4.3 Trek the remaining 130 feet and 0.2 mile to the peak.

4.5 Reach the peak. Return via the same route.

9.0 Arrive back at the trailhead.

Hiking Information

Closest Outfitters

The Trailhead, 707 US 24 N, Buena Vista; (719) 395-8001; thetrailheadco.com

Salida Mountain Sports, 110 North F St., Salida; (719) 539-4400; salidamountain sports.com

Great Pre- or Post-Mountain Eats and Drinks

Eddyline Brewing Restaurant, 926 S Main St., Buena Vista; (719) 966-6017; eddyline brewing.com

Deerhammer Distilling Company, 321 E Main St., Buena Vista; (719) 395-9464; deer hammer.com

Moonlight Pizza & Brewpub, 242 F St., Salida; (719) 539-4277; moonlightpizza.biz

Here's the Scoop, 215 F St., Salida; (719) 539-9727

27 Mount Antero

14,269' (NGVD29), 14,276' (NAVD88), 10th highest

If ever a mountain was a rock star, it would be Mount Antero. Its hit single would be "Act Naturally." That's because the mountain has a starring role in The Weather Channel's *Prospectors* series, which launched in 2013. The mountain doesn't have to do much, since it's known for its gem riches. The several prospectors and rock hounds who have active claims on its flanks provide all the human drama for the show. The cirques, bowls, and granite peak of Mount Antero provide plenty of drama for the eyes.

Start: Baldwin Gulch Trailhead
Distance: 2WD trailhead: 16 miles; 4WD trailhead: 9.4 miles
Hiking time: 2WD trailhead: 10 hours; 4WD trailhead: 6.5 hours
Elevation gain: 2WD trailhead: 5,012 feet; 4WD trailhead: 3,471 feet
Difficulty: Class 1, Class 2
Trail surface: Dirt road, dirt, scree
Trailhead elevation: 9,410 feet
Camping: Backcountry camping
Fees: None

Best seasons: Spring through fall
Maps: USGS Mount Antero, St. Elmo; National Geographic Trails Illustrated #130: Salida, St. Elmo, Shavano Peak Trail Map
Nearest towns: Buena Vista, Salida
Trail contacts: San Isabel National Forest, (719) 553-1400; USDA Forest Service, Salida Ranger District, (719) 539-3591
Special considerations: In late summer Mount Antero is a lightning magnet. It's best to summit early and get down before afternoon storms roll in.

Finding the trailhead: From US 285 (South from Buena Vista and north from Salida) go west on CR 162 toward Mount Princeton. The road is paved for about 10 miles. After a total of 12.5 miles on the road, turn left onto Baldwin Gulch Jeep Road (CR 277). Park here if driving a 2WD vehicle. You can try to venture on, but be aware that the jeep road may be closed by snow as late as June. GPS: 2WD trailhead: N38° 42.60'/W106° 17.5'; 4WD trailhead: N38° 40.95'/W106° 16.37'

The Hike

Mount Antero was surveyed during the Pike Expedition of 1806 and was later named for Unitah Ute Chief Antero. Chief Antero signed the Washington Treaty of 1880 and advocated for peace between the Utes and the United States. The mountain, located in the San Isabel National Forest, is the tenth-highest fourteener in Colorado and the highest peak named for a Native American. It's easily visible in the Arkansas Valley from US 285 between Salida and Buena Vista.

The recent history of Mount Antero is tied to prospecting. Gems were first discovered high on its flanks by Nelson Wanamaker in 1881. It's most famous for its aquamarine and smoky quartz, but prospectors also collect fluorite, phenakite, and topaz. In

Mount Antero from Mount Princeton. Tabeguache is back and to the right.

fact, the mountain is recognized as being the highest-elevation gem site in the United States as well as having the highest concentration of minerals in the nation.

The minerals, particularly beryl (aquamarine is a form of beryl), are also the cause of the 4WD roads that scar the mountain. Baldwin Gulch Jeep Road (FR 277) was created in the 1950s for a beryl mine that never took off. It is also the preferred route for hiking up the mountain—love it or hate it. It makes the hike easier, but 4WD vehicles and ATVs also use it in summer.

There are other routes up Mount Antero—among them Browns Creek, Little Browns Creek, and the Cascade Trails—but the Colorado Fourteeners Initiative recommends using the Baldwin Gulch route because: "Use of this route will help to reduce impacts to this fourteener's fragile alpine environment."

Both the roads and the mineral deposits mean Mount Antero is not a lonely mountain, particularly in the summer months. Baldwin Gulch is not a quiet route, but it is the easiest route up the mountain.

The Baldwin Gulch Trailhead is at 9,420 feet on the mountain's west side. From there the hike is a 16-mile round-trip. It's a long day trip, or hikers can camp off the road, adhering to Leave No Trace standards unless camping in a well-worn campsite.

Those with heavy-duty 4WD vehicles can drive an additional 3 miles to the 4WD trailhead at 10,840 feet, which makes the hike a 10-mile or less round-trip. The Miles and Directions are from the four-wheel-drive trailhead. However, this is a tough, steep road. People report bone-rattling driving times of 1 hour to cover just a few miles. It's actually feasible to drive beyond the four-wheel-drive trailhead, but it is not recommended because there is little to no parking available along the steep one-lane road.

Mount Antero

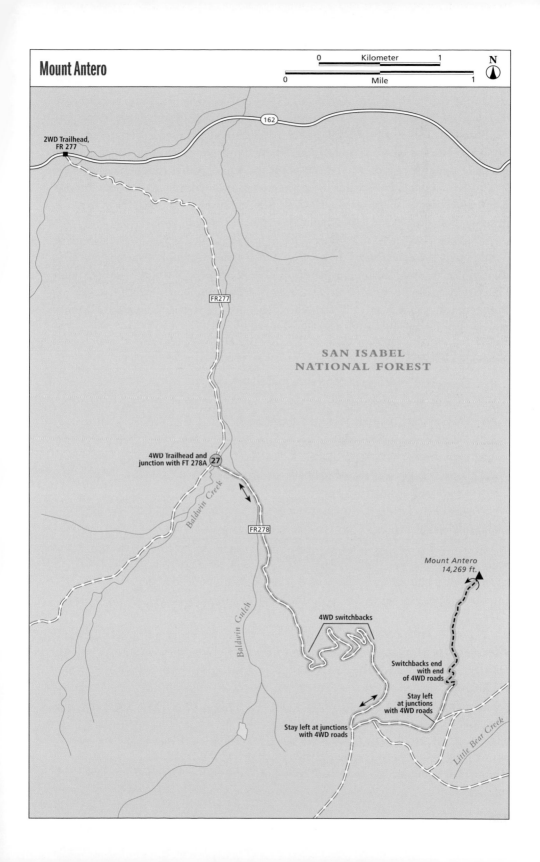

0   Kilometer   1

0   Mile   1

N

162

2WD Trailhead,
FR 277

FR277

SAN ISABEL
NATIONAL FOREST

4WD Trailhead and
junction with FT 278A   27

FR278

Baldwin Creek

Baldwin Gulch

Mount Antero
14,269 ft.

4WD switchbacks

Switchbacks end
with end
of 4WD roads

Stay left
at junctions
with 4WD roads

Stay left at junctions
with 4WD roads

Little Bear Creek

From the Baldwin Gulch Trailhead, follow FR 277 for 3.0 miles, heading southeast and south to a small dirt lot. That point is the 4WD trailhead. From there take FR 278 to the left, heading southeast. Begin climbing some switchbacks on the dirt road in 1 mile. At 3.2 miles go left at a crossing onto FR 278A, heading east. Follow FR 278A until you reach a small saddle at Point 13,820. Follow the road until it ends. The summit of Mount Antero is easily visible to the northeast; if there's no snow, the path is visible along its eastern side. At this point the trail becomes rougher and requires some Class 2 hiking. Follow this trail a little more than 0.5 mile to gain the summit. The trail is hard to see in some areas, but the peak is not. Stay on-trail as much as possible to minimize damage to the fragile alpine ecosystem.

From the peak of Mount Antero hikers can see a plethora of fourteeners. The Collegiate peaks are visible to the north; the iron-rich peaks of Tabeguache and Shavano are to the southwest. From here you can see why the 20-mile-wide, 90-mile-long Sawatch Range is called the "backbone of the continent." Fully fifteen of the fourteeners, including eight of the tallest, are in the Sawatch Range, and Mount Antero provides breathtaking, 360-degree panoramas.

Miles and Directions

0.0 Begin hiking at the 4WD trailhead at Baldwin Gulch on FR 278.

1.4 Begin hiking up switchbacks on FR 278.

2.9 The road begins heading back toward the southwest.

3.2 The road begins switchbacking.

4.0 Begin switchbacks to the summit.

4.7 Reach Mount Antero's summit. Return the way you came.

9.4 Arrive back at the 4WD trailhead.

Hiking Information

Closest Outfitters

The Trailhead, 707 US 24 N, Buena Vista; (719) 395-8001; thetrailheadco.com

Salida Mountain Sports, 110 North F St., Salida; (719) 539-4400; salidamountain sports.com

Great Pre- or Post-Mountain Eats and Drinks

Eddyline Brewing Restaurant, 926 S Main St., Buena Vista; (719) 966-6017; eddyline brewing.com

Deerhammer Distilling Company, 321 E Main St., Buena Vista; (719) 395-9464; deer hammer.com

Moonlight Pizza & Brewpub, 242 F St., Salida; (719) 539-4277; moonlightpizza.biz

Here's the Scoop, 215 F St., Salida; (719) 539-9727

Harder Fourteeners

These mountains require more-strenuous climbing. They're mostly still considered Class 2 scrambling, but many of them have some Class 3 moves, meaning you might be quadrupedal at some points, picking your way through chimneys, climbing over some easy boulders or rock walls. Some of these mountains also have longer trails, making a one-day trek less likely. These are challenging mountains for sure, but you're still relatively protected, and a fall isn't likely to be deadly.

A scree field close to Uncompahgre's summit adds some complexity to the trek (hike 28).

28 Uncompahgre Peak

14,309' (NGVD29), 14,314' (NAVD88), 6th Highest

At 14,309 feet Uncompahgre Peak is the sixth-tallest fourteener in Colorado. It's at least 50 feet taller than the next-tallest fourteener in the range, 14,246-foot Mount Wilson, making it the undisputed monarch of the San Juan Mountains. Thankfully it's a pretty friendly monarch, requiring only Class 1 hiking with a little Class 2 scrambling—though it may require a long pilgrimage for those without access to a good 4WD vehicle. The peak rises out of the alpine meadows like the conning tower of some giant submarine or the nose of a blue whale. Both analogies are fitting since its neighbor, Wetterhorn, has been likened to a shark's nose.

Start: Nellie Creek Trailhead
Distance: 4WD trailhead 7.3 miles (*Option:* 2WD trailhead: 15.3 miles)
Hiking time: 12 hours (*Option:* 2WD trailhead: 24 hours)
Elevation gain: 4WD trailhead: 2,909 feet (*Option:* 2WD trailhead: 5,160 feet)
Difficulty: Class 1, Class 2
Trail surface: Dirt, scree
Trailhead elevation: 4WD trailhead: 11,400 feet (*Option:* 2WD trailhead: 9,320 feet)
Camping: Backcountry camping; camping at trailheads

Fees: None
Best seasons: Spring through fall
Maps: USGS Uncompahgre Peak, Wetterhorn Peak, Lake City, Courthouse Mountain; National Geographic Trails Illustrated #141: Telluride, Silverton, Ouray, Lake City
Nearest towns: Lake City, Ouray
Trail contacts: Bureau of Land Management, Gunnison Field Office, (970) 642-4940; USDA Forest Service, Gunnison Ranger District, (970) 641-0471; Hinsdale County Sheriff's Office, (970) 944-2291

Finding the trailhead: From Bluff and 1st Streets in Lake City—the southwest edge of town—take a slight right, continuing on Bluff Street (CR 20), which becomes the dirt Henson Creek Road, also known as the Alpine Loop Scenic Byway as it exits town. Drive 5.1 miles to the Nellie Creek Trailhead, which is on the right (north) side of the road. The trail also is Nellie Creek Road (FR 877)—the 4WD road that leads to the upper Nellie Creek Trailhead. This is a rough road that can incapacitate passenger vehicles. Hence there is a campsite at the junction. It's the only place on Henson Creek Road where people can camp overnight. This is also as far as the road is plowed during winter. For high-clearance 4WD vehicles, continue 4 miles up Nellie Creek Road (FR 877). Please be wary. Other people may be hiking up or down the road. Drive about 3.4 miles to reach the parking lot and 4WD trailhead. GPS: 2WD: N38° 01.23' / W107° 24.05'; 4WD: N38° 03.74' / W107° 25.31'

The Hike

Uncompahgre Peak was likely first climbed by Utes, and it's the only mountain in the San Juan Range to have a Native American word as its name. The name most likely stems from the Ute word Uncompahgre, which means "red water spring." Lt. E. G. Beck with the Gunnison Expedition of 1853 recorded the mountain's name, but he's not telling anyone where it came from these days. Early prospectors in the region also called it Capitol Mountain or Leaning Tower. A. D. Wilson and Franklin Rhonda made the first recorded ascent of the mountain in 1874 as part of the Hayden Expedition, but they found that grizzly bears had beat them to the summit. (Don't worry; there are no grizzlies in Colorado today.)

The mountain, the highest in the San Juan Range, stands out from the surrounding landscape. The USDA Forest Service recognized this when Uncompahgre became one of the first designated primitive areas in the 1930s.

Since Uncompahgre is one of the more-singular peaks in the San Juans, it shouldn't be a surprise that it's a hike to reach. The most popular and standard route

Uncompahgre Peak from the Ridge Stock Driveway Trail

Hiking back down Uncompahgre

up Uncompahgre is the Nellie Creek Route, which requires a 7.3-mile round-trip hike from the 4WD trailhead or a 15.3-mile round-trip hike from the 2WD trailhead. If hiking from the 2WD trailhead, follow Nellie Creek Road for 3.4 miles to the 4WD parking lot and trailhead.

From the 4WD trailhead pick up the trail (FT 239) at the Nellie Creek Trailhead. The first 0.5 mile of the trail is in forest. After that the hike is above tree line in a lovely alpine basin. As the trail exits tree line, it comes closer to Nellie Creek until 0.8 mile, when it almost touches the creek. At about 11,850 feet the trail makes a quick right (north) up a slope. Reach the top of the slope at 0.9 mile, about 11,900 feet, and turn left at the junction, heading west and slightly south. The path continues on a westerly direction and at 1.9 miles and 12,650 feet crosses Nellie Creek near its headwaters. Shortly thereafter it takes a left, heading south and crossing the basin to Uncompahgre's southern ridge. At 2.4 miles reach a trail junction and go right on the trail to Uncompahgre at 12,950 feet. The trail continues on to the right, gaining what will be the southern ridgeline of Uncompahgre.

At 2.6 miles and 13,160 feet the trail skirts to the right of a high point on the eastern side of the ridge before regaining it 0.1 mile later at 13,300 feet. Here there are some fantastic views of Matterhorn and Wetterhorn to the west. At just over 3.0 miles the trail comes close to some sheer overlooks with drop-offs to the west. Switchback

Uncompahgre Peak

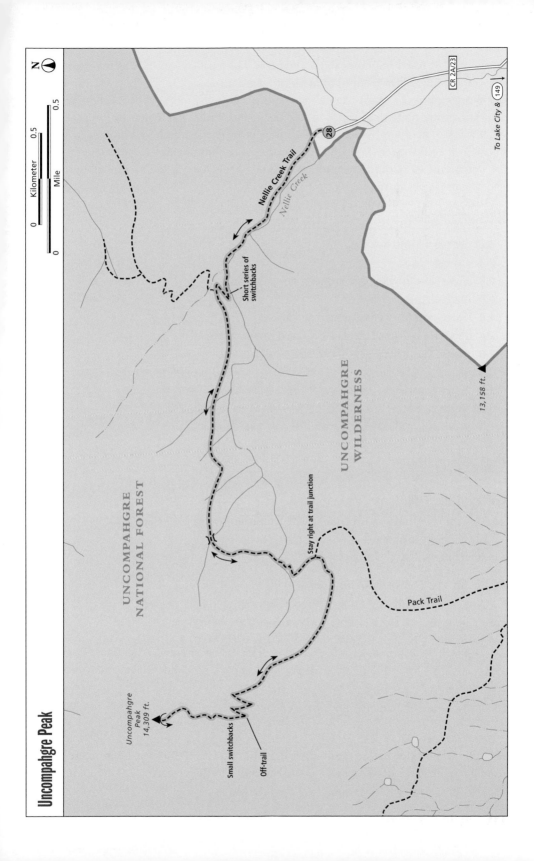

N

Kilometer
0   0.5

Mile
0   0.5

UNCOMPAHGRE
NATIONAL FOREST

UNCOMPAHGRE
WILDERNESS

Nellie Creek Trail

Nellie Creek

Short series of
switchbacks

Stay right at trail junction

Pack Trail

Uncompahgre
Peak
14,309 ft.

Small switchbacks

Off-trail

28

CR 2A/23

To Lake City & (149)

13,158 ft.

up the trail to reach 3.3 miles and 13,800 feet. The trail crosses over to the western side of Uncompahgre's giant summit block. The trail becomes more braided through this short section of Class 2 scrambling as it gains 200 feet in less than 0.1 mile. Over 14,000 feet the trail to the top is visible again, and it's an easy climb to the peak at 14,309 feet. There are numerous rock parapets to shield climbers from the winds on the top of this peak. Though the approach and climb to this mountain are easy, the northern face of this behemoth rises some 700 feet above the basins below on a chossy cliff face. Return via the same route.

Miles and Directions

0.0 Start at the 4WD trailhead.

0.5 Exit tree line.

0.8 Come close to Nellie Creek and cut right to the north.

0.9 The trail cuts left to the west.

1.9 Cross Nellie Creek's headwaters.

2.4 Reach a trail junction; stay to the right and gain the ridgeline.

2.6 Skirt to the right of a 13,320-foot high point.

3.0 The trail regains the ridge then starts switching back to Uncompahgre's southern ridge.

3.3 Begin scrambling to Uncompahgre's large summit block.

3.65 Reach the summit at 14,309 feet. Return via the same route.

7.3 Arrive back at the 4WD trailhead.

Hiking Information

Closest Outfitters

The Sportsman Outdoors & Fly Shop, 238 S Gunnison Ave., Lake City; (970) 944-2526; lakecitysportsman.com

San Juan Sports, 102 S Main St., Creede; (719) 658-2359; sanjuansports.com

Great Pre- or Post-Mountain Spots

Packer Saloon & Cannibal Grill, 310 N Silver St., Lake City; (970) 944-4144

Lake City Cafe, 310 Gunnison Ave., Lake City; (970) 944-0301

San Juan Soda Co., 227 N Silver St., Lake City; (970) 944-0500; sanjuansodacompany .com

29 Tabeguache Peak

14,155' (NGVD29), 14,162' (NAVD88), 25th highest

Unlike Mount Shavano (14,229 feet), Tabeguache Peak hides behind its closest sibling. Like a protective big brother or sister, you've got to go through Shavano to get to Tabeguache because the standard route to the mountain passes over Shavano then goes over a ridge that requires Class 2 scrambling. The two peaks are usually done in one day; however, it's a long day, with an extended period above tree line, and it requires summiting Shavano twice. If attempting to do both in one day, consider hiking up into the forest below Shavano the afternoon before.

Start: Blank Gulch Trailhead
Distance: 10.5 miles
Hiking time: 10 hours
Elevation gain: 4,480 feet
Difficulty: Class 1, Class 2
Trail surface: Dirt, scree
Trailhead elevation: 9,740 feet
Camping: Backcountry camping
Fees: None
Best seasons: Spring through fall

Maps: USGS Mount Antero, St. Elmo, Garfield; National Geographic Trails Illustrated #130: Salida, St. Elmo, Shavano Peak
Nearest towns: Poncha Springs, Salida
Trail contacts: San Isabel National Forest, (719) 553-1400; USDA Forest Service, Salida Ranger District, (719) 539-3591; Chaffee County Sheriff's Office, (719) 539-2596
Trail tips: If you see storm clouds on the horizon while on the way to Tabeguache from Shavano, turn back. The lighting could make for a very hazardous stay above tree line.

Finding the trailhead: From the intersection of US 50 and US 285 near Poncha Springs, head north on US 285 and turn left (west) onto CR 140. At 2.9 miles take a right onto FR 250, heading north. Drive north-northwest for 4 miles and veer left onto FR 252; continue for another 3.2 miles to reach a dirt parking lot. The trail begins at the northeast end of the parking lot. GPS: N38° 35.83'/W106° 11.81'

The Hike

Tabeguache is the third, and most hidden, peak in the Indian Group. The other two, Shavano and Antero, are also its closest neighbors. This mountain was named in honor of the Ute tribe of Tabeguaches led by Chief Shavano. Shavano worked with the U.S. government and Native American nations to help reduce violence between the settlers and the Native American nations. So in some sense the smaller of the two peaks is like a tribe behind its leader. The name Tabeguache translates to "cedar-bark, sunny slope people."

The hike starts just northwest of the parking lot and the restrooms. At 0.1 mile take a right at the junction with the Colorado Trail and hike north along the fence.

Tabeguache just right of the prominent Mount Antero

At 0.25 mile come to a trail junction and turn left, following the sign to Shavano. Continue heading northwest on a wide dirt trail as the trail begins a pretty steady ascent that will continue for most of the climb. Heading farther into the forest, the trail becomes narrower and a little harder to see, but many trees are marked, and the wear of foot traffic is evident on roots and rocks. In some places streams may course across the trail in spring.

At 1.4 miles (10,800 feet) cross Squaw Creek. Cross the creek two more times and head northwest, reaching at 11,000 feet at 1.6 miles. At 11,240 feet come to the first sharp right at a talus field; continue heading northeast before curving back around. At 1.9 miles reach one of the flatter parts of the hike, which might be a good place to camp.

Come close to Shavano's east ridge near a clearing at 2.3 miles and 11,800 feet then make a dramatic cut back to the left (south). Shortly afterward turn right (west) as the trees thin out. At 2.7 miles and 12,220 feet, exit the forest and start hiking across a good but rocky trail that heads toward Shavano's eastern slope. At 3.4 miles and 12,840 feet the trail starts switching back toward the south ridge of Shavano. Take a right and head north at 13,350 feet and 3.7 miles to gain the broad saddle that leads to the top; scramble the last 0.5 mile to Shavano's summit. From the top of Shavano at 4.2 miles, head northwest, descending the scree-covered northwestern

Tabeguache Peak

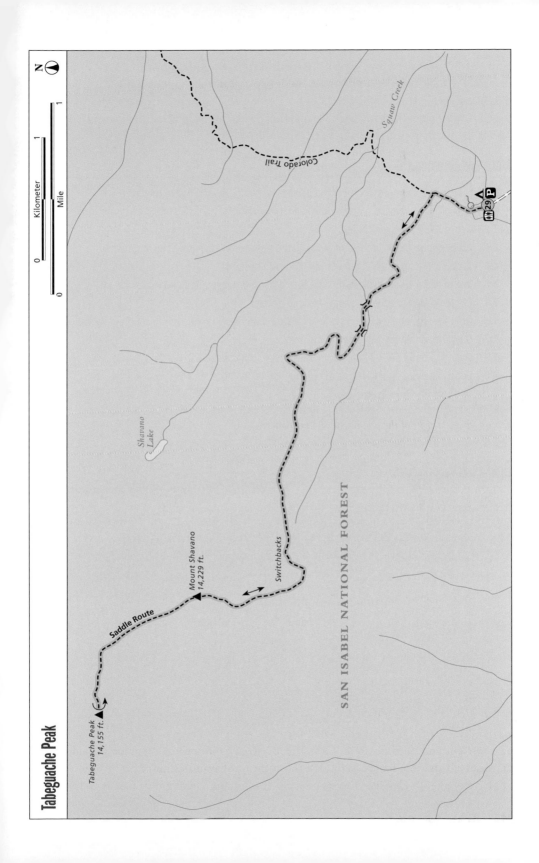

N

0   Kilometer   1

0   Mile   1

Colorado Trail

Squaw Creek

Shavano Lake

SAN ISABEL NATIONAL FOREST

Switchbacks

Mount Shavano
14,229 ft.

Saddle Route

Tabeguache Peak
14,155 ft.

⑮29

P

ridge. At 4.9 miles and roughly 13,710 feet, hit the low point between the two peaks in a small saddle. Turn left to the west and begin ascending the remaining 0.3 mile to Tabeguache's peak. Reach the peak at 5.25 miles. To best enjoy the view, look every way but southeast—the way back to Shavano. Look there too; it's still spectacular, but save it for when you start hiking back in that direction.

Miles and Directions

0.0   Start at the northwest corner of the parking lot and follow the trail to the fence.

0.1   Take a right and join the Colorado Trail heading north.

0.25 Take a left heading northwest.

1.4   Cross Squaw Creek. In the next 0.1 mile the trail crosses the creek two more times.

1.6   Take a sharp right near a talus field and head northeast.

2.3   Take a sharp left heading south then turn back to the right and head west.

2.7   Exit forest and head to Shavano's eastern slope.

3.4   Gain the face of the eastern slope and follow switchbacks to the broad southern saddle.

3.7   Gain the saddle and scramble to the peak.

4.2   Gain Shavano's peak and head northwest over stable scree.

4.9   Reach the low point between the two mountains. Turn west and start ascending Tabeguache.

5.25 Summit Tabeguache Peak. Return via same the route, passing over Shavano a second time.

10.5 Arrive back at the trailhead.

Hiking Information

Closest Outfitters

The Trailhead, 707 US 24 North, Buena Vista; (719) 395-8001; thetrailheadco.com

Salida Mountain Sports, 110 North F St., Salida; (719) 539-4400; salidamountain sports.com

Great Pre- or Post-Mountain Eats and Drinks

Eddyline Brewing Restaurant, 926 S Main St., Buena Vista; (719) 966-6017; eddyline brewing.com

Deerhammer Distilling Company, 321 E Main St., Buena Vista; (719) 395-9464; deer hammer.com

Moonlight Pizza & Brewpub, 242 F St., Salida; (719) 539-4277; moonlightpizza.biz

Here's the Scoop, 215 F St., Salida; (719) 539-9727

30 Mount Harvard

14,420' (NGVD29), 14,427' (NAVD88), 3rd highest

Just like the Ivy League school that shares the name, it takes a little more to get to the top of Mount Harvard. It's a long Class 1 and Class 2 climb to highest peak in Chaffee County—that's not a riff on "420," just fact—and the third tallest in the state. Harvard is one of five collegiate peaks in the San Isabel National Forest's Collegiate Peak Wilderness. Nestled in the Sawatch Range among other fourteeners, it's hard to see its size and mass, but Harvard clearly stands above its peers. Harvard is often climbed with Columbia. Both mountains are accessed from the North Cottonwood Trailhead.

Start: North Cottonwood Trailhead
Distance: 12.8 miles
Hiking time: 12 to 13 hours
Elevation gain: 4,540 feet
Difficulty: Class 2
Trail surface: Dirt, scree
Trailhead elevation: 9,880 feet
Camping: Backcountry camping
Fees: None
Best seasons: Spring through fall

Maps: USGS Mount Harvard, Mount Yale, Harvard Lakes, Buena Vista West; National Geographic Trails Illustrated #129: Buena Vista, Collegiate Peaks
Nearest town: Buena Vista
Trail contacts: San Isabel National Forest, Leadville Ranger District, (719) 486-0749; Chaffee County Sheriff's Office, (719) 539-2596

Finding the trailhead: From the intersection of US 24 and CR 356 in Buena Vista, just north of Buena Vista, go west on CR 356 for 1.6 miles. Turn left onto CR 361 and drive for 3.6 miles. Turn right onto CR 365 and drive 2.3 miles to the end of the road. The trailhead is on the right; the trail takes off from the northwest side of the dirt lot. The road to the trailhead is a dirt road and gets rough, but driven carefully, many 2WD vehicles can make it. GPS: N38° 52.25' / W106° 15.96'

The Hike

Harvard might be the first university in the United States, but it's the second collegiate peak by one day. That's because Harvard University professor and Yale University alum J. D. Whitney and his team summited Mount Yale (14,196 feet) on August 18, 1869. Whitney was head of the Harvard School of Mining, and he and his students were assessing the area on the rumor that there were 17,000-foot mountains in the area. They named the higher of the two for their current university and the other for Whitney's alma mater.

Though Mount Harvard is the third-highest peak in Colorado and the fourth-highest in the lower forty-eight states, some Harvard alumni concocted a plan to elevate Mount Harvard to the second-highest peak in the United States by dragging a 14-foot metal pole to the summit in 1962. They weren't able to reach the peak before

Looking across to Mount Harvard from Mount Belford and Mount Oxford

darkness and abandoned the pole a few hundred yards short of the summit. With the help of a Cornell grad, Harvard alumni and brothers John and Tim Wirth—Tim was later elected US senator from Colorado—carried the pole to the top of Harvard in 1963. The pole disappeared sometime in the 1980s.

From the parking lot, the North Cottonwood Creek Trail (FT 1449) heads west, quickly crossing to the south side of North Cottonwood Creek. Follow this fantastic trail through conifers and the occasional aspen grove for 1.5 miles until coming to a trail junction at 10,320 feet. Stay right at the junction toward Horn Fork Basin and Bear Lake. From here the trail crosses to the north side of the creek then begins heading northwest on the Horn Fork Trail, still FT 1449, which leads to Horn Fork Basin and Bear Lake. Stay on the main trail, avoiding a turnoff for Columbia to the right at 11,400 feet and 3.5 miles. People often camp in this area if taking more than one day to hike Harvard or do both mountains in one day—or two.

Here the trail divides coniferous forest on the east and willow thickets on the west. Follow the trail as it courses to the right of the trees across Horn Fork Basin then heads left (north) on the east side of the basin. Continue hiking on this side of the basin. At 5.0 miles and 12,360 feet a short trail to the left leads to Bear Lake—a good rest and water filtering spot if needed. At 12,500 feet and 5.2 miles the trail

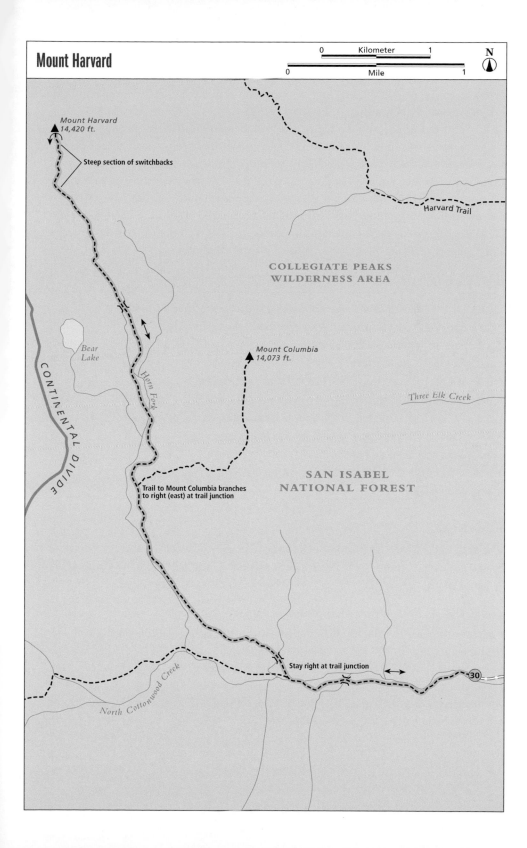

0   Kilometer   1

0   Mile   1

N

Mount Harvard
14,420 ft.

Steep section of switchbacks

Harvard Trail

COLLEGIATE PEAKS
WILDERNESS AREA

Bear
Lake

CONTINENTAL DIVIDE

Horn Fork

Mount Columbia
14,073 ft.

Three Elk Creek

SAN ISABEL
NATIONAL FOREST

Trail to Mount Columbia branches
to right (east) at trail junction

Stay right at trail junction

30

North Cottonwood Creek

becomes steeper and transitions from dirt to scree. Turn right and start ascending a small ridge at 5.4 miles and 12,830 feet. Ascend the ridge and enter into a sub-basin below Harvard. At 13,000 feet and 5.6 miles the trail levels out before making the steepest ascent of the journey to Harvard's peak.

Climb up near the south ridge of Harvard, heading northwest, flirting with the ridgeline but never quite making it. The trail makes some loose switchbacks up the slope to help prevent erosion and fight tedium until it reaches Harvard's southern ridge at 13,600 feet. Follow switchbacks up the ridge northeast to the top, scrambling over ever-rockier terrain. This last part at the base of the summit block, less than 50 feet from the top, requires Class 2 scrambling and maybe even some hands on rocks. However, the rock is stable, and exposure is not great. Reach the summit at 6.4 miles and celebrate reaching 14,420 feet. Return via the same route.

Miles and Directions

0.0 Start at the trailhead and hike west on the North Cottonwood Trail (FT 1449).

1.5 Stay right at the trail junction toward Horn Fork Basin and Bear Lake.

3.5 Pass the junction to Mount Columbia.

5.0 Pass the trail to Bear Lake.

5.2 The trail becomes steeper as it transitions from dirt to scree.

5.4 Cross over small ridge.

5.6 The trail begins switchbacking upslope to the summit.

6.4 Reach the summit. Return to trailhead via same route.

12.8 Arrive back at the trailhead.

Hiking Information

Closest Outfitters

The Trailhead, 707 US 24 North, Buena Vista; (719) 395-8001; thetrailheadco.com

Salida Mountain Sports, 110 North F St., Salida; (719) 539-4400; salidamountain sports.com

Great Pre- or Post-Mountain Eats and Drinks

Eddyline Brewing Restaurant, 926 S Main St., Buena Vista; (719) 966-6017; eddyline brewing.com

Deerhammer Distilling Company, 321 E Main St., Buena Vista; (719) 395-9464; deer hammer.com

Moonlight Pizza & Brewpub, 242 F St., Salida; (719) 539-4277; moonlightpizza.biz

Here's the Scoop, 215 F St., Salida; (719) 539-9727

31 | Humboldt Peak

14,064' (NGVD29), 14,069' (NAVD88), 37th highest

Humboldt Peak is the easiest peak in the Sangre de Cristo Range—for those ready for a long Class 2 hike and scramble with at least 4,000 feet of elevation gain. It's the easiest to climb in the Crestone Group of fourteeners, which is a cluster of five peaks that surpass 14,000 feet. The standard route up Humboldt is from the South Colony Lakes basin. The basin also can serve as a base for those who want to take on Crestone Peak (14,294 feet) and Crestone Needle (14,197 feet) over a few days.

Start: Lower South Colony Trailhead
Distance: 2WD trailhead: 16 miles; 4WD trailhead: 10.8 miles
Hiking time: 2WD trailhead: 10 hours; 4WD trailhead: 7 hours
Elevation gain: 2WD trailhead: 5,264 feet; 4WD trailhead: 4,164 feet
Difficulty: Class 1, Class 2
Trail surface: Dirt, scree
Trailhead elevation: 2WD trailhead: 8,800 feet; 4WD trailhead: 9,900 feet
Camping: Multiple spots at 4WD trailhead; backcountry camping
Fees: None
Best seasons: Late spring through fall

Maps: USGS Crestone Peak, Crestone, Beck Mountain; National Geographic Trails Illustrated #138: Sangre de Cristo Mountains
Nearest towns: Westcliffe, Crestone
Trail contacts: Rio Grande National Forest, Saguache Ranger District, (719) 655-2547; San Isabel National Forest, San Carlos Ranger District, (719) 269-8500; Custer County Sheriff's Office, (719) 783-2270
Trail tips: This might be the easiest fourteener in the Sangre de Cristos, but don't underestimate it—especially if parking at the lower trailhead. It's a long climb with a lot of elevation. Parts of this trail go through the Sangre de Cristo Wilderness; follow local wilderness rules.

Finding the trailhead: From Westcliffe, at the junction of CO 69 and CO 96 (6th and Main Streets in town), drive south on CO 69 for 4.6 miles. Turn right onto CR 119, also called Colfax Lane. Drive to the end of Colfax at 10.2 miles and turn right onto CR 120 (South Colony Road); stay on CR 120 for 1.3 miles and turn right onto Colfax Lane. Drive 5.5 miles to the end of Colfax; turn right (west) and drive 1.5 miles to a 2WD trailhead at the junction of CR 120 and CR 125 on the right. High-clearance and 4WD vehicles can continue on for another 2.4 miles over a rough 4WD road to the upper 4WD trailhead at 9,900 feet. The trailhead is on the southwest side of the parking area, next to a kiosk. *Note:* CR 120 used to go farther up into the Crestone Group but was closed in 2009. GPS: 2WD trailhead: N37° 59.61'/W105° 28.36'; 4WD trailhead: N37° 58.59'/W105° 30.34'

The Hike

Humboldt is a good mountain to start on in the Sangre de Cristos, but it's by no means as easy as Mount Sherman or many Front Range fourteeners. At roughly 11

Hiking toward Humboldt Peak. LEE MAUNEY

miles and at least 4,000 feet of elevation gain from the upper trailhead on a largely Class 2 trail, Humboldt is tiring. However, compared with the sheer walls and Class 3 and 4 climbing required of the other mountains in the Crestone Group, Humboldt is a pussycat. The Rocky Mountain Field Institute has done work to stabilize and make the trail more sustainable since the 1990s. Staying on-trail helps prevent erosion and results in a safer climb.

The peak was named in honor of famed German geographer, explorer, and mountaineer Alexander von Humboldt by Prussian and German settlers who arrived in the region in 1870. Silver was discovered in Wet Mountain Valley in 1874 by Leonard Frederick. Frederick called his mine on the west slope of the valley Humboldt, which led to the mountain sharing the name. The first recorded ascent of the mountain was in 1883, but given that mining was nearby, it's likely prospectors summited the mountain earlier.

The path to Humboldt's peak heads southwest across a lovely forest along the bottom of Humboldt's south slope. From the 4WD trailhead cross a footbridge and hike on the South Colony Lakes Road (CR 120), closed to vehicles. Follow the road for a little more than 2.5 miles and 11,100 feet and find the sign for FT 1339, which heads off to the right (east) on a well-maintained trail. At 3.1 miles and 11,600 feet reach a rocky open area below a long gully. There are some campsites off to the left on dirt trails in this area.

At 3.4 miles and 11,700 feet the trail exits the evergreen forest and into willows as the trail comes close to Lower South Colony Lakes. The trail courses along the north side of the basin; the trail remains relatively level here. As it begins to gain elevation, the trail gradually hooks around to the right in a more northerly direction. At 12,080 feet and 4.1 miles the trail to Humboldt goes to the right at the trail junction and quickly starts switchbacking up the slope to the saddle between Humboldt

Humboldt Peak

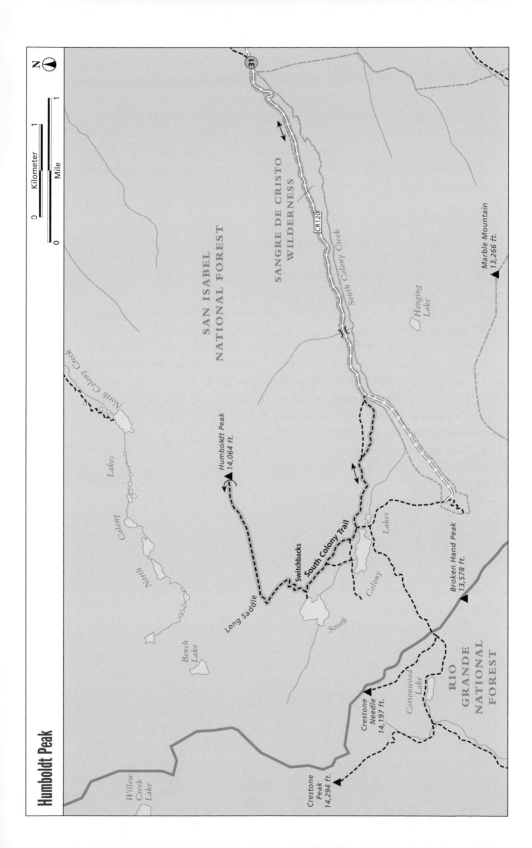

N

SAN ISABEL
NATIONAL FOREST

SANGRE DE CRISTO
WILDERNESS

RIO
GRANDE
NATIONAL
FOREST

Willow
Creek
Lake

North Colony Creek

North
Colony
Lakes

Bench
Lake

Long Saddle

Switchbacks

South Colony Trail

South
Colony
Lakes

Humboldt Peak
14,064 ft.

Crestone Peak
14,294 ft.

Crestone Needle
14,197 ft.

Cottonwood
Lake

Broken Hand Peak
13,578 ft.

CR120

South Colony Creek

Hanging
Lake

Marble Mountain
13,266 ft.

31

0   1   Kilometer

0   1   Mile

and Crestone Peak at 12,820 feet and 4.6 miles. The trail, which becomes harder to track, heads right (east) up Humboldt's west ridge. Scramble up the ridge, staying close to the crest, to a false summit at 13,750 feet and 5.0 miles; skirt to the right and climb east up and over rock to the solid, grassy ridge to Humboldt's peak. Climb the remaining 20 feet and peak out at 14,064 feet and 5.4 miles, gaining a fantastic view of the valley eastern valley. The rest of the Crestones loom to the west, with the San Luis Valley dividing the Crestones themselves from Kit Carson and Challenger. Return via the same route.

Miles and Directions

- **0.0** Start at the 4WD trailhead and cross a footbridge about 150 feet from the trailhead. Hike on the closed CR 120.
- **2.5** Turn right at trail junction to FT 1339.
- **3.1** Cross over rocky area; look for camping spots shortly after.
- **3.4** Exit the forest and enter a willow thicket. Come close to the Lower South Colony Lakes.
- **4.1** Near Upper South Colony Lake take a right at a trail junction, heading north and up a series of switchbacks to the saddle.
- **4.6** Gaining roughly 740 feet, reach the saddle between Humboldt and Crestone Peaks. Turn right (east) and scramble up the ridge, staying close to the crest.
- **5.0** Come to a false summit. Scramble over rock to the right of the false summit and head for the close summit block over a grassy ridge.
- **5.4** Summit Humboldt. Return by the same route.
- **10.8** Arrive back at the trailhead.

Hiking Information

Closest Outfitters
Take a Hike!, 210 Main St., Westcliffe; (719) 783-3771; takeahikewc.com
Edge Ski Paddle & Pack, 107 N Union Ave., Pueblo; (719) 583-2021; edgeskiand paddle.com

Great Pre- or Post-Mountain Spots
Chappy's Mountain View Bar & Grill, 213 Main St., Westcliffe; (719) 783-0813; face book.com/ChappybarandgrillwestcliffeCO
Royal Gorge Brewing Co. & Restaurant, 413 Main St., Cañon City; (719) 345-4141; royalgorgebrewpub.com
Elevation Beer Company, 115 Pahlone Pkwy., Poncha Springs; (719) 539-5258; elevationbeerco.com

32 Challenger Point

14,081' (NGVD29), 14,084' (NAVD88), 34th highest

Nestled on the shoulders of 14,165-foot Kit Carson Peak, Challenger Point makes the cut as a fourteener—just barely. Though Challenger rises 81 feet above the magic threshold, the saddle between it and Kit Carson drops 301 feet, barely surpassing that requirement by just 1 foot. Challenger is a long, challenging Class 2 climb, but it is among the easier peaks in the Sangre De Cristos and much easier than climbing Kit Carson, with which it is commonly climbed.

Start: Willow and South Crestone Trailhead
Distance: 4WD trailhead: 11.6 miles
Hiking time: 4WD trailhead: 11 to 13 hours
Elevation gain: 4WD trailhead: 5,184 feet
Difficulty: Hard Class 2
Trail surface: Dirt, scree, rock
Trailhead elevation: 8,880 feet
Camping: Backcountry camping
Fees: None
Best seasons: Summer through fall

Maps: USGS Crestone Peak, Crestone, Beck Mountain; National Geographic Trails Illustrated #138: Sangre de Cristo Mountains
Nearest towns: Westcliffe, Crestone
Trail contacts: Rio Grande National Forest, Saguache Ranger District, (719) 655-2547; San Isabel National Forest, San Carlos Ranger District, (719) 269-8500; Custer County Sheriff's Office, (719) 783-2270
Trail tips: Don't feed the bighorn sheep or other wildlife.

Finding the trailhead: From the intersection of CO 17 and CR T in Moffat (13.4 miles south of the intersection of US 285 and CO 17), take CR T (Russel Street) east for 11.9 miles. The road turns left as it heads into Crestone and becomes Birch Street (CO 71) for 0.4 mile. Continue 0.2 miles on this main road in Crestone as it turns right and becomes Golden Avenue. Turn left as it becomes Alder Street. In 0.1 mile take the first right onto Galena Street, a dirt 2WD road. Follow that road 2.3 miles over increasingly bad roads (2WD vehicles may opt to park at the forest boundary at 13.8 miles) to the trailhead. GPS: N37° 59.33'/W105° 39.77'

The Hike

Challenger Point got its name as a result of the tragic disintegration of the *Challenger* space shuttle in 1986. The peak bears a plaque commemorating the crew who died in the accident: Francis Scobee, Michael Smith, Judith Resnik, Ronald McNair, Ellison Onizuka, Gregory Jarvis, and Sharon Christa McAuliffe. The name change was suggested by Colorado Springs resident Dennis Williams in 1986 and quickly approved by the US Board on Geographic Names in 1987. Alan Silverstein led an expedition to place the plaque on July 18 that summer. Unfortunately it is not the only plaque in the area placed to commemorate a space shuttle disaster. Columbia Point (13,980

The plaque commemorating space shuttle Challenger's *crew on Challenger Point's peak.*
CHRIS SEAVER

feet) bears a plaque commemorating the crew of the *Columbia* space shuttle, which exploded in 2003.

That somber note aside, this is an awesome place to be remembered! The hike to the peak has amazing meadows, and Willow Lake is a high-altitude oasis with gorgeous waterfalls. The conglomerate rock in the region makes for some interesting and unexpected features like Kit Carson Avenue, and many of the peaks in the Crestone Group jut up toward space. There could be no better place for such explorers and luminaries to be remembered than in a place that, in its own way, reaches to the stars.

Challenger Point requires Class 2 hiking and has some scrambling that may even require the use of hands for balance or climbing. As a more than 11-mile round-trip, it makes for a long day. When paired with Kit Carson, a Class 3 adventure with more exposure and difficult moves, it becomes a very long 13-mile or more trek requiring endurance, stamina, and some mountaineering skill. Thankfully the journey can be broken up into two days by camping near Willow Lake (camp at least 300 feet from it, as required by wilderness rules), allowing climbers to sleep a little higher up on the trail to get a good, early start the next day. The trail is well traveled, and in 2014 the Rocky Mountain Field Institute said it planned to start restoring vegetation and creating a more sustainable path up the mountains.

From the Willow Creek Trailhead head east, straight into the forest. In about 100 yards turn right onto Willow Creek Trail, heading southeast and crossing two small streams. At 0.1 mile take a left, heading east in a clearing as the ridges begin to fold the trail into a small gully. Cross over the gully; at 0.4 mile the trail begins switchbacking up a slope and at 1.3 miles and 9,900 feet reach the ridge crest. From the small ridge, and from there on out, gain an impressive view of the basin, which is bookended by Challenger Point's west face on the southeast side of the basin. Come down into the drainage, descending to about 9,800 feet near Willow Creek Park, which has a beautiful meadow to the right. A smaller trail branches off to the right, close to the meadow at 1.5 miles, but stay left on the main trail. The trail begins a slow ascent, staying on the left side of the small valley through a slightly sparse evergreen forest. At 10,000 feet and 1.8 miles the trail starts going through a series of small switchbacks followed by long, straight stretches of trail.

The trail begins heading southeast, crossing toward the other side of the valley at 2.8 miles and 10,700 feet the trail enters a small clearing and crosses a small gully near a craggy rock face. At 3.1 miles and 10,940 feet, cross over frothy Willow Creek and start up a series of tight switchbacks, entering scree. At 3.3 miles and 11,110 feet come close to the base of Challenger's headwall on the south side of the basin, reentering forest 11,300 feet and 3.6 miles.

From here the trail becomes easier for a period, winding its way through the narrow valley, and at 3.6 miles drop down to cross the stream at about 11,300 feet as the trail cuts back across the valley and heads up a steep incline toward some falls just below the west end of the lake at 4.2 miles. In 0.1 mile reach the west side of Willow Lake in a gorgeous basin, with cliffs and waterfalls on the east end and the craggy gray walls of rock face just beyond. There are many places to camp near Willow Lake, as the many social trails attest; just stay more than 300 feet from the lake and follow wilderness rules.

The main trail wraps around the northern side of the lake, heading east. At 4.4 miles and 11,620 feet it exits the forest abruptly in short willows and begins curving right (south) to gain the top of the cliffs on the east end of the lake. At 11,770 feet and 4.6 miles the trail crosses over upper Willow Creek above the waterfall; Challenger's north slopes are slightly left, and Kit Carson is the impressive block just left and behind Challenger.

From here the grassy trail quickly changes character and gets steeper as it starts climbing out of the basin. At 4.9 miles and 11,900 feet, near a small pond, the trail heads up the grassy slope to the right that starts gaining elevation rapidly, staying just left of a large rock outcropping. From here the trail is harder to find (RMFI's improvements might change that), but follow trail fragments and cairns over scree and rock on this Class 2 segment.

Near 13,200 feet approach the outcropping; just beyond it head left for a couple hundred feet then right up towards the crest. Stay on the right side of the rock gully, scrambling up the steep, difficult slope. At 5.6 miles and 13,890 feet go left, crossing

Challenger Point

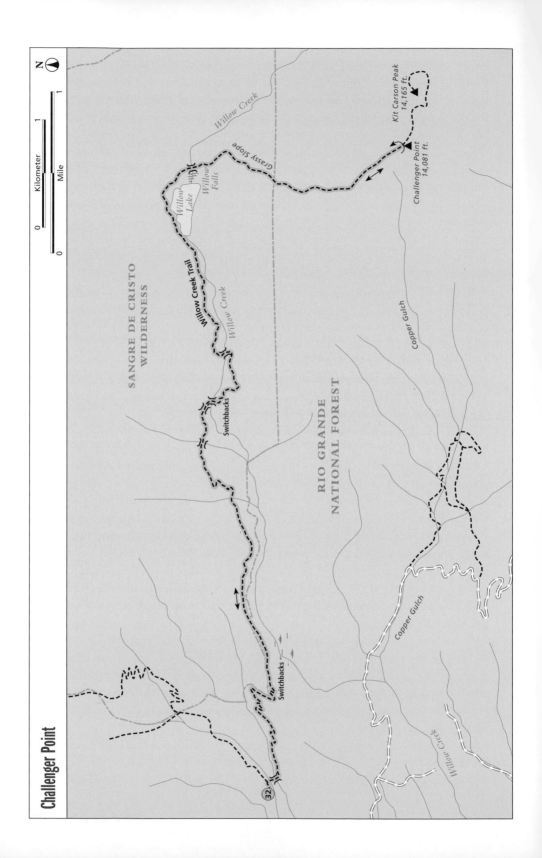

SANGRE DE CRISTO WILDERNESS

RIO GRANDE NATIONAL FOREST

Willow Creek

Willow Creek

Willow Lake

Willow Falls

Grassy Slope

Willow Creek Trail

Switchbacks

Switchbacks

Copper Gulch

Copper Gulch

Willow Creek

Kit Carson Peak
14,165 ft.

Challenger Point
14,081 ft.

32

N

Kilometer
0   1

Mile
0   1

over the top of the gully and gaining the north ridge of Challenger Point. Scramble up the ridge, facing some mild exposure over the last 0.25 mile, and summit at 5.8 miles and 14,081 feet. Return via the same route, or continue on to Kit Carson.

Miles and Directions

0.0 Start at the trailhead and head east. In 100 yards turn right onto Willow Creek Trail.

0.1 Turn left, heading east in a clearing.

0.4 The trail switchbacks up a slope.

1.3 Reach the ridge crest.

1.5 Stay left on the main trail above Willow Creek Park.

1.8 The trail goes through some small switchbacks.

2.8 Reach a small clearing and cross a gully.

3.1 Cross over Willow Creek then hike up tight switchbacks.

3.3 Exit the forest near Challenger's headwall.

3.6 Reenter forest.

4.2 Pass falls just below Willow Lake.

4.4 Exit the forest into willow thickets.

4.6 The trail crosses over upper Willow Creek.

4.9 Head up the grassy slope to the right.

5.6 Reach top of Challenger's north ridge.

5.8 Summit Challenger Point. Return via the same route. (**Option:** Continue on to Kit Carson Peak.)

11.6 Return to trailhead.

Hiking Information

Closest Outfitters

Take a Hike!, 210 Main St., Westcliffe; (719) 783-3771; takeahikewc.com

Chappy's Mountain View Bar & Grill, 213 Main St., Westcliffe; (719) 783-0813; facebook.com/ChappybarandgrillwestcliffeCO

Edge Ski Paddle & Pack, 107 N Union Ave., Pueblo; (719) 583-2021; edgeskiandpaddle.com

Great Pre- or Post-Mountain Spots

Royal Gorge Brewing Co. & Restaurant, 413 Main St., Cañon City; (719) 345-4141; royalgorgebrewpub.com

Elevation Beer Company, 115 Pahlone Pkwy., Poncha Springs; (719) 539-5258; elevationbeerco.com

33 Mount Sneffels

14,150' (NGVD29), 14,155' (NAVD88), 27th highest

Near Ouray and Telluride, Mount Sneffels is the tallest mountain in Ouray County. Sneffels peers over its fellow mountains with a distinctive and oft-photographed summit block. Requiring a difficult Class 2 hike and scramble, it serves as a good entry into climbing Colorado's more difficult fourteeners. Sneffels has a small summit block, but with distinctive neighbors like Teakettle Mountain (Teakettle lost its "spout" during the winter of 1998–99) and Potosi Peak, Sneffels offers a stunning 360-degree panorama with sheer drop-offs.

Start: Blue Lakes Trailhead
Distance: 2WD trailhead: 7.3 miles; 4WD trailhead: 2.3 miles (Don't worry. All the fun, tough stuff is in the last 2.3 miles.)
Hiking time: 3 hours from 4WD trailhead
Elevation gain: 2WD trailhead: 3,450 feet; 4WD trailhead: 1,750 feet
Difficulty: Class 2, Class 3
Trail surface: Dirt, scree, rock
Trailhead elevation: 2WD trailhead: 10,750 feet; 4WD trailhead: 11,850 feet

Camping: Backcountry camping
Fees: None
Best seasons: Spring through fall
Maps: USGS Mount Sneffels, Telluride, Irontown; National Geographic Trails Illustrated #141: Telluride, Silverton, Ouray, Lake City
Nearest town: Ouray
Trail contacts: Uncompahgre National Forest, Ouray Ranger District, (970) 240-5300; Ouray County Sheriff, (970) 325-7272

Finding the trailhead: From the south end of Ouray on US 550 and Ouray CR 361, turn south onto Ouray CR 361 (Camp Bird Road), a dirt road, toward Yankee Boy Basin. At 4.7 miles stay to the right on CR 26 (FR 853). Parts of the road are cut into the rock face, so rock hangs overhead like a partial tunnel. Stay on CR 26 for 1.3 miles, ignoring the turnoff for Imogene Pass. Continue on Yankee Boy Basin Road for another 0.8 miles, passsing through the remnants of the town of Sneffels. Come to a sign with information about Yankee Boy Basin. If driving a low-clearance vehicle, consider parking here. The road gets considerably rougher from this point on. There are decent parking options here. Passenger cars have made it farther, to about 11,200 feet, but their undercarriage will get significantly scraped up.

If continuing in a 4WD vehicle, go right on Yankee Boy Basin Road (FR 853.1B). Reach the lower 4WD trailhead at 11,400 feet and another 1.5 miles. Only tough 4WD vehicles should attempt going beyond this point. For those that do have a rugged 4WD vehicle, stay to the right, traveling just over another 1 mile to reach the upper 4WD trailhead at 12,420 feet. GPS: 2WD trailhead: N37° 58.75'/W107° 45.51'; 4WD trailhead: N37° 59.70'/W107° 47.09'

Hiking toward Mount Sneffels. Peak is left of center.

The Hike

The length of a journey up Mount Sneffels is based on a vehicle's and a driver's ability. The approach to this peak can be a longer hike than climbing the peak itself. From the Yankee Boy Basin Trailhead at 10,700 feet, it's a 5.6-mile round-trip to the upper trailhead—mainly along the 4WD road. From the lower 4WD parking lot, it's a 2.6-mile round-trip to the upper trailhead if you opt to take the lovely trail that courses around Wrights Lake at 12,180 feet. But from the Blue Lake Basin Trailhead in Yankee Boy Basin, it's a tricky, Class 2+ hike bordering on Class 3 scrambling.

Given the limitations of vehicles and drivers, this hike description will start from the only common denominator: the upper 4WD Blue Lakes Trailhead. From there, hike northwest over a solid talus trail, heading toward Blue Lakes Pass and the jagged, colorful southern ridge of Sneffels.

At about 0.25 mile stay to the right at the trail junction, continuing toward Sneffels to the northwest. At just under 0.5 mile the trail starts switchbacking and climbing at a steeper trajectory.

Follow the switchbacks to enter a steep scree-and-gravel-covered slope. In late spring and summer it's a Class 2, 0.4-mile scramble from about 12,800 feet to the 13,500-foot Lavender Couloir saddle between 13,694-foot Kismet Peak and Sneffels.

The couloir is sometimes easier to climb in spring, when it's still covered with snow. Try to stay off the loose dirt by carefully climbing up the rocks on either side of the washed-out gravel in the middle. This goes for descending the route too. The couloir is named for Dwight Lavender, one of the first mountaineers to climb Sneffels' north face.

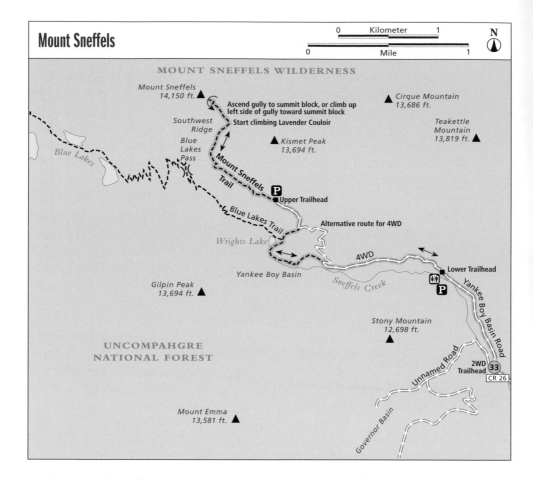

MOUNT SNEFFELS WILDERNESS

Mount Sneffels
14,150 ft.

Ascend gully to summit block, or climb up
left side of gully toward summit block

Cirque Mountain
13,686 ft.

Southwest
Ridge

Start climbing Lavender Couloir

Teakettle
Mountain
13,819 ft.

Blue
Lakes
Pass

Kismet Peak
13,694 ft.

Blue Lakes

Mount Sneffels
Trail

Upper Trailhead

Blue Lakes Trail

Alternative route for 4WD

Wrights Lake

4WD

Yankee Boy Basin

Sneffels Creek

Lower Trailhead

Gilpin Peak
13,694 ft.

Stony Mountain
12,698 ft.

Yankee Boy Basin Road

UNCOMPAHGRE
NATIONAL FOREST

2WD
Trailhead

33

CR 26

Unnamed Road

Mount Emma
13,581 ft.

Governor Basin

Entering the gully on the northwest side of the saddle offers two options to get to the peak: Climb up the talus in the heart of the gully, or ascend the rock face to the left of the gully. Both options offer a decent amount of difficult Class 2 exposure. Snow can persist in this gully into early summer, and a mountaineering ax may be helpful.

If climbing in the gully, the crux move on this peak is the V-notch 20 feet below the top of the gully. Climb up and through the notch to the summit block then scramble over the remaining 200 or so feet to the top to gain some well-earned and amazing views from the top of Colorado.

To the east you are rewarded with views of the silhouette of 14,015-foot Wetterhorn against 14,309-foot Uncompahgre in the distance. To the southeast, across a snaky ridge, are Teakettle Mountain and Potosi Peak. Beyond them the Handies Group marks the horizon. Peaks in the Wilson Group, off to the southwest, are the closest fourteeners. To the north smaller, undulating hills and plateaus show how volcanic action created this landscape.

Impressive rock pinnacles along Mount Sneffels' ridge.

Miles and Directions

0.0   Start at the Blue Lakes Trailhead, the 4WD trailhead.

0.25 Stay to the right at the trail junction.

0.5   Start ascending Lavender Couloir.

0.8   Reach the Lavender Couloir saddle between Kismet and Sneffels. Turn left (northwest) to begin ascending the next scree-filled gully to Sneffels' summit.

0.9   If climbing the gully, climb toward the center and eventually the right side as it narrows. Just shy of the top of the gully, find a notch to the left of the gully (south side) and climb up and over it. The summit is a 200-foot scramble beyond the notch over a rough trail.

1.15 Reach the summit. Return via the same route.

2.3   Arrive back at the Blue Lakes Trailhead and return to where you parked your vehicle.

Hiking Information

Closest Outfitters

Ouray Mountain Sports, 732 Main St., Ouray; (970) 325-4284; ouraysports.com

Great Pre- or Post-Mountain Spots

Ouray Brewing Co., 607 Main St., Ouray; (970) 325-7388; ouraybrewery.com

O'Brien's Pub & Grill, 726 Main St., Ouray; (970) 325-4386; obriensouraycolorado
.com

Buen Tiempo Mexican Restaurant, 515 Main St., Ouray; (970) 325-4544; buentiempo
restaurant.com

34 Mount of the Holy Cross

14,005' (NGVD29), 14,012' (NAVD88), 51st highest

Mount of the Holy Cross is one of Colorado's most famous fourteeners thanks to the iconic cross that graces its east face. Still, this mountain is hidden and by no means the easiest to climb. The standard route is a long Class 2 climb, and climbers have gotten lost coming off this high peak. It's not too far from Denver and is quite close to Vail. This gem is the northern end cap to the Sawatch Range, the greatest concentration of fourteeners in the state.

Start: Halfmoon Trailhead
Distance: 11.4 miles
Hiking time: About 10 hours
Elevation gain: 5,630 feet, including second ascent of Half Moon Pass
Difficulty: Class 2
Trail surface: Dirt, scree
Trailhead elevation: 10,360 feet
Camping: Backcountry camping; camping spots at East Cross Creek
Fees: None

Best seasons: Early summer through fall
Maps: USGS Mount of the Holy Cross, Minturn, Mount Jackson; National Geographic Trails Illustrated #126: Holy Cross, Ruedi Reservoir
Nearest town: Minturn
Trail contacts: White River National Forest, Holy Cross Ranger District, (970) 827-5715; Eagle County Sheriff's Office, (970) 479-2201
Trail tips: Holy Cross is in national wilderness land; follow all regulations. This hike requires a lot of ascension on the return trip.

Finding the trailhead: Take exit 171 off I-70 and head southeast on US 24 East, following signs toward Minturn and Leadville. At 4.9 miles turn right onto Tigiwon Road (also called Notch Mountain Road). Drive 8.3 miles, staying right on this curvy dirt road (most 2WD vehicles can make it), reaching the Halfmoon Trailhead at 13.2 miles. **Note:** This road is closed in the fall through the beginning of summer. Check with the USDA Forest Service for road closure information. GPS: N39° 30.03' / W106° 25.99'

The Hike

The most famous feature of this mountain, its cross, is well hidden and best seen from Notch Mountain (13,237 feet), which is 1.3 miles northeast of Holy Cross's summit. On the standard approach from Half Moon Creek, climbers don't even get a view of the cross on the mountain. The cross is formed by a long, thin rock couloir and a high bench on its east face. It's most apparent when snow remains in the rock features. Snowmelt from the cross fills the "Bowl of Tears," a sapphire lake at the base of the 1,400-foot-tall cross.

The mountain has an interesting history. Prospectors, Native Americans, trappers, and other mountain men reported sighting the mountain in the late 1850s. But since the cross disappears in both summer and winter, it was visible only for a few months.

The path to Mount of the Holy Cross. LEE MAUNEY

A precise location was elusive. Samuel Bowles wrote about seeing it from Grays Peak—about 40 miles away—in his 1869 book, *The Switzerland of America.* The feature was considered a rumor until the Hayden Expedition confirmed it in 1873 with William Henry Jackson's first picture of the cross. Two members of the Hayden team, J. T. Gardner and W. H. Holmes, made the first ascent of the mountain that summer.

The mountain was made a national monument in 1929, and thousands flocked to it annually in the 1930s. But interest waned and the cost of keeping it up as a national monument became too expensive. The mountain lost its designation as a national monument in 1950. In 1980 Congress designated it as the Holy Cross Wilderness Area. It endures as one of Colorado's most-loved fourteeners and draws thousands of summiters a year.

The mountain also has had its share of tragedies. Though it just barely crosses over into fourteener territory, hikers have gotten lost on this wild trail, often requiring search-and-rescue teams to come out. Some of these hikers are never seen again. On the standard route some climbers fail to turn right while descending Holy Cross's northwest ridge, leading them to Cross Creek Valley. Then there's the altitude gain of 970 feet—on the way back from the peak. That feature brings the total round-trip ascent to more than 5,600 feet of elevation gain, which can wear many out-of-shape or inexperienced climbers beyond exhaustion.

On the summit of Mount of the Holy Cross. Lee Mauney

The Trail to Holy Cross begins at the south end of the parking area, heading southwest. Just beyond the parking lot, find a kiosk and fill out a wilderness registration card. Start hiking up Half Moon Trail (FT 2009) and enter a stand of evergreens. Cross over a small stream at 0.1 mile and continue hiking up the solid dirt trail through a sparse forest and green meadow toward Half Moon Pass. At 0.4 mile (10,600 feet) reach two short switchbacks and continue heading in the same direction. At 0.6 mile and 10,860 feet the trail takes a sharp right then fishhooks up in the same direction. This is the first of some long switchbacks that lead to the top of Half Moon Pass at 11,650 feet and 1.6 miles as the forest thins out. This also is the base of Notch Mountain. Continue on as the trail heads west through patches of forest and meadow then south toward East Cross Creek. At 2.8 miles and 11,120 feet begin descending switchbacks as the trail leaves the shoulder of Notch Mountain and descends to 10,690 feet. Remember, you have to go back up this on the way back to the trailhead!

Reach a flat area with some signage about camp spots in the dense evergreen forest in this area. Continuing on the path, cross East Cross Creek at 2.9 miles and 10,700 feet toward the western side of this low area before resuming the climb. The good trail winds through some rockier areas as it starts climbing out of the gully in a southerly direction, but the trail remains solid.

Come to tree line at 11,600 feet and 3.8 miles and follow the trail and directional cairns as the trail continues crisscrossing up the steep ascent toward Holy Cross's north ridge over rocky meadow. Thank the Colorado Fourteeners Initiative (CFI) for working on this trail. The trail continues to roughly 13,400 feet at 5.0 miles, turns left, and crawls up the summit block.

Stay right of the ridge crest, following faint trail segments over lots of talus toward a notch at 13,740 feet. This is the top of Angelica Couloir. Angle left and climb the remaining 260 feet to the summit.

The Bowl of Tears is just southeast of the summit, almost 2,000 feet below. Holy Cross Couloir is just above the lake.

Mount of the Holy Cross

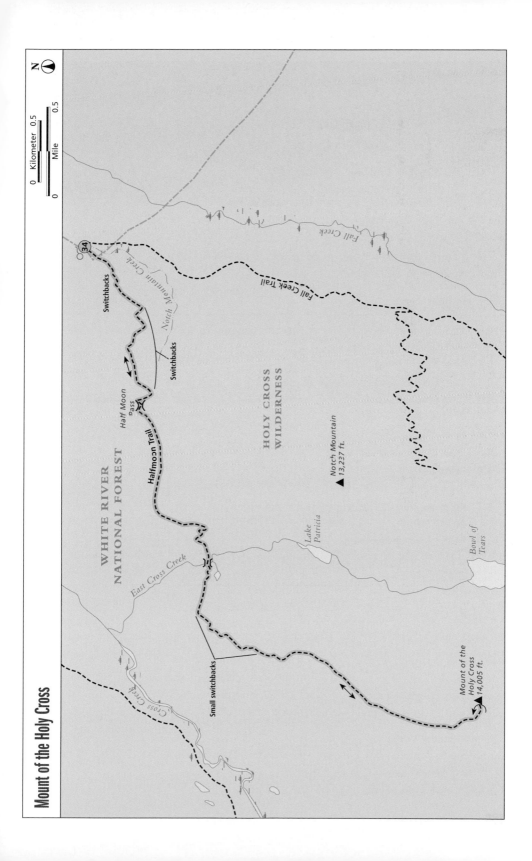

N

0   Kilometer   0.5

0   Mile   0.5

WHITE RIVER
NATIONAL FOREST

HOLY CROSS
WILDERNESS

34

Switchbacks

Notch Mountain Creek

Switchbacks

Half Moon Pass

Halfmoon Trail

Fall Creek Trail

Fall Creek

Notch Mountain
13,227 ft.

East Cross Creek

Lake Patricia

Bowl of Tears

Cross Creek

Small switchbacks

Mount of the
Holy Cross
14,005 ft.

Bowl of tears below Mount of the Holy Cross. LEE MAUNEY

Return via the same route, making sure to stay on-trail, particularly coming off the northern ridge of Holy Cross.

Miles and Directions

0.0 Start at southern end of parking lot. Register at the kiosk for the wilderness area just after leaving the lot.

0.1 Cross a small stream.

0.4 Take two short switchbacks and continue heading in the same direction.

0.6 The trail makes a sharp right then fishhooks before going through a series of spread-out switchbacks.

1.6 Reach the top of Half Moon Pass.

2.9 Cross East Cross Creek.

3.8 Reach tree line.

5.0 Begin the final summit of Holy Cross.

5.7 Reach the summit. Return by the same route, taking special care when coming off the northern ridge.

11.4 Arrive back at the trailhead.

Hiking Information

Closest Outfitters

Alpine Quest Sports, 34510 US 6, Edwards; (970) 926-3867; alpinequestsports.com

Ptarmigan Sports, 137 Main St. #C-104, Edwards; (970) 926-8144; ptarmigansports .com

Great Pre- or Post-Mountain Spots

Crazy Mountain Brewing Co., 439 Edwards Access Rd., Edwards; (970) 926-3009; crazy mountainbrewery.com

Gore Range Brewery, 105 Edwards Village Blvd., Edwards; (970) 926-2739; gorerange brewery.com

Sticky Fingers Cafe & Bakery, 132 Main St., Minturn; (970) 827-5353

35 Castle Peak

14,265' (NGVD29), 14,269' (NAVD88), 12th highest

Castle Peak is the easiest peak in the Elk Range, which should say something, since it's still considered more difficult than every fourteener in the Sawatch Range and almost every mountain in the Front Range. Castle Peak is in the Maroon Bells/Snowmass Wilderness in the White River National Forest near Aspen. This ruddy block of a mountain is a Class 2 hike. More-experienced climbers may opt to also climb Conundrum (14,060 feet), an unofficial fourteener that's a subpeak of Castle but still makes for an impressive climb with some Class 3 scrambling.

Start: Castle Creek Trailhead
Distance: 4WD: 6.2 miles; 2WD: 11.2 miles
Hiking time: 4WD: 6 hours; 2WD: 9 hours
Elevation gain: 4WD: 3,090 feet; 2WD: 4,460 feet
Difficulty: Class 2
Trail surface: Dirt, scree
Trailhead elevation: 4WD: 11,160 feet; 2WD 9,800 feet
Camping: A number of camping spots are close to the 2WD trailhead; backcountry camping

Fees: None
Best seasons: Summer through fall
Maps: USGS Hayden Peak, Maroon Bells, Pearl Pass, Gothic; National Geographic Trails Illustrated #127: Aspen, Independence Pass
Nearest town: Aspen
Trail contacts: White River National Forest, Aspen-Sopris Ranger District, (970) 963-2266; Pitkin County Sheriff's Office, (970) 920-5300

Finding the trailhead: From the roundabout just northwest of Aspen on CO 82, head south on Castle Creek Road to Ashcroft (second exit if coming from the north) for 13 miles. Turn right onto Montezuma Road (FR 102) and look for a place to park a 2WD vehicle in the first mile of this road. At 10,200 feet a creek crossing will likely weed out passenger vehicles from continuing up the mountain road. There are also dispersed camping spots in this area along the road. After that the road is suited for high-clearance vehicles, which should be able to make the upper trailhead at 11,160 feet; the trailhead has space for about six vehicles. Rugged 4WD vehicles may make it as far as 12,800 feet, but the 11,160-foot trailhead is a good place to park and start hiking. GPS: 2WD trailhead: N39° 01.37'/W106° 48.52'; 4WD trailhead: N39° 00.37'/W106° 50.28'

The Hike

Castle Peak is the easiest fourteener to climb in the rugged Elk Range of mountains, which are known for their rotten rock but are also some of the most stunning fourteeners in the state. Though Castle is the tallest mountain in the range and in Elk County, it's also the easiest fourteener in the region to climb. In fact, even

Climbing toward the apex of Castle Peak. CHRIS SEAVER

Conundrum Peak—essentially a subpeak of Castle—has more difficult Class 3 climbing than Castle.

Impressed by its castellated summit, the Hayden Survey Expedition gave Castle Peak its name. The mountain was first summited by Hayden geographer Henry Gannett in 1873. It remains a remote mountain and often is climbed as a warm-up to the more difficult fourteeners in the region, including the Maroon Bells and Capitol Peak.

Conundrum, which is usually climbed with Castle, wasn't named Conundrum over questions of whether or not to call it a fourteener. Rather it takes its name from Conundrum Creek and the hot springs nearby. Apparently, much like Quandary Peak, miners in the region found traces of gold in the creek and followed it upward in the hope of finding a lode. It never happened, and that failure became a name-worthy conundrum.

Starting from the 4WD trailhead at 11,160 feet, hike up Montezuma Basin on FR 102, staying to the right at 0.3 mile as the road passes Pearl Pass Road. Continue up the road until 12,800 feet and 2.2 miles. (**Note:** Rugged 4WD vehicles and experienced drivers may attempt to reach this point in their vehicles.) From this point head southwest up the left side of the basin up a steep slope with snow throughout most of the year. Climb over the snow or—later in summer—scree and at 13,190 feet and 2.4 miles encounter some switchbacks. If climbing snow, cut back and forth as needed. At 13,350 feet and 2.5 miles head left as the trail enters the large basin below Castle Peak.

A trail zigzags up to the northeastern ridge of Castle from here. Climb up to about 13,550 feet at 2.6 miles and cut right over the talus, heading southeast across the slope to the ridge.

Reach the ridge at 13,720 feet and 2.75 miles. From here on out the climbing is more difficult Class 2 scrambling and the trail disappears in some places. Some of the rock is rotten, but with careful stepping and route choice, the route is Class 2. To get around rock outcroppings in this area, drop to the right of the ridge and contour back

Glissading into the basin below Capitol Peak. CHRIS SEAVER

Castle Peak

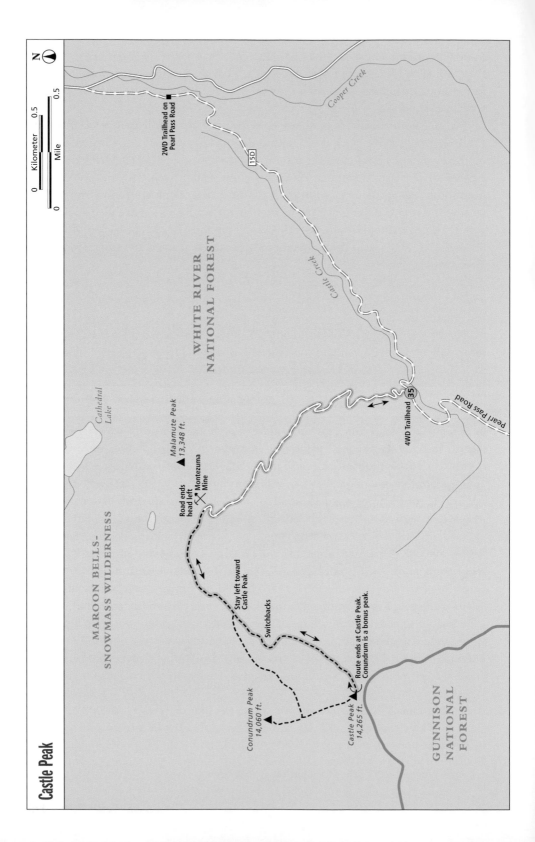

N

0   Kilometer   0.5

0   Mile   0.5

MAROON BELLS-
SNOWMASS WILDERNESS

Cathedral
Lake

Conundrum Peak
14,060 ft.

Castle Peak
14,265 ft.

Route ends at Castle Peak.
Conundrum is a bonus peak.

Switchbacks

Stay left toward
Castle Peak

Road ends
head left

Montezuma
Mine

▲ Malamute Peak
13,348 ft.

WHITE RIVER
NATIONAL FOREST

Castle Creek

4WD Trailhead

35

Pearl Pass Road

15D

Castle Creek

2WD Trailhead on
Pearl Pass Road

Cooper Creek

GUNNISON
NATIONAL
FOREST

up. The trail is solid here. At 3.1 miles and 14,010 feet the remaining route is in view. The final pitch is a little steeper and has some exposure, but it's an epic final approach.

At 3.1 miles reach the summit and get stunning views in all directions as basins spread out toward each compass point, divided by Castle's ridges.

Return via the same route, or hike north down the saddle to Conundrum and climb up the Class 3 route to the top.

Miles and Directions

0.0 Start at the 4WD parking at 11,160 feet.

0.3 Stay right as the road passes Pearl Pass Road.

2.2 Reach the end of the 4WD road and head up a steep slope on the left.

2.4 Climb up some switchbacks if scree is apparent, or cut back and forth as needed if on snow.

2.5 Enter the basin below Castle Peak; head left.

2.6 Climb on talus, heading southeast toward Castle's ridge.

2.75 Begin a difficult Class 2 scramble up Castle's northeast ridge, skirting to the right of most obstacles and regaining the ridge as needed.

3.1 Gain the summit at 14,265 feet. Return via same route. (**Option:** Head on to Conundrum.)

6.2 Arrive back at the 4WD parking.

Hiking Information

Closest Outfitters

Ute Mountaineer, 210 S. Galena St., Aspen; (970) 925-2849; utemountaineer.com

Bristlecone Mountain Sports, 781 E Valley Rd., Basalt; (970) 927-1492; bristlecone mountainsports.com

Great Pre- or Post-Mountain Spots

Aspen Brewing Co., 304 E Hopkins Ave., Aspen; (970) 920-BREW (2739); aspenbrewing company.com

Woody Creek Tavern, 2858 Upper River Rd., Woody Creek; (970) 923-4585; woody creektavern.com; a favorite haunt of the late Hunter S. Thompson

Belly Up Aspen, 450 S Galena St., Aspen; (970) 544-9800; bellyupaspen.com

J-Bar at Hotel Jerome, 330 E Main St., Aspen; (970) 925-3721; hoteljerome.auberge resorts.com/dining/

36 Mount Lindsey

14,042' (NGVD29), 14,047' (NAVD88), 42nd highest

Mount Lindsey is a big, beautiful mound of fourteener glory in the Blanca Group of the Sangre de Cristos. It's one of five fourteeners in the area with a lot of prominence as the hills in the region quickly fade into high plains. Located in Costilla County, just barely outside San Isabel National Forest, the peak is on private property. Thankfully the owners allow access. The standard route is a difficult Class 2 trek, although some may opt to climb up a solid Class 3 ridge to avoid a Class 2 scramble up a couloir with loose, raggedy scree. Some recommend bringing a helmet for the scree and Class 3 moves on this peak.

Start: Lilly Lake Trailhead
Distance: 8.0 miles
Hiking time: 7 to 9 hours, depending on experience
Elevation gain: 3,412 feet
Difficulty: Difficult Class 2, some easy Class 3, depending on route
Trail surface: Dirt, scree, rock
Trailhead elevation: 10,626 feet
Camping: No camping on road; backcountry camping
Fees: None
Best seasons: Spring through fall (backcountry winter sports in the area)

Maps: USGS Blanca Peak, Mosca Pass; National Geographic Trails Illustrated #138: Sangre de Cristo Mountains
Nearest towns: Walsenburg, Alamosa
Trail contacts: Rio Grande National Forest, Conejos Ranger District, (719) 274-8971; Huerfano County Sheriff, (719) 738-1600; Costilla County Sheriff, (719) 672-3302
Trail tips: The landowner requests that dogs be leashed at all times. Dogs won't be able to make the scramble and will have to travel up the scree. Please close all ranch gates after passing through them.

Finding the trailhead: From the intersection of CO 69 and CR 545 in Gardner, head west on CO 69 for 0.8 mile. Turn left onto Mosca Pass Road (CR 550). USDA Forest Service signs should show mileage for Upper Huerfano and Lily Lake Trailheads at 21.5 miles and 22.5 miles, respectively. Stay on this road until the end, but note the following mileage marks. Mosca Pass Road becomes a dirt road at 7 miles. Stay on Mosca Pass Road as it passes CR 570 and the road becomes FR 580. At 12.8 miles stay left at a junction. Reach the entrance to the Singing River Ranch at a total of 16.5 miles. At this point the road becomes rougher, but a 2WD vehicle can still make it to the trailhead. Continue for 0.9 mile, entering the Aspen River Ranch at 17.4 miles. In 3.4 more miles reach San Isabel National Forest. Continue on the narrow road for 1.8 more miles to reach the Lily Lake Trailhead. GPS: N37° 37.42'/W105° 28.38'

Mount Lindsey. CHRIS SEAVER ▶

The Hike

Mount Lindsey straddles public and private land. In fact, its summit is on private property, but landowners allow people to summit the fourteener. Please respect private property; stay on the established trail and keep it clean. The approach from Lily Lake Trailhead is in the San Isabel National Forest and the Sangre de Cristo Wilderness, but at 3.1 miles and 12,900 feet the route becomes private property.

Of the Blanca Group of fourteeners, Lindsey is the most isolated, giving it some fantastic views, not just of the Blanca Group but also of how the Sangre de Cristos stretch out like some rocky isthmus above the valley basins.

The mountain was called "Old Baldy" thanks to its large, rocky peak until 1953. That year the Colorado Mountain Club proposed the name change to the US Board on Geographic Names to honor Malcolm Lindsey, a past CMC president who passed away in 1951. The peak was his favorite, and he led many junior expeditions up this mountain and others. There's no indication whether or not Mr. Lindsey also was bald.

The trail heads south from the parking area through a forest and parallels the Huerfano River. The first 1.4 miles of this trail are relatively flat, allowing for excellent views of a classic alpine valley, trees below and sheer rock faces above. It all terminates with Blanca Peak (14,345 feet), directly ahead to the south.

After 0.2 mile of forest, the trail reaches a meadow. The trail cuts across the meadow and stays to the right along the forest's edge, reentering the forest at roughly

Climbing down Mount Lindsey. CHRIS SEAVER

0.5 mile. At 1.0 mile come to a trail junction for Lily Lake. Keep going straight. Shortly thereafter cross Huerfano River at 1.1 miles and 10,780 feet. The river is easily crossable in August, but earlier in the year it might be a little less tame because of snowmelt.

On the other side of the river, the trail curls left around the base of a boulder field. At 1.4 miles and 10,880 feet the trail begins its ascent toward Lindsey in earnest as it heads southeast, climbing into a shallow gully. At 11,560 feet and 1.9 miles cross over the bottom of the gully and a small stream then climb up the other side of the gully and into the trees, exiting the gully at 11,990 feet and 2.2 miles and coming into the basin between Lindsey and Blanca. Up to the left (east) is a feature called the Iron Nipple (13,500 feet). Ahead is the summit of Lindsey.

Hike southeast across the basin and start ascending the good trail that snakes up the easy slope to the 13,140-foot saddle between Iron Nipple and Lindsey's north-western ridge. The trail gets rockier closer to the ridge.

Ascend to the top of the ridge at 3.3 miles and cross over to the other side of the saddle. This is where the fun begins. The large, northwest gully—a scree chute—ahead is the standard Class 2 route to Lindsey's peak. (If you prefer solid Class 3 climbing to hiking on scree, consider tackling the northwest ridge instead of dipping down on the trail. It's a straight shot to the top and might be an easier alternative for people comfortable with some mild exposure. This route is even more appealing when the couloir isn't snow covered.)

To reach the gully, follow the trail that cuts below Lindsey's northwest ridge on good scree. Reach the base of the gully at 13,340 feet and 3.6 miles. To avoid the worst of the scree and prevent more erosion, try climbing closer to either side of the

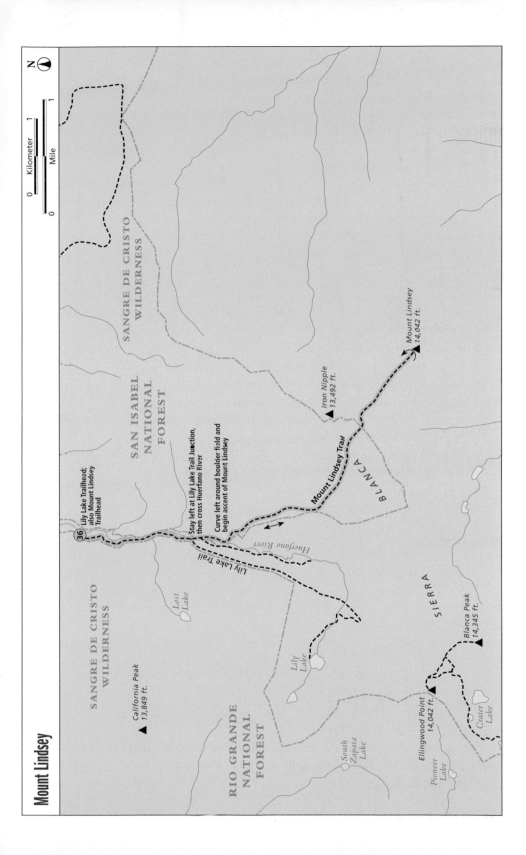

Mount Lindsey

N

0   Kilometer   1

0   Mile   1

SANGRE DE CRISTO
WILDERNESS

▲ California Peak
13,849 ft.

RIO GRANDE
NATIONAL
FOREST

Lost
Lake

Lily Lake Trail

Lily
Lake

South
Zapata Lake

Pioneer
Lake

▲ Ellingwood Point
14,042 ft.

SIERRA

Crater
Lake

▲ Blanca Peak
14,345 ft.

BLANCA

SAN ISABEL
NATIONAL
FOREST

SANGRE DE CRISTO
WILDERNESS

36   Lily Lake Trailhead;
also Mount Lindsey
Trailhead

Stay left at Lily Lake Trail Junction,
then cross Huerfano River

Curve left around boulder field and
begin ascent of Mount Lindsey

Huerfano River

Mount Lindsey Trail

▲ Iron Nipple
13,492 ft.

▲ Mount Lindsey
14,042 ft.

gully. Toward the top the gully, at 3.7 miles and 13,600 feet, the gully narrows and some scrambling over rocks might be necessary.

Passing through a notch, at 13,650 feet reach the top of gully—only to find more gullies, albeit shorter, shallower ones. There isn't much of a solid trail here, but there are some trail segments and cairns to guide the way.

Reach the northwest ridge crest at 13,950 feet, and hike the remaining 300 yards and 90 or so vertical feet to the top.

From the top you've got a stunning view of Blanca Peak and its little buddy Ellingwood Point (14,042 feet). To the north the Crestone Group of mountains crops up from the plains like a giant caldera. To the south you get a great view of Colorado's agrarian side, with circular crop fields and plains that stretch to the horizon.

Return via the same route.

Miles and Directions

0.0   Start at the Lilly Lake Trailhead, heading south on a trail that parallels the Huerfano River.

1.0   Go straight at the trail junction for Lily Lake.

1.1   Cross the Huerfano River.

1.4   The trail begins an ascent toward Lindsey, climbing up a shallow gully.

1.9   Cross over the bottom of the gully and a small stream.

2.2   Climb out of the basin between Lindsey and Blanca and head up to the left.

3.3   Ascend to the top of the ridge and cross over to the other side of the saddle.

3.6   Reach the base of the gully, climbing up to either side.

3.7   Reach the top the gully. Scramble over some rocks and cross over some more gullies, following cairns, that go through sections of trail leading to the top.

4.0   Reach the peak. Return via the same route.

8.0   Arrive back at the trailhead.

Hiking Information

Closest Outfitters

Kristi Mountain Sports, 3223 Main St., Alamosa; (719) 589-9759; kristimountain
  sports.com

Great Pre- or Post-Mountain Spots

San Luis Valley Brewing Co., 631 Main St., Alamosa; (719) 587-2337; slvbrewco.com

Calvillo's Mexican Restaurant, 400 Main St., Alamosa; (719) 587-5500; calvillos
  .qwestoffice.net

The Rubi Slipper, 506 State Ave., Alamosa; (719) 589-2641

37 Ellingwood Point

14,042' (NGVD29), 14,049' (NAVD88), 43rd highest

Ellingwood, Blanca Peak (14,345 feet), and Little Bear (14,037 feet) share the Lake Como Trailhead, which is up the long, gnarled, difficult Lake Como ATV road. Depending on how far up the road you're able to drive, it will add 6 to 8 miles of hiking each way to your adventure. But this is a great, beautiful basin for camping out for a night or two to make it worthwhile to conquer one, two, or all three peaks.

The standard route to Ellingwood Point is a Class 2 summit that shares almost all its route with the trail to Blanca. It's a rough push over scree to the peak. The peak shares a short, exciting Class 3 saddle with Ellingwood, and both can be had in a glorious day by adventurous climbers. Snow can persist into summer on this mountain, and a mountaineering ax may come in handy.

If you drive a rock-crawler, extremely modified 4WD, ATV, or perhaps a horse, you may make it up to the Lake Como trailhead (about 10 miles from the highway junction). A 4WD vehicle with high clearance might be able to travel as far as 3.25 miles from the junction with CO 150 at about 8,800 feet. This is a notoriously difficult road with a series of moves called "Jaws" that will chew up and spit out an SUV's undersides.

Start: Lake Como
Distance: 5.2 miles
Hiking time: About 5 hours
Elevation gain: 2,292 feet
Difficulty: Difficult Class 2
Trail surface: Dirt, scree, rock
Trailhead elevation: 11,750 feet
Camping: Camping by Lake Como and by Blue Lakes
Fees: None
Best seasons: Spring through fall (backcountry winter sports in the area)

Maps: USGS Blanca Peak, Mosca Pass, Twin Peaks; National Geographic Trails Illustrated #138: Sangre de Cristo Mountains
Nearest towns: Fort Garland, Alamosa
Trail contacts: Pike San Isabel National Forest, San Carlos Ranger District, (719) 269-8500; Rio Grande National Forest, Conejos Ranger District, (719) 274-8971; Huerfano County Sheriff, (719) 738-1600; Costilla County Sheriff, (719) 672-3302
Trail tips: Start the hike early. Weather can build quickly, and it's hard to see it rolling in when lower in the climb.

Finding the trailhead: Take CO 150 north toward Great Sand Dunes National Park from the junction of US 160 and CO 150, west of Fort Garland and Blanca and east of Alamosa. Go 3.2 miles on CO 150, passing CR 4S on the left and taking the next right, which becomes Lake Como Road. The Lake Como Trailhead is 7.2 miles from the highway junction along this 4WD road. Most people will have to park their vehicles at about 1.6 to 1.8 miles on Lake Como Road. Those who have a 4WD vehicle with good clearance can make it about 3.25 miles on the road, finding parking along the road or one of the switchbacks—make sure other vehicles can pass your vehicle on the road and that other vehicles can turn around on a switchback. Park your vehicle and begin hiking up the 4WD drive road to Lake Como. If you plan on driving an ATV or rock crawler to Lake Como, check out some videos of the obstacles first. GPS: 2WD Trailhead: N37° 32.27'/W105° 34.64'; 4WD Trailhead: N37° 33.04'/W105° 33.54'; Lake Como: N37° 34.20'/W105° 30.92'

The Hike

Ellingwood is one of Colorado's more-contentious fourteeners. The peak has only 342 feet of prominence from the saddle with Blanca, making it close to the 300-foot prominence rule so some have bridled at calling it a fourteener. However, this is still a challenging summit. Thanks to that same saddle, it can also be climbed with Blanca in one day, for a nearly 6-mile round-trip with a lot of elevation gain.

Despite the controversy, Ellingwood was named in good faith in honor of Albert Ellingwood, one of the first people to ascend all of Colorado's fourteeners and who achieved numerous first ascents in Colorado and Wyoming, including the first summit of Crestone Peak in 1916—the last fourteener climbed in the state—when he was a professor at Colorado College. It's no surprise he was a pioneering member of the Colorado Mountain Club, founded in 1912. Colorado recognized it as Ellingwood Peak in 1969, with federal recognition coming the year after.

It's a Class 1 hike to Lake Como Trailhead on the rutty Lake Como Road, with some jagged rocks that are easy to hike on but murder on a vehicle. The elevation gain isn't too bad, but it is a pretty steady incline to the lake. The hike itself is lovely after you reach the shade of trees in Chokecherry Canyon at about 8,800 feet. From there the road heads northeast toward Holbrook Creek, crossing it at 10,700 feet. From there the road parallels the creek until it reaches Lake Como at 11,760 feet.

The standard route to Ellingwood and Blanca continues up the same "road" that brought you to Lake Como. From the trailhead hike northeast then east around Lake Como's western shores along what's still called Lake Como Road. The road crosses a meadow then enters an evergreen forest at 11,760 feet and nearly 0.25 mile. Continue through the forest on the road, passing near some ruins about 100 yards into the forest. Exit the forest in 100 more yards and start climbing up the improbable road as you come close to the base of Little Bear's western ridge. Pass some small lakes near the ruins of the Blanca Mine and continue up the curling road, crossing a stream at 0.8 mile and 12,090 feet as the road ascends towards Blue Lakes at 12,100 feet and finally peters out. There are some good camping spots near the lakes, though they're largely above tree line.

Although the road dies around Blue Lakes, a good trail continues to lead up and out of the basin, crossing a stream beneath a waterfall at 1.0 mile and 12,160 feet. Shortly after, it climbs up a scree field that turns into a series of ledges and scree that cross over the stream that feeds the waterfall at 1.3 miles and 12,490 feet close to a small lake. The trail goes around the lake's southeast side then heads northeast, passing over its tributary stream at 12,570 feet and 1.4 miles. The trail skirts to the

Ellingwood Point from Little Bear Peak. CHRIS SEAVER

northwest side of another small lake at 12,650 feet then heads east up a scree field. At 1.7 miles and 12,730 feet come close to Crater Lake's northwest edge. Continue heading northeast across scree. Above the lake at roughly 2.0 miles and 12,950 feet, the trail encounters some ledges and begins switchbacking up the slope. Cairns help guide the way.

At 13,340 feet the trail levels out for a short spot before heading north up scree to Ellingwood's southern ridge. From here it's a 0.25-mile scamper to the top.

From the peak it looks as though the other peaks in the group are ganging up on Ellingwood: Blanca dominates to the southwest, while Mount Lindsey flanks its left shoulder to the east and Little Bear flanks its right shoulder to the west. The west offers great views of the San Luis Valley, and the Crestones are visible in the north.

Ellingwood Point

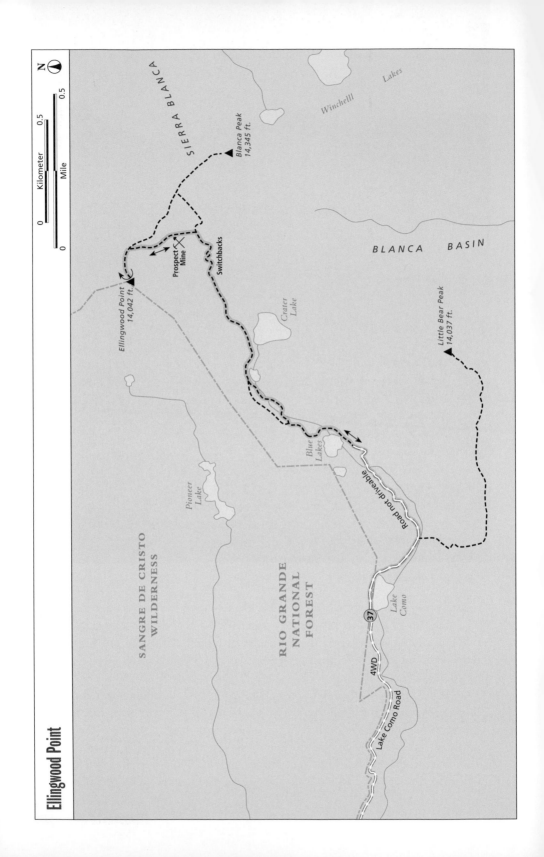

SANGRE DE CRISTO WILDERNESS

RIO GRANDE NATIONAL FOREST

Pioneer Lake

Blue Lakes

Crater Lake

Ellingwood Point 14,042 ft.

Prospect Mine

Switchbacks

SIERRA BLANCA

Blanca Peak 14,345 ft.

Winchelll Lakes

BLANCA BASIN

Little Bear Peak 14,037 ft.

Road not driveable

Lake Como

37

4WD

Lake Como Road

N

Kilometer
0   0.5

Mile
0   0.5

Ellingwood Point from Blanca Peak. CHRIS SEAVER

Miles and Directions

0.0 Start at Lake Como and head back over to Lake Como Road to the north of signage at the lake. Head northeast then east.

0.25 Enter the forest.

0.4 Exit the forest.

0.8 Cross a small stream as the road becomes a trail.

1.0 After passing Blue Lakes, cross over a trail under a waterfall. Start climbing a scree field that leads to some ledges.

1.3 Recross the same stream above the waterfall.

1.4 Cross a stream above a small lake.

1.7 Come close to Crater Lake's north edge.

2.0 Following cairns, switchback up the scree-and-ledge-filled slope.

2.2 Start heading left (northwest) toward Ellingwood at roughly 13,330 feet.

2.3 Turn left below an old mine, heading north across a relatively flat spot, then hike up talus to Ellingwood's southern ridge and scamper to the top.

2.6 Reach the summit. Return by the same route.

5.2 Arrive back at Lake Como.

Hiking Information

Closest Outfitters

Kristi Mountain Sports, 3223 Main St., Alamosa; (719) 589-9759; kristimountain sports.com

Great Pre- or Post-Mountain Spots

San Luis Valley Brewing Co., 631 Main St., Alamosa; (719) 587-2337; slvbrewco.com

Calvillo's Mexican Restaurant, 400 Main St., Alamosa; (719) 587-5500; calvillos .qwestoffice.net

The Rubi Slipper, 506 State Ave., Alamosa; (719) 589-2641

38 Blanca Peak

14,345' (NGVD29), 14,349' (NAVD88), 4th highest

Blanca, Ellingwood Point (14,042 feet), and Little Bear (14,037 feet) share the Lake Como Trailhead, which is up the long, gnarled, difficult Lake Como ATV road. Depending on where you park on that road, it will add a total of 8 to 10 miles to your adventure. This is definitely a place to camp out for a night or two and do one, two, or all three peaks!

Blanca is the fourth-tallest peak in Colorado. It's the tallest peak in its four-pack of fourteeners, but it's not the hardest among them. Compared to Little Bear, Blanca's tough Class 2 summit will seem like a walk in the park. The peak shares a short, exciting Class 3 saddle with Ellingwood, and both can be had in a glorious day by adventurous climbers. Snow can persist into summer on this mountain, and a mountaineering ax may come in handy.

If you drive a rock-crawler, extremely modified 4WD, ATV, or perhaps a horse, you may make it up to the Lake Como trailhead (about 10 miles from the highway junction). A 4WD vehicle with high clearance might be able to travel as far as 3.25 miles from the junction with CO 150 at about 8,800 feet. This is a notoriously difficult road with a series of moves called "Jaws" that will chew up and spit out an SUV's undersides.

Start: Lake Como
Distance: 5.4 miles from Lake Como
Hiking time: About 5 hours
Elevation gain: 2,595 feet
Difficulty: Difficult Class 2
Trail surface: Dirt, scree, rock
Trailhead elevation: 11,750 feet
Camping: Camping by Lake Como and Blue Lakes
Fees: None
Best seasons: Spring through fall (backcountry winter sports in the area)

Maps: USGS Blanca Peak, Mosca Pass, Twin Peaks; National Geographic Trails Illustrated #138: Sangre de Cristo Mountains
Nearest towns: Fort Garland, Alamosa
Trail contacts: Pike San Isabel National Forest, San Carlos Ranger District, (719) 269-8500; Rio Grande National Forest, Conejos Ranger District, (719) 274-8971; Huerfano County Sheriff, (719) 738-1600; Costilla County Sheriff, (719) 672-3302
Trail tips: Start the hike early. Weather can build quickly, and it's hard to see it rolling in when lower in the climb.

Finding the trailhead: Take CO 150 north toward Great Sand Dunes National Park from the junction of US 160 and CO 150, west of Fort Garland and Blanca and east of Alamosa. Go 3.2 miles on CO 150, passing CR 4S on the left and taking the next right, which becomes Lake Como Road. The Lake Como Trailhead is 7.2 miles from the highway junction along this 4WD road. Most people will have to park their vehicles at about 1.6 to 1.8 miles on Lake Como Road. Those who have a 4WD vehicle with good clearance can make it about 3.25 miles on the road, finding parking along the road or one of the switchbacks—make sure other vehicles can pass your vehicle on the road and that other vehicles can turn around on a switchback. Park your vehicle and begin hiking up the 4WD drive road to Lake Como. If you plan to drive an ATV or rock crawler to Lake Como, check out some videos of the obstacles first. GPS: 2WD Trailhead: N37° 32.27'/W105° 34.64'; 4WD Trailhead: N37° 33.04'/W105° 33.54'; Lake Como: N37° 34.20'/W105° 30.92'

The Hike

By almost all measures, Blanca Peak is an ancient giant. The stone that makes up its impressive peak is 1.8 billion year-old Precambrian rock. Its neighbors, both north and south, in the Sangre de Cristos are only 250 million to 300 million years old. Despite its age, Blanca is one of three ultra-prominent peaks in Colorado and the fourth highest in the state. It's the tallest peak in the Sierra Blanca Massif and indeed the whole Sangre de Cristo mountain range. The peak also serves as the apex for three Colorado counties: Alamosa, Costilla, and Huerfano.

Lt. E. G. Beckwith of the 1853 Gunnison Expedition referred to the range as Sierra Blanca, Spanish for "white sawtooth," and named the tallest mountain Blanca Peak. Long before Europeans came to the area, the mountain was regarded as sacred. The Navajo call it the Sacred Mountain of the East: Sisnaajiní, which translates to the "Dawn or White Shell Mountain," and consider it the eastern boundary of Dinetah, their ancestral homeland.

When Gilbert Thompson and Frank Carpenter of the Wheeler Survey made the first recorded ascent on August 14, 1874, they found man-made stoneworks on the peak. They surmised they had been made by Utes or perhaps wandering Spaniards.

Hiking to the Lake Como Trailhead is a Class 1 hike on the rutty, dirt Lake Como Road interspersed with some jagged rocks that are easy to hike on but murder on a vehicle. The elevation gain isn't too bad, but it is a pretty steady incline to the lake. The hike itself is lovely too after you reach the shade of trees in Chokecherry Canyon at about 8,800 feet. From there the road heads northeast toward Holbrook Creek, crossing it at 10,700 feet. From there the road parallels the creek until it reaches Lake Como at 11,760 feet.

The standard route to Blanca—as well as Ellingwood—uses that selfsame "road" that brought you to Lake Como. The road crosses a meadow then enters an evergreen forest at 11,760 feet and nearly 0.25 mile. Continue through the forest on the road, passing near some ruins about 100 yards into the forest. Exit the forest in 100 more yards and start climbing up the improbable road as you come close to the base of Little Bear's western ridge. Pass some small lakes near the ruins of the Blanca Mine and continue up the curling road, crossing a stream at 0.8 mile and 12,090 feet as the road ascends toward Blue Lakes at 12,100 feet and finally peters out. There are some good camping spots near the lakes, though they're largely above tree line.

Although the road dies around Blue Lakes, a good trail continues to lead up and out of the basin, crossing a stream beneath a waterfall at 1.0 mile and 12,160 feet. Shortly after, it climbs up a scree field that turns into a series of ledges and scree

Blanca Peak from the bottom of Lake Como Road. CHRIS SEAVER

that cross over the stream that feeds the waterfall at 1.3 miles and 12,490 feet, close to a small lake. The trail goes around the lake's southeast side then heads northeast, passing over its tributary stream at 12,570 feet and 1.4 miles. The trail skirts to the northwest side of another small lake at 12,650 feet then heads east up a scree field. At 1.7 miles and 12,730 feet come close to Crater Lake's northwest edge. Continue heading northeast across scree. Above the lake, at roughly 2.0 miles and 12,950 feet, the trail encounters some ledges and begins switchbacking up the slope. Cairns help guide the way.

At roughly 13,300 feet and 2.2 miles on this long slope, look for a trail that goes northeast to the peak on the right, which is Blanca. Continue to the ridge crest at 13,775 feet and 2.5 miles and head right up the ridge crest. Stay on the right (south) side of the ridge, scrambling over and around some bigger pieces of rock, and gain the peak at 2.7 miles from Lake Como.

From Blanca's peak it's clear that this is the king of the range. All the other mountains in the range appear much lower from this vantage point, including the shark fin of Ellingwood immediately to the northwest. To the north, beyond a series of smaller mountains, the Crestone Group is visible. Mount Lindsey is clear to the east, and Little Bear's ragged peak is across a sharp ridge to the southwest.

Blanca Peak

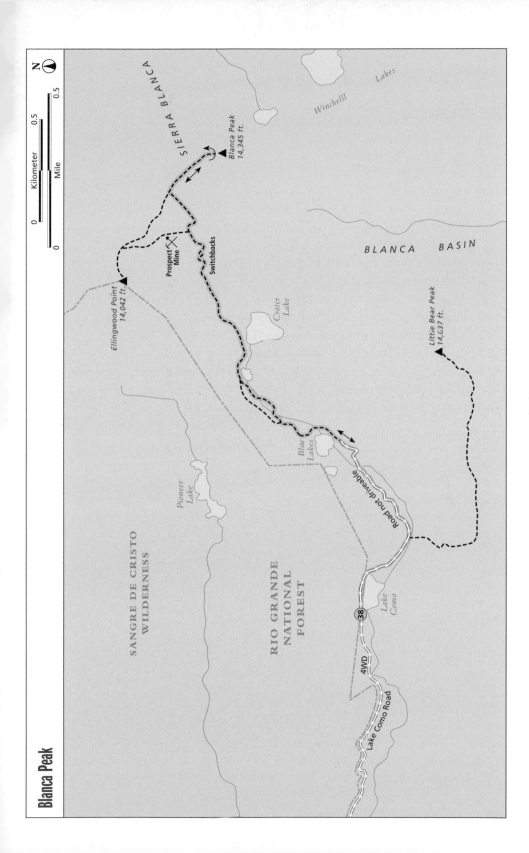

N

Kilometer
0   0.5

0   0.5
Mile

SANGRE DE CRISTO
WILDERNESS

SIERRA BLANCA

Winchell
Lakes

Blanca Peak
14,345 ft.

Ellingwood Point
14,042 ft.

Prospect
Mine

Switchbacks

BLANCA   BASIN

Pioneer
Lake

Crater
Lake

RIO GRANDE
NATIONAL
FOREST

Blue
Lakes

Little Bear Peak
14,037 ft.

Road not driveable

38

Lake
Como

4WD

Lake Como Road

Return via the same route. Or take on the Class 3 saddle to gain Ellingwood's peak as well then head down and rejoin the same trail.

Miles and Directions

0.0 Start at Lake Como and head back over to Lake Como Road to the north of signage at the lake. Head northeast then east.

0.25 Enter the forest.

0.4 Exit the forest.

0.8 Cross a small stream as the road becomes a trail.

1.0 After passing Blue Lakes, cross over a trail under a waterfall. Start climbing a scree field that leads to some ledges.

1.3 Recross the same stream above the waterfall.

1.4 Cross stream above small lake

1.7 Come close to Crater Lake's north edge.

2.0 Following cairns, switchback up the scree-and-ledge-filled slope.

2.2 Start heading right (northeast) toward Blanca Peak at roughly 13,330 feet.

2.5 Reach a saddle and head right up Blanca Peak, staying on the right side of the ridge.

2.7 Gain Blanca's impressive peak. Return via the same route. (**Option:** Stay right across the saddle to ascend Ellingwood.)

5.4 Arrive back at Lake Como.

Hiking Information

Closest Outfitters

Kristi Mountain Sports, 3223 Main St., Alamosa; (719) 589-9759; kristimountain sports.com

Great Pre- or Post-Mountain Spots

San Luis Valley Brewing Co., 631 Main St., Alamosa; (719) 587-2337; slvbrewco.com

Calvillo's Mexican Restaurant, 400 Main St., Alamosa; (719) 587-5500; calvillos .qwestoffice.net

The Rubi Slipper, 506 State Ave., Alamosa; (719) 589-2641

THOUGHTS ON THE 2015 FOURTEENER SPEED RECORD

Despite snow and other bad weather, and some nagging injuries, in spring 2015 Colorado's Andrew Hamilton completed an epic climb of all fifty-eight Colorado fourteeners—official and unofficial, just to make sure—in 9 days, 21 hours, and 51 minutes. He surpassed the previous record of 10 days, 20 hours, and 26 minutes set by Teddy "Cave Dog" Keizer fifteen years prior. It's a unique, extremely challenging record that requires endurance, climbing skills, weather windows, patience, and friends and family. It's an unofficial race with a lot of variables, but it's something that could only happen in Colorado. Here's what he had to say about the adventure.

Inspiration to Go for the Fourteener Record—Again

Hiking the fourteeners is just something I have done since I was a kid. Now I'm lucky enough to take my kids on fourteeners. This year wasn't the first or even second time I went for the record. I won it in 1999, without the benefit of a 4WD vehicle or a support crew or even good research into climbing and driving strategies. Despite all that, I still managed to take an hour off the record.

Something about finishing it in record time gave me a new sense of self-confidence, something I had always lacked. I proved I could pull through even though everything seemed stacked against me.

A year later a much better organized Teddy Keizer (aka Cave Dog) chopped three days off the record. I was amazed by his route planning, crew efficiency, and ability to go and go without sleep. The record stood for twelve years. Nobody went for it. There was talk that it could never be broken.

In 2012 John Prater made an attempt. He posted a note on fourteeners.com that he was going to go for it and included a link to his satellite tracker, allowing people to watch his progress. It hooked me. I had fun refreshing my browser, calculating his speed, speculating on the next peak.

When his crew called for volunteer hikers to join him, I volunteered for the Big Elks day, a critical day to make the record. He got hurt before that, but just following his effort spurred me to think about the record again.

I gave it a shot in 2014. Everything was going great until an injury took me out just a few days from the finish. Otherwise it went so well that I was planning this year's attempt even on the way to the hospital!

(continued on next page)

Planning

The fourteener speed record is a unique speed record. It is long enough that you can't rely on fitness alone to get you through it. There is no set route. You have to study the mountains, study previous attempts, and piece together the most efficient route you can utilizing trails, bushwhacking, roads, crew, light, dark—myriad features that fit you. A fast runner might choose routes with longer mileage but better trails, whereas a slow runner might choose to cut distance by going off-trail.

The possibilities are endless. Planning to take on this type of record ends up as a planning and logistical challenge as much as it is a fitness challenge. In this scope, my failed attempt in 2014 is an invaluable resource of knowledge.

After all the paper planning, you have to physically access all the routes you plan to use before taking on the challenge. Good decision making is much harder when you are several days into something this exhausting on just a few hours of sleep. Trusting just your map and compass skills in dark or rain may screw you up. I've climbed all the fourteeners at least ten times—except Culebra—and I still manage to get lost when something unexpected happens. Familiarizing yourself with them in as many ways as is possible is important.

The final time came in at about 9.91 days, only .03 day longer than the plan called for. And I came out of it in pretty good shape. Unlike 1999, where I lost over 20 pounds, this year I only lost 3 pounds overall.

Potential to Beat the Record

Can the new record be broken? Yes. I'm a lousy runner. Someone could take time off any of my hiking splits. Ricky Denesik held the record before me and spent 24 hours less time on trails than I did in 2015. I beat his record by resting way less! If Ricky or Brett Maune, who also tried to set the record in 2014, did it with less rest, he could handily beat my time. If you compared his times to mine after just two days in 2014, he was more than 10 hours ahead.

Seasonality is one of the hardest factors to plan for. I had terrible luck with that in 2015. Late-season snowpack hanging over from winter forced me to use a pack laden with crampons, an ice ax, snowshoes, microspikes, heavy winter gloves, a heavy winter jacket, and more. That weather, coupled with an early monsoon season, meant I would face terrifying alpine lightning storms, while heavy rain brought mudslides in certain regions.

All these factors, including several days of moderate rain and thick fog, mean there are numerous ways to beat the record. And of course someone may come along and think of some great new innovation, like a new route, that could shave time off the record.

39 Windom Peak

14,082' (NGVD29), 14,092' (NAVD88), 32nd highest

Windom Peak (14,087 feet), Sunlight Peak (14,059 feet), and Mount Eolus (14,084 feet) are climbed via the Chicago Basin. The standard route to the basin is by hiking in from the Durango and Silverton Narrow Gauge Railroad stop at Needleton. From there it is a 6.2-mile hike to the Chicago Basin.

Windom and the accompanying mountains in the Weminuche Wilderness of the San Juan National Forest will take climbers back to Earth's earliest epochs. The mountains in the Needle Range are composed of Precambrian era Eolus Granite, a hornblende. The rocky heart of these mountains has endured time immemorial, even as layers of younger rock have eroded. Windom and Sunlight are commonly climbed together. Consider climbing Sunlight, the harder peak, before climbing the taller Windom.

The standard route to Windom Peak, Sunlight Peak, and Mount Eolus involves a train ride—and not just any Amtrak train, it's a narrow gauge train—lucky you! These peaks are the farthest from any road—the closest approach by foot via the Purgatory Flats Trailhead requires a 15-mile hike just to get to Chicago Basin. It's a beautiful hike, much of it along the Animas River, but the train offers a unique approach to ascending a peak that's akin to how the miners and settlers of yesteryear did it. Even with the ride in on the train, a 6.2-mile trek still remains—again a beautiful hike—to the start of this hike, the Chicago Basin!

Start: Chicago Basin
Distance: 5.2 miles from Chicago Basin
Hiking time: 5 to 6 hours
Elevation gain: 2,980 feet
Difficulty: Class 2
Trail surface: Dirt, scree, rock
Trailhead elevation: 11,110 feet
Camping: Backcountry camping in wilderness
Fees: None
Best seasons: Spring through fall
Maps: USGS Columbine Pass, Electra Lake, Engineer Mountain, Mountain View Crest, Snowdon Peak, Storm King Peak, Vallecito Reservoir; National Geographic Trails Illustrated #140: Weminuche Wilderness

Nearest towns: Durango, Silverton
Trail contacts: San Juan National Forest, Columbine Ranger District, (970) 884-2512; La Plata County Sheriff's Office, (970) 247-1157
Trail tips: Dogs are not allowed on the train. If bringing a pet, you must hike in. The Chicago Basin is lousy with mountain goats. These goats will approach you. They want your pee (well, the salt in it anyway) and your food. Don't feed them. The more used to humans they become, the more likely they are to eat tents, clothes, and food. Hang a bear bag when camping at night and when climbing in the daytime.

Finding the trailhead: Access to the Needleton/Chicago Basin Trailhead is via the Durango and Silverton Narrow Gauge Railroad. The train picks up passengers at 479 Main Ave. in Durango. That's the main station. It also picks up passengers at 10th St. and Animas St. in Silverton. It drops off hikers at a suspension footbridge across the Animas River. Check the schedule online at www.durangotrain.com. For special pricing check the "Wilderness Access" section under the Ride With Us tab for information. The site also recommends calling for booking information and specials at (888) 872-4607 or (970) 387-5416.

From the drop-off point, hike across the bridge. Straight ahead are some cabins built in the 1950s. Head south on the obvious, excellent dirt trail that turns right from the bridge to follow the river and enter forest. The trail turns to the left moving away from the river at 0.4 mile, at about the same time it hits the first junction. Stay to the left toward Needle Creek as the trail moves away from the river. At 0.5 mile pass the Weminuche Wilderness sign and register for the area. From here the trail begins a gradual ascent toward Chicago Basin. It also echoes the southeasterly path of Needle Creek even though the creek is not always visible from the trail. At 1.9 miles the trail crosses over New York Creek on a footbridge. At 4.5 miles and 10,460 feet the forest starts to thin a little and at 5 miles and 10,675 feet the forest is noticeably thinner. At this point the trail turns slightly left and heads around the base of a hill before heading northeast. Look for the remains of old cabins along this stretch. Pass a tan gully on your right with an intermittent stream at 6 miles and 11,000 feet. Chicago Basin is a couple hundred yards beyond that. There is no well-defined trailhead here. But a good reference point is where the trail intersects some old tire ruts near a small stand of trees. GPS: Approach Trailhead at Needleton: N37° 38.01'/W107° 41.57'; Chicago Basin: N37° 36.52'/W107° 37.06'

The Hike

Windom and the Needle Mountains were first surveyed by the Hayden Expedition in 1874. It's unclear who first climbed these well-hidden and remote mountains, but prospectors found their way to the region after the survey and were likely the first to reach the summit of each of these peaks in their quest for fortune.

The US Geological Survey named the mountain Windom in 1902 when it surveyed the region. The mountain was named for William Windom—not the actor, who passed away in 2012, but his great-grandfather, who was a senator for Minnesota before becoming secretary of the treasury under President James Garfield. Windom was a supporter of most Native Americans—he disliked the Sioux apparently—and vehemently opposed the Sand Creek Massacre. He called it the start of a "most unnecessary war," adding, "from that most atrocious act it has grown to its present proportions."

From the Chicago Basin hike east across the meadow on a solid trail. At 0.4 mile and 11,210 feet stay left at a trail junction heading toward Twin Lakes and enter a stand of trees. Follow the trail as it heads northeast out of the basin through trees and meadows. The path continues northeast as it crosses over a good rock slab at 0.6 mile and 11,400 feet. Exiting the short section of slab and gaining tree line, the trail turns left and heads north out of the basin. The excellent trail goes straight up the slope, paralleling a stream to the right. At 0.8 mile and 11,700 feet the trail crosses a tributary to the stream on the left side, just above where it joins the stream. The trail zags to the right and then cuts back to the left. From here it zigzags up the slope, crossing

Windom Peak swathed in clouds

the stream once more before reaching 12,500 feet at 1.5 miles and just south of Twin Lakes. The trail to Eolus leads off to the left.

Turn right (northeast), staying south of the lake. Contour around lower Twin Lake and begin heading right near its northern shore. From here there are numerous ways to begin tackling Windom's peak. The trail that branches to the left at 12,590 feet and 1.6 miles is better suited for Sunlight Peak.

Turn right on a trail that heads southeast then horseshoes back up to the northeast and goes over a slope. At 2.1 miles and 13,050 feet reach the top of this slope and enter an upper basin with Sunlight on the north end, the impressive, jagged teeth of Sunlight Spire (13,995 feet) to Sunlight's right, and Windom south and right of the spire. Head east toward the right side of the basin and the western ridge of Windom, reaching a saddle between it and 13,472-foot Peak 18 at 2.3 miles and 13,480 feet. From here it's a pretty straight shot to Windom's apex. Follow trail fragments and cairns as you see them, but the trail basically snakes up the Class 2 ridge until 13,800 feet, when it reaches a notch. Ascend over the notch and scamper, scramble, and climb the remaining 250-plus feet to gain the top. Staying left at the top of the ridge is easier. Reach the peak at 2.6 miles and 14,087 feet.

Return via the same route. Or continue north and west along an exciting Class 3 and Class 4 ridge to Sunlight Peak.

Windom Peak

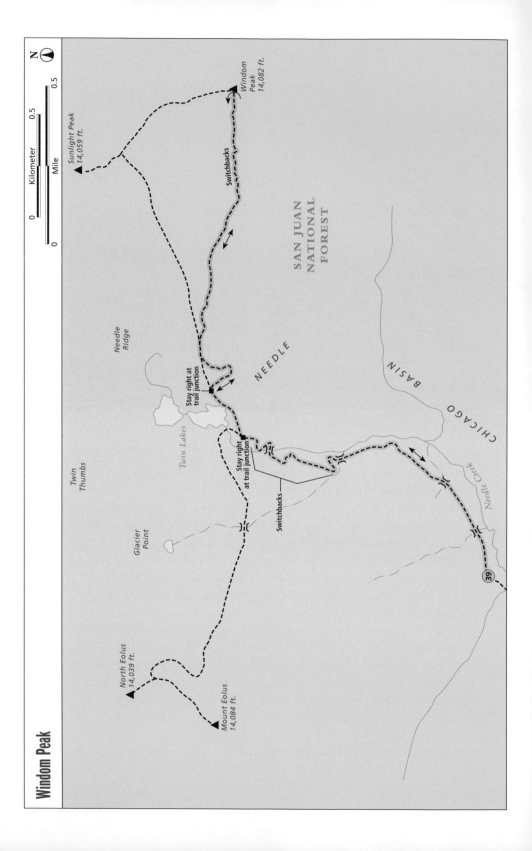

Sunlight Peak
14,059 ft.

Windom Peak
14,082 ft.

Switchbacks

SAN JUAN
NATIONAL
FOREST

Needle Ridge

NEEDLE

Stay right at trail junction

Twin Lakes

Twin Thumbs

Stay right at trail junction

Switchbacks

CHICAGO BASIN

Needle Creek

Glacier Point

North Eolus
14,039 ft.

Mount Eolus
14,084 ft.

39

N

Kilometer
0   0.5

Mile
0   0.5

Miles and Directions

0.0 Start at the Chicago Basin coordinates above, hiking east.

0.4 Stay left at the trail junction, heading toward Twin Lakes.

0.6 Cross over a slab and reach tree line.

0.8 Cross over a stream.

1.25 Cross over another stream.

1.5 A faint trail leads off to Mount Eolus. Stay right, on the south side of lower Twin Lake, heading northeast.

1.6 At a trail junction stay right and head southeast for a short bit before turning back toward the northeast.

2.1 Reach the base of the upper basin between Sunlight (north) and Windom (south), staying on the south side of the basin.

2.3 Heading east, gain the western ridge of Windom and start the final ascent.

2.6 Reach Windom's peak. Return via the same route.

5.2 Arrive back at Chicago Basin.

Hiking Information

Closest Outfitters

Backcountry Experience, 1205 Camino del Rio, Durango; (970) 247-5830; bcexp .com

Pine Needle Mountaineering, 835 Main Ave., Durango; (970) 247-8728; pineneedle .com

Great Pre- or Post-Mountain Spots

Avalanche Brewing Company, 1067 Notorious Blair St., Silverton; (970) 387-5282; avalanchebrewing.com

Brew Pub & Kitchen, 117 West College Drive, Durango; 970-259-5959; brewpub kitchen.com/

Ska Brewing Co., 225 Girard St., Durango; (970) 247-5792; skabrewing.com

Steamworks Brewing Co., 801 E Second Ave., Durango; (970) 259-9200; steam worksbrewing.com

Handlebars Food & Saloon, 117 W 13th St., Silverton; (970) 387-5395; handlebars silverton.com

Hardest Fourteeners

These are the hardest, most dangerous fourteeners in Colorado. These mountains require a combination of Class 3 and Class 4 climbing skills and have difficult moves and/or are exceedingly long. People have been injured or died on each of these peaks. They are dangerous, even for experienced climbers. Care should be taken in learning more about these peaks and routes, as well as in preparing to climb them. While some of the state's most famous mountains are on this list, such as Longs Peak and the Maroon Bells, if you're just starting to climb mountains, these are not the peaks to try first. You should bring a helmet on most of these mountains. On some you could even use ropes and harnesses for safety—if you know how to use a rope and harness.

The route to Wilson Peak requires significant exposure and Class 3 climbing moves near the peak.

40 Wilson Peak

14,017' (NGVD29), 14,024' (NAVD88), 48th highest

Though it's more than 200 feet shorter than its 14,246-foot neighbor, Mount Wilson, Wilson Peak is the tallest mountain in San Miguel County. Both mountains were named for A. D. Wilson, the chief topographer with the Hayden Expedition of 1874. Wilson is not an easy climb. It's a long Class 1 hike across shifting talus. And that's before the Class 3 traverses and climb to the peak. Bring a helmet to wear for the final ascent to Wilson Peak's summit block. Much of the approach is on or close to mining claims, so it's important to stay on-trail.

Start: Rock of Ages Trailhead
Distance: 9.2 miles
Hiking time: About 12 hours
Elevation gain: 3,670 feet
Difficulty: Class 3
Trail surface: Scree, rock
Trailhead elevation: 10,350 feet
Camping: Camping near trailhead in designated camping spots
Fees: None
Best seasons: Late spring through early fall

Maps: USGS Mount Wilson, Delores Peak, Little Cone, Gray Head; National Geographic Trails Illustrated #141: Telluride, Silverton, Ouray, Lake City
Nearest towns: Placerville, Telluride
Trail contacts: Uncompahgre and San Juan National Forests, Norwood Ranger District, (970) 327-4261; San Miguel County Sheriff, (970) 728-4442; Dolores County Sheriff, (970) 677-2257

Finding the trailhead: From the junction of CO 145 and Silver Pick Road (also called CR 60M) in Telluride, immediately cross the San Miguel River. Shortly thereafter the road becomes a good dirt road. Continue on this road for 3.3 miles then turn left to stay on the road, which becomes FR 622. In 0.8 mile turn right to stay on FR 622 for another 1.6 miles. Turn right to stay on FR 622 and continue 0.7 mile. Turn right onto FR 645 and travel another 2.2 miles, crossing a stream at about 1 mile. GPS: N37° 52.99' / W108° 01.11'

The Hike

The Rock of Ages Trailhead was recently reopened thanks to efforts by the Colorado Fourteeners Initiative, the Trust for Public Land, the USDA Forest Service, and others. The trail courses through the Uncompahgre National Forest—though with the amount of rock hiked over, it's hard to call it forest. It also passes through the Lizard Head Wilderness and by mines. There are a number of restrictions, including no camping at the trailhead (luckily there are plenty of established camping spots on the road to the trailhead). No dogs are allowed on part of the trail, and they must be on-leash where they are permitted.

Wilson Peak in the morning sun

The Rock of Ages Trail (FT 429) heads south from the parking lot. Shortly after leaving the parking lot, come to a gate and a sign for Elk Creek Trail. Go around the gate and stay left on the Rock of Ages Trail. At 0.5 mile the trail begins a series of short switchbacks in the woods. At 1.0 mile it exits the woods, taking a hard left. From here on out the hike is mainly across scree and large gravel. There's only one more small spot where the trail passes through trees and over the ridge that separates Elk Creek and Silver Pick Basins. At 1.9 miles exit the last of the forest and start the ascent up Silver Pick Basin, following the trail. Wilson Peak is in front and across the basin to the southeast.

This part of the trail passes through a mine site and partly on old mine roads. At 2.2 miles cross over a fence warning that no dogs are allowed on the trail. Hike across the basin and come close to Big Bear Creek. At 2.5 miles continue south, leaving the creek. At 2.8 miles find the remains of a mine, including the ruins of a building made out of rock. It's on private property, so leave it alone. Follow the trail as it goes east then southeast.

At 3.25 miles the trail cuts back to the west for about 0.2 mile then resumes its southeastern trajectory as it crosses through the remains of the Silver Pick Mine at 12,700 feet. Then the trail begins the talus-filled ascent to the Rock of Ages saddle at

Wilson Peak off to the left behind its ridge

13,000 feet and 3.8 miles. Cross over the saddle to the east, facing some easy Class 3 exposure. Looking down into Navajo Basin reveals the remains of the Rock of Ages Mine, including an old mine cart. Directly ahead, across from the basin, is 14,246-foot Mount Wilson; 14,159-foot El Diente is to the right along the ridge.

After crossing the saddle turn northeast at 4.1 miles and begin ascending Wilson Peak's southwest ridge. Stay close to the ridge, following cairns as you see them. It's possible to traverse a lower trail, but scrambling a bit closer to the east side of the ridge line is easier.

Gain the ridgeline at 4.25 miles and about 13,500 feet and continue to work up the ridge, following the trail. Shortly thereafter reach a gendarme-guarded gap that allows for great views of the mines and Rock of Ages Trail.

In another 0.25 mile (14,850 feet) reach the false summit. It's also helmet time—climbers above could inadvertently kick rock loose. Carefully climb up and then descend the false summit to see the true summit just beyond. Cross just below the small summit ridge downclimbing about 50 feet on solid but exposed rock. Next climb up the difficult Class 3 rock to the summit block. The peak is just a quick 150-foot scramble from the top of the crux.

Take some time on the top of this beautiful peak. Though Mount Wilson and El Diente are both taller peaks south and west of Wilson Peak, views are stunning in every direction. To the northwest Mount Sneffels (14,150 feet) is the next closest and

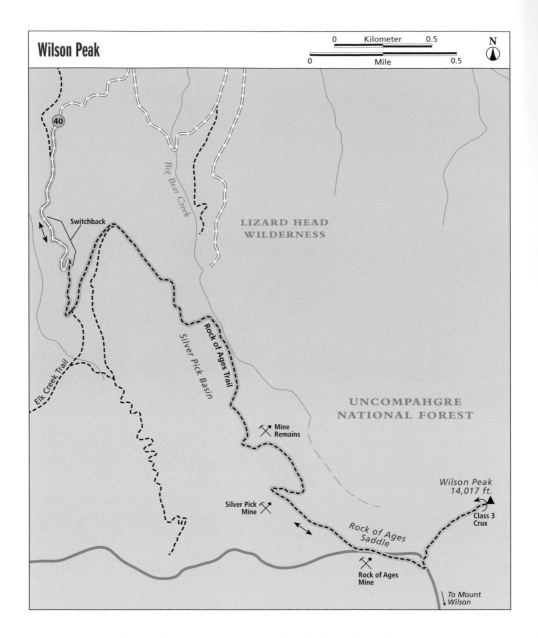

0   Kilometer   0.5

0   Mile   0.5

N

40

Big Bear Creek

Switchback

LIZARD HEAD
WILDERNESS

Rock of Ages Trail

Silver Pick Basin

Elk Creek Trail

UNCOMPAHGRE
NATIONAL FOREST

Mine
Remains

Wilson Peak
14,017 ft.

Silver Pick
Mine

Class 3
Crux

Rock of Ages
Saddle

Rock of Ages
Mine

To Mount
Wilson

looks somewhat like a British royal crown. Telluride is in the valley directly below
Sneffels. Teakettle Mount (13,819 feet) also is visible nearby. Other mountains in
the San Juans are farther off and appear as jagged teeth on the horizon. Lizard Head
(13,130 feet) is one of the more interesting nearby peaks.

Miles and Directions

0.0 Start from the parking lot on Rock of Ages Trail (FT 429).

0.6 Reach small switchbacks in forest.

1.1 Exit the forest and turn left on scree.

1.4 Reenter a small patch of trees as you cross from the Elk Creek Basin to the Silver Pick Basin.

1.9 Exit the woods, enter Silver Pick Basin, and begin the ascent up the basin. Stay right, following all signs.

2.2 Pass a fence and then cross over Silver Pick Basin, coming close to Big Bear Creek.

2.5 Move away from the creek.

2.8 Pass to the right of some old mine ruins, including cables for an old aerial tram.

3.25 The trail cuts back to the west then resumes going southeast.

3.8 Reach Rock of Ages Saddle, heading east.

4.1 Reach the end of the saddle and start heading left (northeast).

4.25 Gain the southwest ridge of Wilson Peak.

4.5 Climb and descend the false summit. Then climb the crux to the summit.

4.6 Reach Wilson Peak. Celebrate before returning via the same route.

9.2 Arrive back at the parking lot.

Hiking Information

Closest Outfitters

Jagged Edge Mountain Gear, 223 E Colorado Ave., Telluride; 970-728-9307; jagged -edge-telluride.com

Great Pre- or Post-Mountain Spots

Telluride Brewing Co., 156 Society Dr., Telluride; (970) 728-5094; telluridebrewing co.com

Smuggler's Brewpub, 225 S Pine St., Telluride; (970) 728-5620; smugglersbrewpub .com

Last Dollar Saloon, 100 E Colorado Ave., Telluride; (970) 728-4800; lastdollarsaloon .com

Brown Dog Pizza, 110 E Colorado Ave., Telluride; (970) 728-8046; browndogpizza .com

41 Wetterhorn Peak

14,015' (NGVD29), 14,020' (NAVD88), 49th highest

Wetterhorn Peak is a beautiful beast named for the more famous Wetterhorn in the Swiss Alps. While hidden from roads, this idyllic Class 3+ peak in the Uncompahgre Wilderness juts out of the landscape like the nose of some giant, fearsome shark. A nearby rock fin creates the bottom of its maw from certain angles. This is a great, solid mountain to climb with some fun Class 3 moves near the top that will challenge climbers and reward them with a small summit block with inspiring views.

Start: Matterhorn Creek Trailhead
Distance: 4WD trailhead: 7.0 miles
Hiking time: 7 hours
Elevation gain: 3,605 feet
Difficulty: Class 3
Trail surface: Dirt, scree, rock
Trailhead elevation: 4WD trailhead: 10,410 feet
Camping: At trailheads; backcountry camping
Fees: None
Best seasons: Spring through fall

Maps: USGS: Uncompahgre Peak, Wetterhorn Peak, Lake City, Courthouse Mountain; National Geographic Trails Illustrated #141: Telluride, Silverton, Ouray, Lake City
Nearest towns: Lake City, Ouray
Trail contacts: Bureau of Land Management, Gunnison Field Office, (970) 642-4940; USDA Forest Service, Gunnison Ranger District, (970) 641-0471; Hinsdale County Sheriff's Office, (970) 944-2291

Finding the trailhead: From Bluff and 1st Streets in Lake City, the southwest edge of town, take a slight right, continuing on Bluff Street (CR 20), which becomes the dirt Henson Creek Road, also known as the Alpine Loop Scenic Byway, as it exits town. At about 9 miles turn right onto North Henson Creek Road (CR 24). The road becomes rougher here, but passenger cars can make the 1.5-mile drive to the trailhead. There is a sign for the trail and parking here. If you have a 4WD vehicle, you can drive up FR 970.2A (also the trail) another 0.6 mile to the 4WD trailhead, which has ample parking. GPS: N38° 01.83'/W107° 29.48'

The Hike

Wetterhorn, German for "weather peak," is a great fourteener for those who already have some decent experience climbing mountains in Colorado or elsewhere. The mountain was named during the Wheeler Survey in 1874 by Lt. William Marshall. He observed: "The Wetterhorn to the south of west a few miles from Uncompahgre Peak is a nose in form and its ascent being unnecessary for topographical purposes was attempted. It exceeds 14,000 feet in altitude and appears inaccessible." That held true until 1906, when George Barnard, C. Smedley, W. P. Smedley, and D. Utter made the first ascent. Since the region is rich in minerals, prospectors may have made undocumented climbs of the mountain in search of riches.

Wetterhorn Peak looking stately from Ridge Stock Driveway Trail as wispy clouds roll by

Both Wetterhorn and its bigger brother Uncompahgre (14,309 feet) are in the Uncompahgre Wilderness and the Uncompahgre Peak Butterfly Closure—an area dedicated to preserving the habitat of the Uncompahgre fritillary butterfly, an endangered species put at risk by sheep grazing, collection, and climate change. Signs at the trailheads warn users of the fragility of the environment. Please stay on-trail as much as possible to protect this habitat.

The hike to Wetterhorn from the 4WD trailhead starts at 10,850 feet, 0.6 mile and about 400 vertical feet north of the turnoff at CR 24. Start the trail at the signage and fence. About 350 feet beyond the fence, sign in at the registry in a lovely forest grove.

At a little over 0.25 mile the trail crosses an intermittent stream as it comes closer to Matterhorn Creek. These streams are mineral rich, with rock stained brownish red by iron or white by zinc and aluminum.

At 0.6 mile come to a junction where Wetterhorn pokes out from behind a grassy mound. Take Ridge Stock Trail (FT 233) to the right. Switch back to the right, heading east over a small hill and then north. At 1.1 miles and 11,600 feet, enter into the Uncompahgre Wilderness, exiting the forest into a fantastic alpine basin.

Cross a couple of intermittent streams as the trail gains altitude relatively slowly. At 1.6 miles and 12,065 feet, take the trail left to Wetterhorn Peak, crossing a couple of

Wetterhorn Peak Trail sign. Wetterhorn is to the left.

good intermittent streams—a good place to filter and replenish water if needed—and over moraines, leading to the northwestern side of the basin with Wetterhorn at the apex of the basin. Matterhorn is directly north from the junction.

The trail gets steeper as it crosses the valley and ends up in a giant's rock garden, winding its way through large rocks that are home to pikas and marmots. Leave the boulder field at 2.6 miles and 12,900 feet. Shortly thereafter reach the southeastern ridge that takes climbers to the top.

At 2.9 miles the hiking gets a little tougher, hiking up a bald, pebbly slope, where it's easy to slip on the way down. At 13,400 feet you'll start passing some towers that foreshadow what awaits on the peak block.

The trail becomes rockier from this point on. The Ships Prow, a prominent tower to the left of the summit, comes into view. The trail remains a decent Class 2 hike through here, with some scrambling over rock as it climbs. Stay to the left of the ridge (west) and turn right at some rock ribs around 13,600 feet and 3.2 miles, climbing to the right to regain the ridgeline. There are a number of ways to do this. Find one that feels safest.

At 13,800 feet ascend around the prow, now to the west, and climb the notch closest to the summit block, to the northeast ahead. Climb up and over the notch, head north for about 15 feet, then climb roughly 150 feet up a shallow gully to gain the summit. This is Class 3 climbing with some exposure, but most of the rock is good and solid.

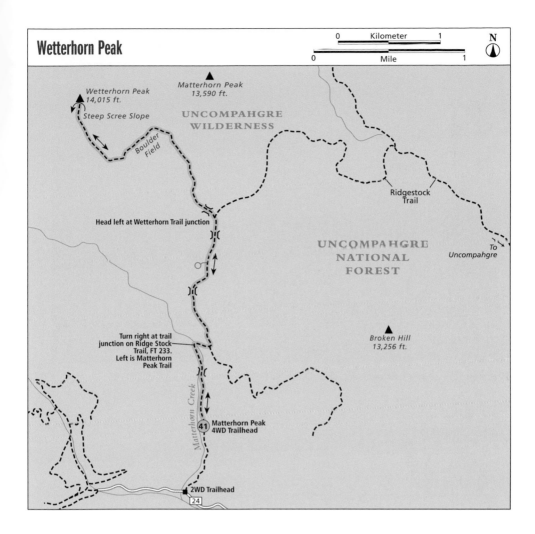

Wetterhorn Peak

0   Kilometer   1

0   Mile   1

N

Wetterhorn Peak
14,015 ft.

Matterhorn Peak
13,590 ft.

Steep Scree Slope

UNCOMPAHGRE
WILDERNESS

Boulder
Field

Head left at Wetterhorn Trail junction

Ridgestock
Trail

UNCOMPAHGRE
NATIONAL
FOREST

To
Uncompahgre

Turn right at trail
junction on Ridge Stock
Trail, FT 233.
Left is Matterhorn
Peak Trail

Broken Hill
13,256 ft.

Matterhorn Creek

41   Matterhorn Peak
4WD Trailhead

2WD Trailhead

24

Miles and Directions

0.0   Start at the 4WD trailhead.

0.25 Cross an intermittent stream.

0.6   Turn right at junction on the Ridge Stock Trail (FT 233).

1.0   Enter the Uncompahgre Wilderness.

1.6   Take the trail to the left toward Wetterhorn.

2.2   The trail gets steeper and enters a section of boulders.

2.6   Exit the boulder field and see the southeast ridge of Wetterhorn.

2.8   Gain the southeastern ridge of Wetterhorn.

2.9   Climbing becomes a little more difficult.

3.2   Climb and scramble over rock, coursing around the rock rib and under the prow.

Deer near the Matterhorn trailhead on the route to Wetterhorn

3.3 Reach the V-notch.

3.5 Summit! Return via the same route.

7.0 Arrive back at the trailhead.

Hiking Information

Closest Outfitters

The Sportsman Outdoors & Fly Shop, 238 S Gunnison Ave., Lake City; (970) 944-2526; lakecitysportsman.com

San Juan Sports, 102 S Main St., Creede; (719) 658-2359; sanjuansports.com

Great Pre- or Post-Mountain Spots

Packer Saloon & Cannibal Grill, 310 N Silver St., Lake City; (970) 944-4144

Lake City Cafe, 310 Gunnison Ave., Lake City; (970) 944-0301

San Juan Soda Co., 227 N Silver St., Lake City; (970) 944-0500; sanjuansodacompany .com

42 Kit Carson Peak

14,165' (NGVD29), 14,169' (NAVD88), 23rd highest

At 14,165 feet Kit Carson Peak is Challenger Point's (14,081 feet) tough big brother. It's a Class 3 climb with good, solid rock to hold onto and some surprising features thanks to the conglomerate rock that makes up this winsome peak in the Sangre de Cristo Range. Due to their proximity, Kit Carson and Challenger are commonly climbed together. Usually the larger mountain is climbed first, but in this case the trail to Kit Carson goes over Challenger, and this route requires a double summit of the point.

Start: Willow and South Crestone Trailhead
Distance: 4WD trailhead: 12.8 miles
Hiking time: 4WD trailhead: 11 to 13 hours
Elevation gain: 4WD trailhead: 6,240 feet
Difficulty: Class 3
Trail surface: Dirt, scree, rock
Trailhead elevation: 8,880 feet
Camping: Backcountry camping
Fees: None
Best seasons: Summer through fall

Maps: USGS Crestone Peak, Crestone, Beck Mountain; National Geographic Trails Illustrated #138: Sangre de Cristo Mountains
Nearest towns: Westcliffe, Crestone
Trail contacts: Rio Grande National Forest, Saguache Ranger District, (719) 655-2547; San Isabel National Forest, San Carlos Ranger District, (719) 269-8500; Custer County Sheriff's Office, (719) 783-2270
Trail tips: Don't feed the bighorn sheep or other wildlife.

Finding the trailhead: From the intersection of CO 17 and CR T in Moffat (13.4 miles south of the intersection of US 285 and CO 17), take CR T (Russel Street) east for 11.9 miles. The road turns left as it heads into Crestone and becomes Birch Street (CO 71) for 0.4 mile. Continue 0.2 miles on this main road in Crestone as it turns right and becomes Golden Avenue. Turn left as it becomes Alder Street. In 0.1 mile take the first right onto Galena Street, a dirt 2WD road. Follow that road 2.3 miles over increasingly bad roads (2WD vehicles may opt to park at the forest boundary at 13.8 miles) to the trailhead. GPS: N37° 59.33'/W105° 39.77'

The Hike

Kit Carson is an interesting peak. With cliffs on all sides, it could be a much more challenging mountain, but a series of good ledges make it easier to summit than it could be. Still, it's a much more strenuous climb than Challenger and requires some decent Class 3 moves, which can challenge less-experienced climbers. The Rocky Mountain Field Institute said in 2014 that it planned to start restoring vegetation and creating a more sustainable path up Kit Carson and Challenger.

Kit Carson has been a peak of many names. Early settlers to the region called it Crestone, but it also had some more colorful names, among them Haystack Baldy and

Kit Carson Peak from Willow Lakes. CHRIS SEAVER

Frustum. The Hayden Survey gave it its current name in 1874. Carson was a guide, fur-trapper, and scout in this region in the mid-1800s. Poorly educated by traditional measures, he spoke Apache, Arapaho, Blackfoot, Cheyenne, Comanche, Crow, French, Piute, Shoshone, Spanish, Ute, and Plains Indians sign language. Legend has it that he lived at the base of his namesake peak in a cabin for years. A US Army colonel, he commanded Fort Garland from 1866 to 1867, where he negotiated settlements with the Utes. He was an unassuming mountain man who wasn't tall but sported a red mustache. His friend Tom Tobin summed him up once: "Kit never cussed more'n was necessary."

From the top of Challenger, Kit Carson looms like the crown of an old cowboy hat. You've got to saddle up to make that traverse. From Challenger's peak head southeast down its western ridge, dropping below the ridge to a point 6 miles from trailhead and 13,860 feet, where the trail passes a steep gully in a small saddle.

The miraculous Kit Carson Avenue, a solid ledge, begins on the other side of the saddle, curling south to Carson's southeast ridge. At the ridge crest follow the ledge left, heading northeast and crossing the peak's southern face. Ascend to the wee saddle at 13,940 feet between Kit Carson's south ridge and the fin called The Prow at 6.1 miles; then descend to 13,670 feet at 6.2 miles. The trail turns left and heads up a steep gully just before encountering a large rock outcropping. This is a good spot to turn back and familiarize yourself and your team with where to catch the avenue on

Kit Carson Peak

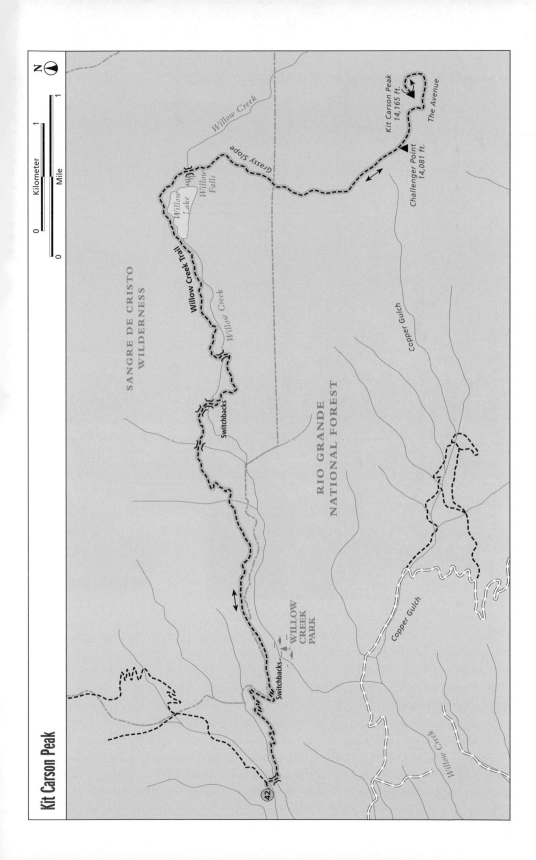

SANGRE DE CRISTO
WILDERNESS

Willow Creek Trail

Willow Lake

Willow Falls

Willow Creek

Grassy Slope

Willow Creek

Switchbacks

Switchbacks

WILLOW
CREEK
PARK

Switchbacks

42

RIO GRANDE
NATIONAL FOREST

Copper Gulch

Copper Gulch

Willow Creek

Kit Carson Peak
14,165 ft.

Challenger Point
14,081 ft.

The Avenue

N

Kilometer

Mile

0   1

0   1

Climbing up the couloir to Kit Carson Peak. CHRIS SEAVER

the way back down—maybe even snap a picture for reference. Climb up the gully, following trail segments and scrambling over some easy Class 3 rock heading northwest. Ascend the gully, avoiding some large rocks near the top by angling left. Above the gully the ascent eases as the trail continues left toward the summit. Reach the summit at 6.4 miles from the trailhead and 0.6 mile from Challenger's Peak. Return via the same route.

Challenger Point looks significantly smaller from Kit Carson. The Crestone Needle (14,197 feet) and Peak (14,294 feet) are the closest peaks beside Challenger. From Carson's top their summits, on steep blocks of solid rock, look foreboding.

Miles and Directions

0.0   Start at the 4WD trailhead and head east on the trail. In 110 yards turn right onto the Willow Creek Trail.

0.1   Take a left, heading east in a clearing.

0.4   The trail switchbacks up a slope.

1.3   Reach the ridge crest.

1.5   Stay left on main trail above Willow Creek Park.

1.8   The trail goes through some small switchbacks.

2.8   Reach a small clearing and cross a gully.

3.1   Cross over Willow Creek then hike up tight switchbacks.

3.3   Exit the forest near Challenger's headwall.

3.6   Reenter the forest.

4.2   Pass falls just below Willow Lake.

4.4   Exit the forest into willow thickets.

4.6   The trail crosses over upper Willow Creek.

4.9   Head up the grassy slope to the right.

5.6   Reach top of Challenger's north ridge.

5.7   Summit Challenger Point and head southeast.

6.0   Pass a steep gully; continue descending down the avenue.

6.1   Turn left and ascend to the saddle of The Prow.

6.2   Descend close to a rock outcropping and head left up a steep gully.

6.4   Reach Kit Carson Peak. Return via same route.

12.8   Arrive back at the trailhead.

Hiking Information

Closest Outfitters

Take a Hike!, 210 Main St., Westcliffe; (719) 783-3771; takeahikewc.com

Chappy's Mountain View Bar & Grill, 213 Main St., Westcliffe; (719) 783-0813; face book.com/ChappybarandgrillwestcliffeCO

Edge Ski Paddle & Pack, 107 N Union Ave., Pueblo; (719) 583-2021; edgeskiand paddle.com

Great Pre- or Post-Mountain Spots

Royal Gorge Brewing Co. & Restaurant, 413 Main St., Cañon City; (719) 345-4141; royalgorgebrewpub.com

Elevation Beer Company, 115 Pahlone Pkwy., Poncha Springs; (719) 539-5258; elevation beerco.com

43 Longs Peak

14,255' (NGVD29), 14,261' (NAVD88), 15th highest

Longs Peak is the northernmost fourteener in Colorado, and one of the most isolated. Longs Peak, in Rocky Mountain National Park, also is the only fourteener on national parkland. While thousands flock to this mountain every year, it's a difficult climb—not merely a hike. People die or are severely injured on this mountain every year—often on the way down. All this makes the views from the top of this king above the plains as well deserved as they are unparalleled.

Start: Longs Peak Trailhead

Distance: 14 miles (2.6-mile round-trip from the Boulder Field)

Elevation change: 5,100 feet

Hiking time: 10 to 15 hours

Difficulty: Class 3

Trail surface: Mixed. Starts out as an easy trail; turns into Class 2 talus hiking then Class 3 scrambling.

Trailhead elevation: 9,400 feet

Camping: Fee (Call ahead for availability.)

Fees: Per-car fee to enter Rocky Mountain National Park (seven-day pass)

Best seasons: Summer and fall

Maps: USGS Longs Peak, McHenrys Peak, Isolation Peak, Allens Park; National Geographic Trails Illustrated #200: Rocky Mountain National Park; #301: Longs Peak, Bear Lake, Wild Basin, Sky Terrain; Southern Rocky Mountain National Park Indian Peaks Wilderness trail map

Nearest town: Estes Park

Trail contacts: Rocky Mountain National Park, Public Land National Park Service, (970) 586-1206; Rocky Mountain National Park, National Park Service Backcountry Office, (970) 586-1242 (camping permits); Larimer County Sheriff's Office, (970) 577-2070; Boulder County Sheriff's Office, (303) 441-3600

Trail tips: If taking on Longs in one day, be prepared for a long day of hiking and scrambling.

Special considerations: Bring plenty of food, water, and water treatment if you have it. Start out early, roughly 3 a.m., to make the hike in one day. Turn back if a storm is coming in and you're above tree line. The climb isn't done when you reach this peak. Descend carefully; it doesn't get easy until you're past the boulder field on the way down.

Finding the trailhead: From the north, take CO 7 south from its junction with CO 36. Drive 9.2 miles to reach the Longs Peak Ranger Station turnoff. From the south, take CO 7 from its junction with CO 72 for 10 miles to the Longs Peak Ranger Station turnoff. The station and parking lot is 1 mile west of the turnoff. Car camping isn't allowed, but there are other campsites nearby. GPS: N40° 16.34'/W105° 33.42'

The Hike

Major Stephen Long recorded the first official US sighting of the peak on June 30, 1820. The Arapaho called Longs and neighboring Mount Meeker (13,911 feet)

Longs Peak's summit block in the morning sun from the Boulder Field

Nesotaieux, meaning the "Two Guides." Early French traders called them Les Deux Orielles, the Two Ears. Though it was named for him, Long did not summit the peak. Arapaho, among them one called Old Man Gun, were said to have trapped eagles on its summit. The first documented climb of Longs was by John Wesley Powell, who led a party to the summit on August 23, 1868.

This giant, 1.4-billion-year-old granite and gneiss slab of a peak is a huge draw to visitors of Colorado and Rocky Mountain National Park, as well as a favorite of many locals. From its peak climbers can see the curvature of the Earth to the east, to the north as far as Wyoming and Nebraska, and Pikes Peak 102 miles to the south.

According to the National Park Service, in 2002 more than 9,000 people summited and thousands more turned around at the Keyhole Gap. The number of people summiting fourteeners has only grown since then, and some have estimated that more than 20,000 people attempt Longs each year. There are roughly 175 routes up Longs and its features, such as The Diamond. These are mostly Class 5+ routes that require extensive rock-climbing experience and gear.

The vast majority of climbers use the Keyhole Route. However, it's not an easy route. Climbers face significant exposure, and ice and snow can persist on this peak throughout summer.

With thousands of other climbers taking on Longs, anticipate crowded conditions, especially in summer and on the more difficult sections of the climb above the Keyhole Gap. It won't feel like being stuck on I-70 East toward Denver on a Sunday, but there's almost always some waiting involved, whether you're going down or coming up.

When climbing the upper parts of Longs, particularly in areas like The Trough, be wary of those above you as well as those below. Kicking rock loose can result in falls or rocks hitting other climbers. If you kick anything significant loose, warn others by shouting "Rock!"

Longs has no regular access to water above the Boulder Field. The park service recommends bringing 3 to 4 quarts (3 to 4 liters) of water per person, particularly if you don't have water treatment with you.

If you plan on summiting in one day, start early. How early? The park service recommends 3 a.m. Storms, particularly afternoon storms, are frequent on Longs in the summer months and can arrive extremely quickly.

Another option is camping in the Boulder Field below the Keyhole Gap. There are a few camping spots nestled in the field of craggy rocks there. Since Longs is on National Park Service land, backcountry camping permits (fee) are required. As soon as you know you're planning to camp on Longs, call the backcountry office at (970) 586-1242 to secure one or more of the few spots in the Boulder Field or below at Goblin's Forest. These go quickly in summer, so make reservations as soon as you know you're climbing. Failing to do so could result in a ticket and some other, really pissed off climbers and campers.

The climb to Longs Peak begins at the eponymous Longs Peak Ranger Station and Longs Peak Trailhead as a beguiling hike through a spruce-and-pine forest at 9,400 feet. Take the East Longs Peak Trail 0.5 mile to a trail junction and bear left up the main trail. At 1.2 miles and 10,120 feet pass Goblin's Forest, a campsite. Continue on the trail through the forest and some switchbacks; then walk across Alpine Brook on a log bridge at about 1.8 miles and 10,600 feet. At about 2.5 miles and 10,975 feet, just after exiting the forest and getting your first good glimpse of Longs, pass a trail sign to Battle Mountain. Continue on the Longs Peak Trail.

At 3.5 miles and 11,500 feet reach Mills Moraine and the junction for Chasm Lake. It's a good place to view Longs and for you and your group to relieve yourselves at the toilet just east of the trail. Continue to the right on the trail and hike northwest across Mount Lady Washington's slopes and on to the Granite Pass Junction at 4.1 miles and 12,080 feet. Stay left on East Longs Peak Trail, heading toward the Boulder Field. Walk through some switchbacks as the terrain becomes increasingly rocky. At about 12,400 feet and 4.8 miles you'll enter the north end of the Boulder Field and gain glimpses of Longs, which rises more than 1,000 feet from the rock-strewn valley. Continue on the trail through the Boulder Field. At roughly 12,660 feet there are some permitted campsites and some open-air toilets for a last pit stop before the real scrambling begins.

The trail gradually peters out as you approach The Keyhole on Longs' northwest ridge. Follow cairns to The Keyhole, passing a conical shelter commemorating Agnes

Climbing across The Narrows, one of the Class 3 parts of Longs Peak.

Vaille and her would-be rescuer, who also died in January 1925. Vaille and Walter Keiner were returning from the first winter ascent of Longs' East Face. He made it, with severe frostbite. She did not.

Reach The Keyhole at 13,150 feet and about 6.0 miles and gain the dizzying ridge between Longs' east and west sides. This is the last really easy part of the climb and a good place for you or part of your group to turn back if you need to. Also, since climbers are scrambling from here on out, mileage is more approximate.

Look for the painted yellow-and-red bull's-eyes. These mark the safest path from here on out. If you lose sight of them, carefully retrace your steps until you see one.

The first section, known as The Ledges, goes left, cutting across the southeastern slope of Longs' ridge. It requires a roughly 50-foot climb before dipping down about 100 feet. At about 13,300 feet and 6.2 miles, gain the large couloir called The Trough, which offers great views of Glacier Gorge to the northeast. Ascend the talus slopes of The Trough carefully—it's an easy place to kick rock on people below—and follow the bull's-eyes when available. If it's snowy, stay to the north side of The Trough. Climb to 13,850 feet, where you'll encounter a large chockstone; climb carefully around it.

Upon exiting The Trough you come to the next challenge, the 250-yard Narrows, a ledge that crosses the south side of Longs. It offers dramatic views and steep, steep cliffs above and below. You'll encounter a couple of big rocks obscuring the path that you have to climb around. Climb up and out, scrambling The Narrows and scrambling onto the Home Stretch, a Class 3 climb. Climb about 300 feet to reach the abrupt, large flat peak and gain some of the most amazing views of your life! The high point on the large, flat summit is a boulder on the north side of the peak.

Longs Peak

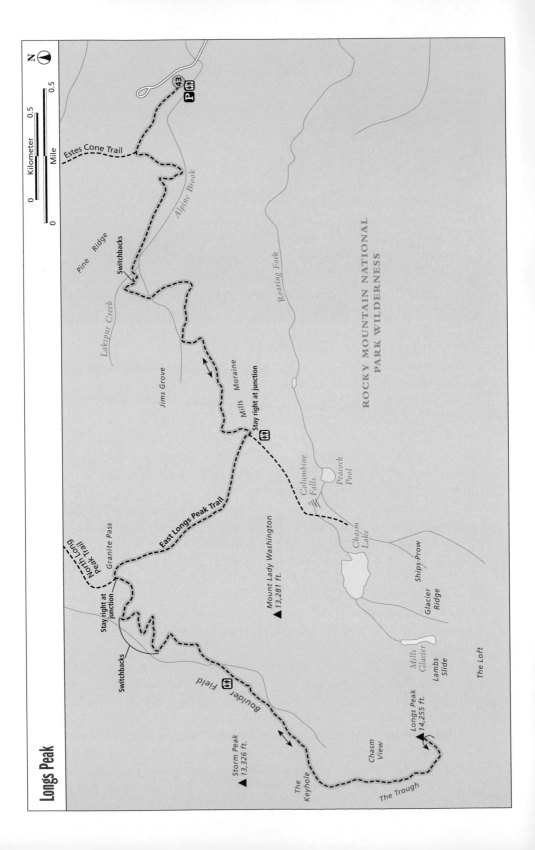

Estes Cone Trail

Pine Ridge

Switchbacks

Alpine Brook

Larkspur Creek

Jims Grove

Mills Moraine

Stay right at junction

North Longs Peak Trail

Granite Pass

East Longs Peak Trail

Stay right at junction

Switchbacks

Storm Peak
▲ 13,326 ft.

Boulder Field

The Keyhole

Chasm View

The Trough

Mount Lady Washington
▲ 13,281 ft.

Columbine Falls

Peacock Pool

Roaring Fork

Chasm Lake

Ships Prow

Glacier Ridge

Mills Glacier

Lambs Slide

Longs Peak
▲ 14,255 ft.

The Loft

ROCKY MOUNTAIN NATIONAL
PARK WILDERNESS

N

Kilometer   0   0.5
Mile   0   0.5

P   43

Watch for clouds, and return via the same route before they can swoop in and douse you or cover you in snow. Be cautious on the descent through to The Keyhole—it can be as dangerous as climbing up.

Miles and Directions

0.0 Start at the Long Peak Trail Trailhead.

0.5 Bear left at a trail junction.

1.2 Pass Goblin's Forest.

1.8 Cross Alpine Brook.

2.5 Exit the forest, entering the tundra.

3.5 Reach the junction for Chasm Lake (use toilet if needed). Continue to the right.

4.1 At Granite Pass Junction stay left on East Longs Peak Trail.

4.8 Enter the north end of the Boulder Field.

6.0 Enter The Keyhole Gap and start crossing The Ledges, following painted red-and-yellow bull's-eyes.

6.2 Enter The Trough.

6.6 Exit The Trough and enter the 300-foot Home Stretch to the peak.

7.0 Gain the flat peak. The high point is on a boulder on the north side of the peak. Return via the same route.

14.0 Arrive back at the trailhead.

Hiking Information

Closest Outfitters

Mountain Man Gear, 20 Lakeview Dr. #111, Nederland; (303) 258-3295; mountainmangear.com

Estes Park Mountain Shop, 2050 Big Thompson Ave., Estes Park; (970) 586-6548; estesparkmountainshop.com

The Hiking Hut, 184 E Elkhorn Ave., Estes Park; (970) 586-0708; enjoyestespark.com

Great Pre- or Post-Mountain Spots

The Stanley Hotel, 333 Wonderview Ave., Estes Park; (800) 976-1377; stanleyhotel.com
In case Longs Peak wasn't scary enough, check out the inspiration for Steven King's *The Shining.*

Smokin' Dave's BBQ and Taphouse, 820 Moraine Ave., Estes Park; (970) 577-7427; www.smokindavesq.com

Wild Mountain Smokehouse & Brewery, 70 E 1st St., Nederland; (303) 258-9453; wildmountainsb.com

Oskar Blues Brewery, 303 Main St., Lyons; (303) 823-6685; oskarblues.com

44 Mount Eolus and North Eolus

14,084' (NGVD29), 14,089' (NAVD88), 33rd highest

Sunlight, Mount Eolus (14,084 feet), and Windom (14,087 feet) are climbed via the Chicago Basin. The standard route to the basin is by hiking in from the Durango and Silverton Narrow Gauge Railroad stop at Needleton. From there it is a 6.2-mile hike to the Chicago Basin. Mount Eolus is the easternmost fourteener in the Windom Group. It's the second-highest mountain in the group, though some have debated that since it's only a few feet shorter than Windom. A Class 2 ascent to the saddle between Eolus and North Eolus (14,039 feet) leads to Class 3 scrambling to its apex. The mountain offers a view south into New Mexico, and Ship Rock can be seen from its summit. The mountain is somewhat isolated from Sunlight and Windom, but ambitious, experienced climbers can summit all three—four if including North Eolus—in one day.

Now you can hike the 9 miles from Durango or Silverton via the Purgatory Flats Trailhead to the train station, or you can take the train—and not just any Amtrak train. It's a narrow gauge train—lucky you! These peaks are the farthest from any road. While it's a beautiful hike, much of it along the Animas River, the train offers a unique approach to ascending a peak that's reminiscent of how the miners and settlers of yesteryear did it.

Start: Chicago Basin
Distance: 5.4 miles
Hiking time: 6 hours
Elevation gain: 2,947 feet
Difficulty: Class 2, Class 3
Trail surface: Dirt, scree, rock
Trailhead elevation: 11,110 feet
Camping: Backcountry camping in wilderness
Fees: None
Best seasons: Spring through fall
Maps: USGS Columbine Pass, Electra Lake, Engineer Mountain, Mountain View Crest, Snowdon Peak, Storm King Peak, Vallecito Reservoir; National Geographic Trails Illustrated #140: Weminuche Wilderness

Nearest towns: Durango, Silverton
Trail contacts: San Juan National Forest, Columbine Ranger District, (970) 884-2512; La Plata County Sheriff's Office, (970) 247-1157
Trail tips: No dogs are allowed on the train; if bringing a pet, you must hike in. The Chicago Basin is lousy with mountain goats. These goats will approach you. They want your pee (well, the salt in it anyway) and your food. Don't feed them. The more used to humans they become, the more likely they are to eat tents, clothes, and food. Hang a bear bag when camping at night and when climbing in the daytime.

Finding the trailhead: Access to the Needleton/Chicago Basin Trailhead is via the Durango and Silverton Narrow Gauge Railroad. The train picks up passengers at 479 Main Ave. in Durango. That's the main station. It also picks up passengers at 10th St. and Animas St. in Silverton. It drops off hikers at a suspension footbridge across the Animas River. Check the schedule online at www.durangotrain.com. For special pricing check the "Wilderness Access" section under the Ride With Us tab for information. The site also recommends calling for booking information and specials at (888) 872-4607 or (970) 387-5416.

From the drop-off point, hike across the bridge. Straight ahead are some cabins built in the 1950s. Head south on the obvious, excellent dirt trail that turns right from the bridge to follow the river and enter forest. The trail turns to the left moving away from the river at 0.4 mile, at about the same time it hits the first junction. Stay to the left toward Needle Creek as the trail moves away from the river. At 0.5 mile pass the Weminuche Wilderness sign and register for the area. From here the trail begins a gradual ascent toward Chicago Basin. It also echoes the southeasterly path of Needle Creek even though the creek is not always visible from the trail. At 1.9 miles the trail crosses over New York Creek on a footbridge. At 4.5 miles and 10,460 feet the forest starts to thin a little and at 5 miles and 10,675 feet the forest is noticeably thinner. At this point the trail turns slightly left and heads around the base of a hill before heading northeast. Look for the remains of old cabins along this stretch. Pass a tan gully on your right with an intermittent stream at 6 miles and 11,000 feet. Chicago Basin is a couple hundred yards beyond that. There is no well-defined trailhead here. But a good reference point is where the trail intersects some old tire ruts near a small stand of trees. GPS: Approach Trailhead at Needleton: N37° 38.01'/W107° 41.57'; Chicago Basin: N37° 36.52'/W107° 37.06'

The Hike

Mount Eolus is at the western prow of the Windom Group. The only fourteener farther west is Wilson Peak (14,017 feet), about 25 miles away. Eolus is a weather breaker. As clouds travel east across the continent, they must travel up and over Colorado's formidable mountains. Those peaks, like Eolus, that face farthest west bear the brunt of clouds grumbling toward higher altitudes.

The name Eolus comes from the Hayden Survey of 1874. During that assessment, chief topographer Franklin Rhoda called the Needle Mountains a "regular manufactory of storms" and named the mountain Æolus for the Greek god of the winds. The Wheeler Survey later changed it to the Americanized Eolus.

North Eolus isn't officially a fourteener, but it is named. From the saddle between the two Eolus peaks, North Eolus's peak is just 200 yards away to the northwest. Weather and time permitting, it's a fun Class 3 scramble to the peak from the 13,800-foot saddle. It can be used to help climbers figure out their approach to Eolus or can be summited after Eolus.

From the Chicago Basin hike east across the meadow on a solid trail. At 0.4 mile and 11,210 feet stay left at a trail junction heading toward Twin Lakes and enter a stand of trees. Follow the trail as it heads northeast out of the basin through trees and meadows. The path continues northeast as it crosses over a good rock slab at 0.6 mile and 11,400 feet. Exiting the short section of slab and gaining tree line, the trail turns left and heads north out of the basin. The excellent trail goes straight up the slope, paralleling a stream to the right. At 0.8 mile and 11,700 feet the trail crosses a tributary to the stream on the left side, just above where it joins the stream. The trail

Looking at Mount Eolus on the left and North Eolus on the right

zags to the right and then cuts back to the left. From here it zigzags up the slope, crossing the stream once more before reaching 12,500 feet at 1.5 miles and just south of Twin Lakes.

The trail to Eolus leads off to the left (north) and quickly crosses a stream near the south end of Twin Lakes. The good dirt trail continues around a left curve as it heads southwest, climbing up the slopes under Eolus. At 12,775 feet and 1.9 miles the trail comes close to large cliffs as the elevation steepens, and it begins to climb out of the valley toward the saddle between the Eolus peaks.

The trail climbs toward the center of the slope, snaking through some slabs of rock on a solid ramp that starts around 13,350 feet and 2.25 miles. Follow the ramp as it switchbacks up the slope and heads toward a basin on the east side with a high alpine lake. At 13,680 feet the route begins to turn northwest up a short Class 3 section to the saddle. You can climb just north of a small gully or straight up the gully to reach the saddle at 2.5 miles and 13,820 feet. North Eolus is a short, Class 3 jaunt straight ahead; Eolus, the main prize, is off to the southwest on the left.

Heading toward Eolus, climb up and over the notch at the top of the ridge to gain the narrow Class 2 and Class 3 "catwalk" ridge. The majority of the ridge is Class 2, but some dips between the larger, flatter rocks require easy Class 3 moves with hands.

Beyond the catwalk the ascent becomes easier, but there's not much of a defined trail. Skirt to the left of the northeast ridge on a large ledge. Look for a break in the face or for trail segments that look doable, and zigzag up ledges to the steep summit block. Take your time finding the route that best fits your skills and ability, staying relatively close to the center of the slope. The final moves to this peak are Class 3, with some exposure.

Mount Eolus and North Eolus

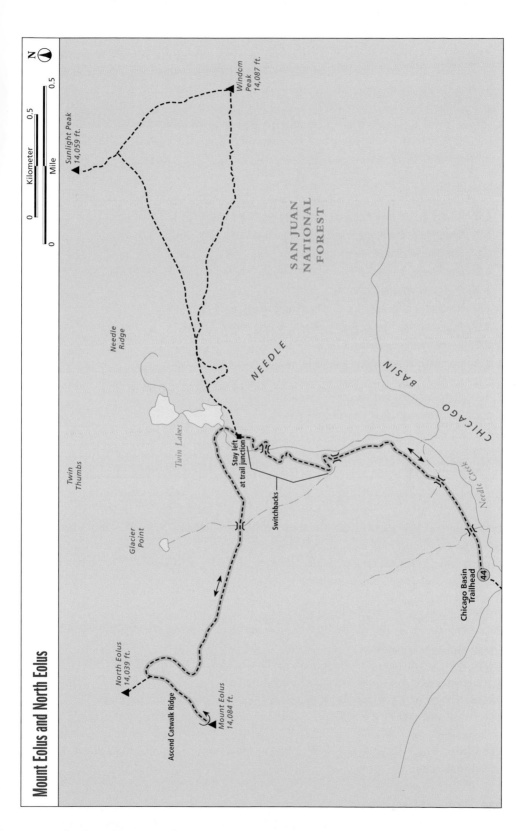

San Juan National Forest

NEEDLE

CHICAGO BASIN

Needle Creek

Chicago Basin Trailhead

44

Switchbacks

Stay left at trail junction

Twin Lakes

Glacier Point

Twin Thumbs

Needle Ridge

North Eolus
14,039 ft.

Ascend Catwalk Ridge

Mount Eolus
14,084 ft.

Sunlight Peak
14,059 ft.

Windom Peak
14,087 ft.

N

0   0.5   Kilometer
0   0.5   Mile

Reach the summit and gain an awesome view to the south into New Mexico. Closer by see Windom and Sunlight to the east. To the northeast get a good idea of why they call it the Needle Mountains as you view a sea of peaks that terminate in sharp points.

Return via the same route. Carefully navigate the summit descent and catwalk traverse. Back in the saddle you can choose, once again, to summit North Eolus or head back to Chicago Basin.

Miles and Directions

0.0 Start at the Chicago Basin coordinates above hiking east.

0.4 Stay left at a trail junction, heading toward Twin Lakes.

0.6 Cross over a slab and reach tree line.

0.8 Cross over a stream.

1.25 Cross over another stream.

1.5 Head left near the south end of Twin Lakes toward a stream; cross it.

1.9 Come near the base of large cliffs on a steeper section of trail.

2.25 Reach a ramp up the slope under the saddle.

2.5 Clamber over the catwalk ridge and head toward the summit block.

2.6 Follow the ledge underneath the summit block on its eastern side. Find and climb ledges that lead to the summit, carefully picking the way.

2.7 Reach summit. Return via the same route.

5.4 Arrive back at Chicago Basin.

Hiking Information

Closest Outfitters

Backcountry Experience, 1205 Camino del Rio, Durango; (970) 247-5830; bcexp .com

Pine Needle Mountaineering, 835 Main Ave., Durango; (970) 247-8728; pineneedle .com

Great Pre- or Post-Mountain Spots

Avalanche Brewing Company, 1067 Notorious Blair St., Silverton; (970) 387-5282; avalanchebrewing.com

Brew Pub & Kitchen, 117 West College Drive, Durango; 970-259-5959; brewpub kitchen.com/

Ska Brewing Co., 225 Girard St., Durango; (970) 247-5792; skabrewing.com

Steamworks Brewing Co., 801 E Second Ave., Durango; (970) 259-9200; steam worksbrewing.com

Handlebars Food & Saloon, 117 W 13th St., Silverton; (970) 387-5395; handlebars silverton.com

45 Mount Wilson

14,246' (NGVD29), 14,250' (NAVD88), 16th highest

At 14,246 feet, Mount Wilson claims a number of titles. It is the westernmost official fourteener (14,159-foot El Diente Peak is farther west, but as the saddle between the two drops less than 300 feet, it's not considered a fourteener by some criteria). It's the tallest peak in Delores County and the Lizard Head Wilderness. It's also a Class 4 beast with rotten (loose, unstable) rock, meaning it requires some advanced climbing skills. A helmet and mountaineering ax are always good ideas to use on this monster. Climbing parties often bring a rope to use for crux moves near the summit.

Start: Navajo Lake Trailhead
Distance: 15.2 miles
Hiking time: 12 hours
Elevation gain: 3,670 feet
Difficulty: Class 3
Trail surface: Scree, rock
Trailhead elevation: 10,350 feet
Camping: Camping near trailhead in designated camping spots
Fees: None
Best seasons: Late spring through early fall
Maps: USGS Mount Wilson, Delores Peak, Little Cone, Gray Head; National Geographic Trails Illustrated #141: Telluride, Silverton, Ouray, Lake City
Nearest towns: Placerville, Telluride
Trail contacts: Uncompahgre and San Juan National Forests, Norwood Ranger District, (970) 327-4261; San Miguel County Sheriff, (970) 728-4442; Dolores County Sheriff, (970) 677-2257
Special considerations: Restrictions apply. Check with the USDA Forest Service regarding party size and pets in Lizard Head Wilderness.

Finding the trailhead: Navajo Lake Trail (15.2 miles round-trip) up Mount Wilson's north slope is considered the standard approach for Mount Wilson and 14,159-foot El Diente.

From CO 145 heading south, turn right onto Dunton Road (FR 535), a dirt road, and stay on the road for 7 miles to reach the trailhead. Immediately after turning onto Dunton Road, cross Coke Oven Creek. The road goes west then switches back until it comes close to Coal Creek. It then turns right (north) and follows Coal Creek. At 4.3 miles stay straight, ignoring the road to the left. Shortly thereafter, as the road continues to the west, it passes the private Morgan Camp and the Kilpacker Trailhead. The Navajo Lake Trailhead is about 2.8 miles beyond Morgan Camp. GPS: N37° 48.20'/W108° 03.83'

The Hike

Mount Wilson was named for A. D. Wilson, as was its shorter sibling, 14,017-foot Wilson Peak, just an arduous 1.0 mile away. Wilson was the main topographer for the Hayden Surveys in 1874. He and Franklin Rhoda made the first recorded successful summit of Mount Wilson on September 13, 1874.

Mount Wilson's stately, jagged summit from Wilson Peak

Mount Wilson's majesty becomes more apparent once you're in the backcountry. The peak has vertigo-inducing drop-offs and a small summit block, making it an exciting, rewarding, and less-traveled peak with significant exposure at the top. From Navajo Lake Basin the majority of the climb is over talus along an ill-defined trail. Snow on the north face of Mount Wilson persists into summer, which makes a mountaineering ax handy throughout the year. However, the majority of the hike, particularly if you stay under the mountain's northeast ridge, requires just Class 2 scrambling. As the peak is approached, it requires some Class 3 scrambling and Class 4 climbing.

Access to the standard north slope route is from the upper reaches of the Navajo Lake Basin. It's 6.4 miles from the Navajo Lake Trailhead, at roughly 12,290 feet.

Begin the easy part of this ascent by crossing a stream and hiking up onto an easy shoulder leading to the north slope of the mountain. Continue on the shoulder until 6.5 miles and 13,300 feet. Climb up over a solid rock ridge at 13,400 feet and reach some easier Class 2 scrambling above 13,500 feet. Climb over the ridge to a broad face of the mountain before crossing a series of gullies. There are some small cairns to help guide hikers through this section of talus. Staying lower through this section while gaining altitude is easier. Cross the last gully near 14,100 feet at 7.3 miles. Scramble across the gully to reach a notch close to 14,150 feet and head left up the ridgeline, climbing Class 3 rock. Stay near the ridge, climbing over the rock. The final move is up over a Class 4 block with significant exposure on either side. The left side affords a little more protection, but not much.

From the summit gain sweeping, eye-popping views where El Diente's jagged canine cuts the western view as the last peak over 14,000 feet to the west. Wilson Peak is just east of north; the crown of Mount Sneffels is to the northeast, towering on the horizon almost directly over 13,913-foot Gladstone Peak. To the east, far beyond the eponymous 13,113-foot Lizard Head Peak, Uncompahgre is sometimes visible on the horizon.

Miles and Directions

0.0 Start at the Navajo Lake Trailhead and follow the good trail northeast.

0.9 Cross the Delores River.

1.3 Enter a small meadow.

1.75 Cross an intermittent creek that feeds into the Delores River.

2.3 Enter forest.

3.25 Cross the first of two intermittent streams.

3.4 Cross second intermittent stream, exiting the forest.

3.7 Following a short series of switchbacks, the trail goes right, heading east toward the lake.

3.9 The trail begins a short switchback, gaining elevation quickly to the ridge that makes up the western perimeter of Navajo Basin.

4.5 Reach the western edge of Navajo Lake. Camp near here or just above the lake in the basin.

4.7 Leave the northeastern edge of lake and hike though meadow.

5.0 The trail exits the meadow to become talus trail as it starts to gain more elevation.

5.2 The trail begins heading southeast.

5.75 The rail comes close to West Delores River.

6.4 Reach the northern edge of Navajo Basin and a trail junction. Head right (southeast) toward Mount Wilson's north slope.

6.5 Cross a stream and start climbing the shoulder of Mount Wilson.

6.8 Pass a permanent snowfield sometimes called Navajo Glacier. In summer you can avoid most or all of it.

7.1 Ascend over a ridge as the route becomes steeper. Continue angling up across the face of the mountain, staying well under the ridge and crossing a series of gullies. Cut over to the southwest slightly and begin angling upward over a series of shallow gullies.

7.3 Come close to the ridge at about 13,900 feet heading more westerly toward a gap. Snowfields may persist until summer in this area.

7.4 Come close to the ridge and scramble toward a notch on the south end of the summit ridge.

7.5 Climb out of the notch headed left and up to the summit block, climbing over Class 3 rock.

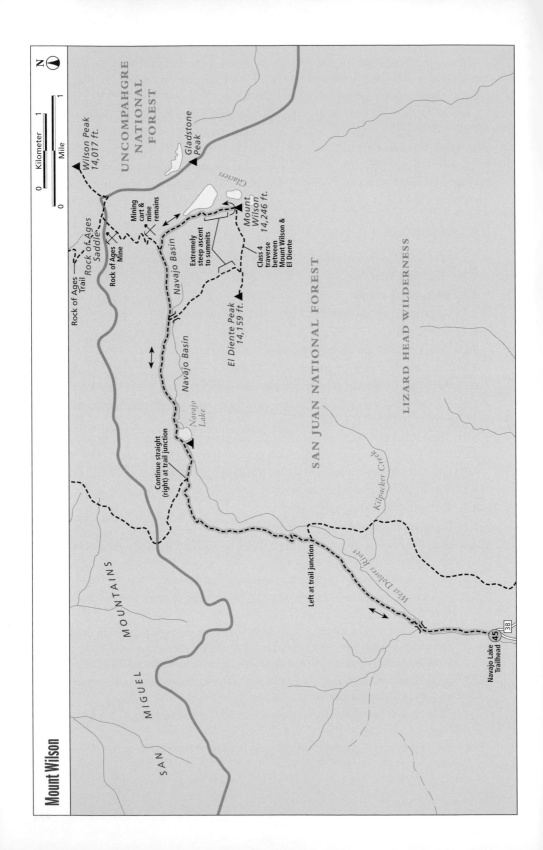

Mount Wilson

N

Wilson Peak
14,017 ft.

Gladstone
Peak

UNCOMPAHGRE
NATIONAL
FOREST

Rock of Ages
Trail

Rock of Ages
Saddle

Mining
cart & mine
remains

Rock of Ages Mine

Navajo Basin

Glaciers

Mount
Wilson
14,246 ft.

Extremely
steep ascent
to summits

Navajo Basin

Class 4
traverse
between
Mount Wilson &
El Diente

El Diente Peak
14,159 ft.

Continue straight
(right) at trail junction

Navajo
Lake

SAN JUAN NATIONAL FOREST

LIZARD HEAD WILDERNESS

SAN
MIGUEL
MOUNTAINS

Kilpacker Creek

West Dolores River

Left at trail junction

Navajo Lake
Trailhead

45
38

0   Kilometer   1

0   Mile   1

7.6 Shortly after reach the crux—a large, stable block with significant exposure. A climb to the left is slightly easier; a climb to the right has more exposure. Both sides require some Class 4 exposure, and a rope can be used here. Reach the summit and return via same route.

15.2 Arrive back at the trailhead.

Option: Starting from the Rock of Ages Trailhead provides a 10.2-mile round-trip. From the junction of CO 145 and Silver Pick Road (also called CR 60M) in Telluride, immediately cross the San Miguel River. Shortly thereafter the road becomes a good dirt road. Continue on this road for 3.3 miles then turn left to stay on the road, which becomes FR 622. In 0.8 mile turn right to stay on FR 622 for another 1.6 miles. Turn right to stay on FR 622 and continue 0.7 mile. Turn right onto FR 645 and travel another 2.2 miles, crossing a stream at about 1 mile. GPS: N37° 52.99'/W108° 01.11'

Hiking Information

Closest Outfitters

Jagged Edge Mountain Gear, 223 E Colorado Ave., Telluride; 970-728-9307; jagged -edge-telluride.com

Great Pre- or Post Mountain Spots

Telluride Brewing Co., 156 Society Dr., Telluride; (970) 728-5094; telluridebrewing co.com

Smuggler's Brewpub, 225 S Pine St., Telluride; (970) 728-5620; smugglersbrewpub .com

Last Dollar Saloon, 100 E Colorado Ave., Telluride; (970) 728-4800; lastdollarsaloon .com

Brown Dog Pizza, 110 E Colorado Ave., Telluride; (970) 728-8046; browndogpizza .com

46 Pyramid Peak

14,018' (NGVD29), 14,023' (NAVD88), 47th highest

Pyramid Peak is typical of mountains in the Elk Range: beautiful, steep, rugged, rotten—and dangerous. Located in the Maroon Bells—Snowmass Wilderness, this mountain is difficult to climb from any angle and deserves climbers' respect. The easiest path to the peak requires Class 4 moves and a fair amount of route finding. The rotten sedimentary rock means you should bring a helmet. The rate of ascent is tough too. The standard trail gains more than 4,400 feet in less than 4 miles.

Start: Maroon Lake Trailhead
Distance: 7.8 miles
Hiking time: 8 hours
Elevation gain: 4,460 feet
Difficulty: Class 4
Trail surface: Dirt, scree, rock
Trailhead elevation: 9,560 feet
Camping: Backcountry camping; Maroon Lake Campground
Fees: Entry fee for vehicles
Best seasons: Mid-June through Oct
Maps: USGS Maroon Bells; National Geographic Trails Illustrated #128: Maroon Bells, Redstone, Marble

Nearest town: Aspen
Trail contacts: White River National Forest, Aspen Ranger District, (970) 925-3445; Pitkin County Sheriff's Office, (970) 920-5300
Trail tips: The USDA Forest Service now requires the use of bear canisters for overnight camping in the warmer months. Every person in the party should carry a wilderness tag. Timed right in fall, this route offers not only stunning views of the peaks but also the golden flames of aspen trees changing colors in alpine valleys.

Finding the trailhead: From the large roundabout on CO 82 northwest of Aspen, head southwest on Maroon Creek Road for 9.5 miles. At 4.8 miles reach the Maroon Bells Welcome Station; continue on to the trailhead at 9.5 miles. The road is closed at the T-Lazy-7 Guest Ranch (3.2 miles) in winter and usually reopens around Memorial Day. Day traffic in the summer months is limited to overnight campers and backpackers. The Roaring Fork Transportation Authority (RFTA) also runs shuttles from Aspen to Maroon Lake. Visit rfta.com for information and prices. GPS: N39° 05.92'/W106° 56.46'

The Hike

Originally dubbed Black Pyramid by the Hayden Survey in 1874, the mountain came to be known as Pyramid Peak. This aptly named monolith is a real challenge for climbers. Whereas many fourteeners in other Colorado ranges had already seen prospectors come and go by the late 1800s, the first recorded ascent of Pyramid Peak didn't occur until August 22, 1909, when Harold Clark and Percy Hagerman reached the summit.

Pyramid Peak's massive ridge taken from the Snowmass Wilderness

The mountain is composed of sedimentary rock from the Permian period, rock it shares with the Maroon Bells. The crumbly sedimentary rock was carved into its current shape by glaciers and refined by continual erosion, characterizing these red, rugged, and rotten mountains. Still, this handsome mountain and its singular peak beg to be climbed, and experienced climbers take up this challenge every year.

Begin at the Crater Lake Trailhead (FT 1975) on the northeast side of Maroon Lake, and follow the trail along the north side amid stunning views of these iconic mountains. Enter the forest on the northwest side of the lake at 0.3 mile. Hike into an aspen grove as the trail begins gaining elevation slowly, beguilingly. At 1.3 miles and 10,130 feet reach a trail junction and head left (southeast) on the Pyramid Peak Trail. At this spot you can see Pyramid towering behind some shorter peaks. Most of the route to the top is up the left side of the peak. Hike into a relatively flat basin and cross over West Maroon Creek at 1.4 miles. At 1.6 miles and 10,230 feet begin ascending south up a talus slope on a good trail. The Colorado Fourteeners Initiative (CFI) built the trail, designed to be sustainable, in 2006. Follow its switchbacks as it rises above the basin floor and into the Pyramid Peak Amphitheater, a hanging basin with Pyramid's north face sitting stately at the end, like a monarch. At roughly 2.4 miles and 11.270 feet the trail ends.

Looking down the ridge from Pyramid Peak. CHRIS SEAVER

With a rock glacier on the left and a steep slope on the right, hike south into the scree-filled basin. At 11,960 feet go left, climbing east up the rock glacier and under Pyramid's mighty gaze. Continue heading southeast and find a trail at roughly 3.1 miles and 11,980 feet at the base of the slope. Find trail fragments heading up through scree-filled gullies that lead to Pyramid's northeast ridge. Reach the ridge at 3.4 miles and 13,025 feet and head right (south and southwest) along a small trail. Most of the remainder of the route is visible from here.

Shortly thereafter pass around a notch at 13,060 feet by climbing around its north side. Regain the ridge by going south and begin the final 1,000-foot ascent up the rough Class 3 and Class 4 northeast ridge of Pyramid. This is a good time to put a helmet on if it isn't on already. Climb back over the ridge on steeper terrain and onto the south side at 3.5 miles. Climb under the ridge on the south side and over two rock ribs, following cairns. Reach the Cliff Traverse, a ledge that gets really narrow in the middle, requiring some Class 3 moves.

Beyond the ledge, follow cairns that guide up the traverse, across a small gully, and over another rock rib. Around this rock rib, enter another gully, the Green Wall. The base of this gully is a good spot to take note of—it's easy to miss during a descent. Staying south of the ridge crest, climb up the gully on Class 3 and Class 4 rock, following cairns as you see them. Exit the gully near 13,600 feet and 3.7 miles. The remaining 400 feet of the route requires route finding over steep, chossy red rock and Class 3 scrambling with some occasional Class 4 moves below the ridge crest. The pitch should ease near 13,900 feet. Climb the remaining 100 feet and find yourself rewarded at 14,018 feet and 3.9 miles with some of the most awe-inspiring vistas available—anywhere!

Pyramid Peak

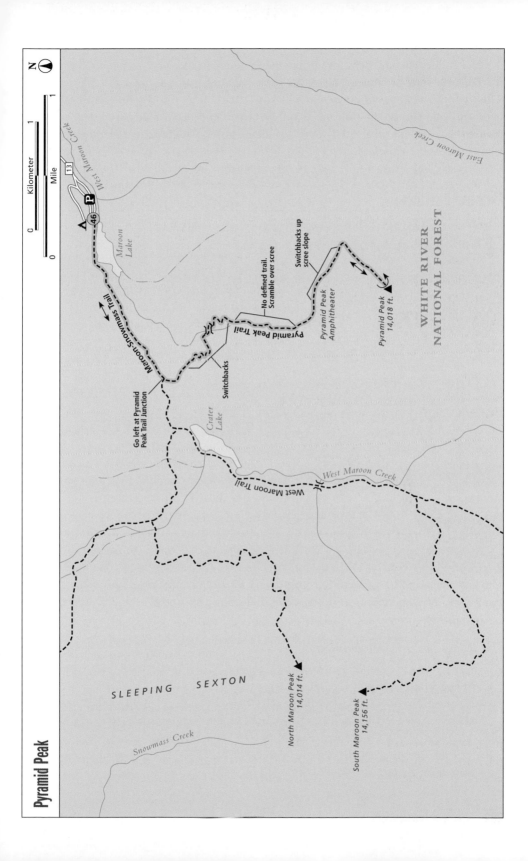

West Maroon Creek

13

P

46

Maroon Lake

Maroon-Snowmass Trail

N

Kilometer

Mile

Go left at Pyramid Peak Trail Junction

Switchbacks

Crater Lake

West Maroon Trail

West Maroon Creek

Pyramid Peak Trail

No defined trail. Scramble over scree

Pyramid Peak Amphitheater

Switchbacks up scree slope

Pyramid Peak 14,018 ft.

WHITE RIVER NATIONAL FOREST

East Maroon Creek

SLEEPING SEXTON

Snowmass Creek

North Maroon Peak 14,014 ft.

South Maroon Peak 14,156 ft.

The ruddy Maroon Bells jut up like sharks' teeth to the west. Just beyond them is a fantastic view of Snowmass (14,092 feet) and to its right, Capitol (14,130 feet). Their whitish peaks stand out against the ruddy rock of the nearby Elks, even more hyper-realistic against the rich greens of evergreen and aspen below. You may find yourself sharing this peak with some mountain goats. Don't feed or bother them. They deserve the vista too!

Return via the same route, taking care to exit the Green Wall where you entered.

Miles and Directions

0.0 Start at the Maroon Lake Trailhead and head west on the Crater Lake Trail (FT 1975).

0.3 Enter forest and the Maroon Bells–Snowmass Wilderness as the trail begins a gradual ascent.

1.3 Reach a trail junction. Head left (southeast) onto the Pyramid Trail.

1.4 Cross West Maroon Creek.

1.6 Begin climbing a scree slope.

2.4 The trail ends in the Pyramid Peak Amphitheater.

3.1 At the southeast end of the basin, reach a trail switchbacking up a gully to Pyramid's northeast ridge.

3.4 Reach a ridge below Pyramid's peak. Pass around notch to the right of the ridge then cross back over to the left side of the ridge at 3.5 miles.

3.6 Climb across the Cliff Traverse on narrow ledge then encounter two successive gullies. Climb 300 feet to the top of the second, the Green Wall.

3.7 Exit the top of the gully and scramble for the top.

3.9 Achieve the summit. Return via same route.

7.8 Arrive back at the trailhead.

Hiking Information

Closest Outfitters

Ute Mountaineer, 210 S. Galena St., Aspen; (970) 925-2849; utemountaineer.com

Bristlecone Mountain Sports, 781 E Valley Rd., Basalt; (970) 927-1492; bristlecone mountainsports.com

Great Pre- or Post-Mountain Spots

Aspen Brewing Co., 304 E Hopkins Ave., Aspen; (970) 920-BREW (2739); aspen brewingcompany.com

Woody Creek Tavern, 2858 Upper River Rd., Woody Creek; (970) 923-4585; woody creektavern.com. A favorite haunt of the late Hunter S. Thompson.

Belly Up Aspen, 450 S Galena St. Aspen; (970) 544-9800; bellyupaspen.com

J-Bar at Hotel Jerome, 330 E Main St., Aspen; (970) 925-3721; hoteljerome.auberge resorts.com/dining/

47 South Maroon Peak and North Maroon Peak

South Maroon Peak: 14,156' (NGVD29), 14,162' (NAVD88), 24th highest

North Maroon Peak: 14,014' (NGVD29), 14,019' (NAVD88), unranked

These mountains are the belles of the Rockies. They grace postcards, posters, and books and are known the world over. Located in the Maroon Bells–Snowmass Wilderness, they are remote, deadly beasts full of rotten red sedimentary rock that demands Class 3 and Class 4 climbing. At 14,156 feet, Maroon Peak is the taller of the two. North Maroon (14,014 feet) is actually a northern subpeak, rising only 234 feet above a tough saddle that connects them. They can be climbed together across a Class 4 saddle by experienced climbers, but that is not addressed here.

Start: Maroon Lake Trailhead
Distance: South Maroon Peak: 10.6 miles out and back; North Maroon Peak: 8.2 miles out and back
Hiking time: South Maroon Peak: 12 hours; North Maroon Peak: 8 hours
Elevation gain: South Maroon Peak: 4,600 feet; North Maroon Peak: 4,450 feet
Difficulty: Class 4
Trail surface: Dirt, scree, rock
Trailhead elevation: 9,560 feet
Camping: Backcountry camping; Maroon Lake Campground
Fees: Entry for vehicles
Best seasons: Mid-June through Oct

Maps: USGS Maroon Bells; National Geographic Trails Illustrated #128: Maroon Bells, Redstone, Marble
Nearest town: Aspen
Trail contacts: White River National Forest, Aspen Ranger District, (970) 925-3445; Pitkin County Sheriff's Office, (970) 920-5300
Trail tips: The USDA Forest Service now requires the use of bear canisters for overnight camping in the warmer months. Every person in the party should carry a wilderness tag. Timed right in fall, this route offers not only stunning views of the peaks but also the golden flames of aspen trees changing colors in alpine valleys.

Finding the trailhead: From the large roundabout on CO 82 northwest of Aspen, head southwest on Maroon Creek Road for 9.5 miles. At 4.8 miles reach the Maroon Bells Welcome Station; continue on to the trailhead at 9.5 miles. The road is closed at the T-Lazy-7 Guest Ranch (3.2 miles) in winter and usually reopens around Memorial Day. Day traffic in the summer months is limited to overnight campers and backpackers. The Roaring Fork Transportation Authority (RFTA) also runs shuttles from Aspen to Maroon Lake. Visit rfta.com for information about prices and times. GPS: N39° 05.92' / W106° 56.46'

The Hike

The Maroon Bells have attracted people to Colorado since it was still a territory. They're stunning throughout the year, whether graced by snow in winter or by great green valleys that become even brighter as leaves return to the aspens in spring. Those

The Maroon Bells, taken from close to Snowmass

same aspens become even more breathtaking as they flame gold and red almost simultaneously in huge fingers throughout the high mountain valleys in fall.

The Hayden Survey of 1874 named it Maroon Mountain and observed that North Maroon was a subpeak. Locals dubbed them the Maroon Bells, referring to their bell-shaped domes and started calling them North Maroon Peak and South Maroon Peak to distinguish between the two.

North Maroon Peak was climbed first by Percy Hagerman and Harold Clark on August 25, 1908. Hagerman made the first ascent of South Maroon Peak on a solo journey a few days later on August 28.

People fall on these mountains almost every year. Indeed a forest service sign calls them "The Deadly Bells." It warns: "The rock is downsloping, rotten, loose, and unstable. It kills quickly without warning. The snowfields are treacherous, poorly consolidated and no place for a novice climber." The sign ends: "DO NOT CLIMB IF NOT QUALIFIED."

Careful route finding and smart choices can help you avoid this fate. Bring a helmet. Ropes may not be advisable, as there aren't many reliable places to anchor into. Helmets not only protect you during a fall but also protect you when others kick rocks loose and from random rocks falling. Since the rock is rotten, falling rock has a habit of covering up parts of the trail. Thankfully the routes have cairns to help guide climbers. Still, use them cautiously. Overzealous climbers may have created their own cairns when off-trail.

Because of their proximity and difficulty and their enduring popularity, both routes are described here, even though North Maroon isn't an official fourteener in everyone's book.

South Maroon Peak (South Ridge)

From the Maroon Lake Trailhead, head out on the Maroon-Snowmass Trail (FT 1975), on the northeast side of Maroon Lake. Follow the trail along the north side of the lake amid stunning views of these iconic mountains. Enter an aspen grove on the northwest side of the lake at 0.3 mile.

At 1.3 miles and 10,130 feet reach a trail junction and continue on the main trail to Crater Lake. At 1.7 miles and 10,140 feet reach the junction with West Maroon Creek Trail (FT 1970). The Maroon-Snowmass Trail branches off to North Maroon. Take the West Maroon Creek Trail as it stays low and passes Crater Lake to the left, heading southwest. The first 3.0 miles of this trail are relatively flat and offer fantastic views of the Maroon Bells as well as 14,018-foot Pyramid Peak.

Cross Minnehaha Gulch and Minnehaha Creek at 2.0 miles and 10,019 feet. At 2.3 miles and 10,140 feet hike into a small talus field on a good rock trail. From here forests become interspersed with scree fields. At the end of this first scree field, reenter low vegetation and cross over a ditch and intermittent stream at 2.4 miles. At 3.3 miles and 10,450 feet reach a trail junction and head right (southwest) on the Maroon Peak Trail.

The ascent begins in earnest here as the trail starts climbing Maroon's east slopes. Begin a steeper ascent at 3.7 miles and 10,770 feet as the trail turns west. From here the trail starts snaking through, over, and around various rock outcroppings as it traverses below Maroon's east slope through alpine meadow.

At 11,200 feet and 3.9 miles turn left to cross a small gully that's often snow filled. On the other side of the gully, the trail turns back to the right. A little farther up, around 11,550 feet and 4.0 miles, the trail arches left and begins its final ascent toward Maroon's southern ridge, crossing over several cliff bands as the trail worsens into fragments. Start looking to cairns for guidance. Reach a low ridge crest at 12,950 feet and 4.6 miles. Follow a well-cairned route toward Point 13,300 and gain the southern ridge of Maroon Peak.

This is a good time to take stock of the situation. The peak is less than 1 mile away, but with climbing maneuvers and route finding, it's still roughly two more hours to the peak. If anyone is too tired to go on or is suffering from altitude sickness, make sure they have an option to turn back. If clouds are rolling in, turn back. Rotten rock gets worse in weather.

If conditions are good and you and/or your group are in good shape, keep going, staying west of the ridge and taking time to study the mountain for the best possible route.

South Maroon Peak and North Maroon Peak

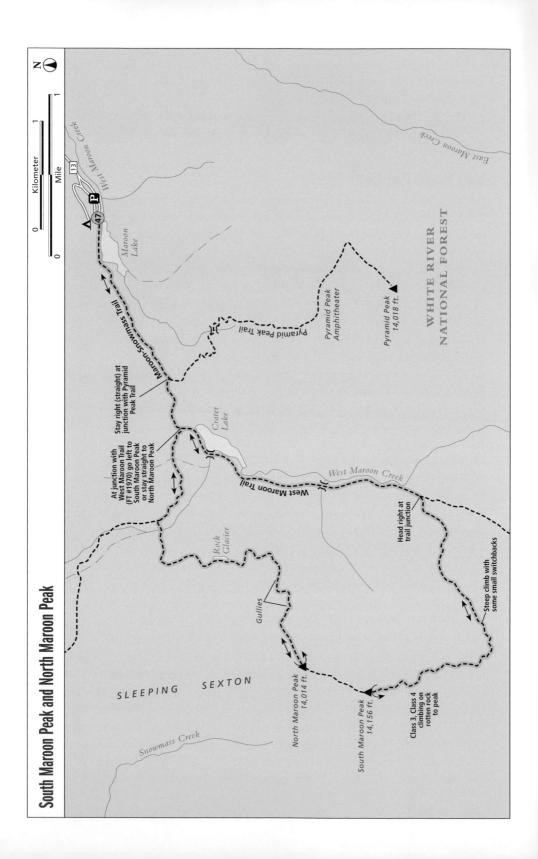

N

Kilometer 0 1
Mile 0 1

13

47 P

West Maroon Creek

Maroon Lake

Maroon-Snowmass Trail

Stay right (straight) at junction with Pyramid Peak Trail

Pyramid Peak Trail

Pyramid Peak Amphitheater

Pyramid Peak 14,018 ft.

WHITE RIVER NATIONAL FOREST

East Maroon Creek

At junction with West Maroon Trail (FT #1970) go left to South Maroon Peak or stay straight to North Maroon Peak

Crater Lake

West Maroon Trail

West Maroon Creek

Head right at trail junction

Steep climb with some small switchbacks

Rock Glacier

Gullies

SLEEPING   SEXTON

Snowmass Creek

North Maroon Peak 14,014 ft.

South Maroon Peak 14,156 ft.

Class 3, Class 4 climbing on rotten rock to peak

At 13,300 feet and 5.1 miles begin ascending a gully, following cairns into a Class 3 chimney that ends in a climb up to the left through a notch. The terrain relents slightly as it curls around ledges. Find two steep, nasty gullies ahead and choose one, following cairns to climb over the best of loose scree. Find a ledge about halfway up and turn left. Continue climbing on ledges, finding a larger ledge that takes you around Point 13,753.

On the northwest side of the point, at 13,400 feet and 5.2 miles, find a large couloir and carefully climb the loose scree. Find a ledge that leads left out of the gully at 13,680 feet and 5.3 miles. Follow the ridge to Maroon's southwest face. The well-deserved prize is close, but still a difficult climb away. There are numerous routes up the remaining 400 feet. Following the best cairned paths, the route can be kept to a Class 3 climb on a series of ledges and short vertical scrambles. Alternatively, climbers can opt to gain the south ridge and climb it to the summit. The summit is severe and shear, but it offers amazing views in every direction.

Miles and Directions: South Maroon Peak

0.0 Start at the Maroon Lake Trailhead and head west on the Maroon-Snowmass Trail (FT 1975).

0.3 Enter forest and the Maroon Bells–Snowmass Wilderness as the trail begins a gradual ascension.

1.3 Reach a trail junction and continue straight on the Maroon-Snowmass Trail.

1.7 Take the West Maroon Creek Trail (FT 1970), to the left (south) at the junction with Maroon-Snowmass Trail.

2.0 Cross Minnehaha Gulch and Minnehaha Creek

2.3 Enter a talus field on a good rock trail. From here forests become interspersed with scree fields.

3.3 Head southwest on the Maroon Peak Trail at the trail junction.

3.7 Start a steeper climb, heading west.

3.9 Turn left and cross a small gully

4.0 Begin the final ascent toward South Maroon's southern ridge. The trail worsens.

4.6 Reach a low ridge crest at follow cairns to Maroon Peak's southern ridge and assess the situation. Consider turning back if you're tired or bad weather is coming.

5.1 Ascend a gully, following cairns to a Class 3 chimney. Climb out to the left. After the chimney, choose one of two steep gullies to ascend.

5.2 Climb a couloir on loose scree.

5.3 Find a ledge leading left out of the gully. Carefully pick a route to climb the remaining 400 feet to the peak. Return via same route.

10.6 Arrive back at the trailhead.

North Maroon Peak

From the Maroon Lake Trailhead, head out on Maroon–Snowmass Trail (FT 1975), on the northeast side of Maroon Lake. Follow the trail along the north side of the lake amid stunning views of these iconic mountains. Enter an aspen grove on the northwest side of the lake at 0.3 mile.

At 1.3 miles and 10,130 feet reach a trail junction; continue on the main trail to Crater Lake. At 1.7 miles and 10,140 feet reach another trail junction. Take the right trail to North Maroon, moving away from Crater Lake. (The left, West Maroon Creek Trail, goes to South Maroon Peak.) The trail climbs through a forest that opens up into a grassy area just before crossing Minnehaha Gulch and Minnehaha Stream at 2.5 miles and 10,740 feet. Almost immediately after crossing the creek, climb up a scree field and turn left at the base of a rock face at 2.75 miles and 11,150 feet, contouring south across North Maroon's western face. Enter another gray scree field at 2.9 miles and follow the trail as it passes under some cliff bands then into a short alpine meadow. At 3.2 miles and 11,155 feet enter a scree field where the rock has become red at the bottom of a rock glacier. Climb up and over the rock glacier, following cairns to the base of cliffs under North Maroon's eastern ridge—it's as though a massive cleaver chopped off the rest of the ridge. Find a better trail close to the cliff and follow it as it curls around to the south side of the ridge.

At 3.6 miles and 11,850 feet the final, tough climb to the peak begins in earnest as you begin climbing into a steep, grassy gully that gains 600 feet in 0.1 mile. Note that this is close to tree line; on the way down, this will help you find where to exit the gully. Cross over to the west side of the couloir and begin climbing at 3.7 miles and 12,150 feet. It's a steep, Class 2 segment of climbing. The trail becomes fragmented the farther up you go.

At 12,400 feet, under a massive rock formation, exit the left side of the gully on a trail. Follow the trail over rock ledges under cliff bands to enter another gully near 12,600 feet and 3.9 miles. This is a steep gully with loose rock and grass ledges. Traverse to its western side and encounter a steep cliff band that forces you back into the gully. From here on out the rock in the gully becomes more rotten. If clouds are coming in, it's a good time to turn back. Until the snow has cleared from the face above, the gully can be rushing with meltwater. Follow the trail to the top of the ridge crest at 13,310 feet and 4.1 miles. Turn left and begin ascending the remaining 0.25 mile to the summit along or near the ridge. The hardest move is near 13,600 feet at the "Rock Band." Follow cairns to climb a steep chimney and exit to the right. Then climb back toward the ridge crest and climb the remaining 400 feet over loose red rock, taking care not to kick anything loose.

From the apex of this beast, South Maroon Peak is the giant mound of red directly south and Pyramid Peak is just north of due west, Snowmass Mountain (14,092 feet) and Capitol Peak (14,130 feet) rise out of the Elk Range in stark gray contrast to the rest of this reddish range of mountains. In summer the valley around Maroon Lake looks like something from another time.

Miles and Directions: North Maroon Peak

0.0 Start at the Maroon Lake Trailhead and head west on the Maroon-Snowmass Trail (FT 1975).

0.3 Enter forest and the Maroon Bells–Snowmass Wilderness as the trail begins a gradual ascent.

1.3 Reach a trail junction and continue straight on the Maroon-Snowmass Trail.

1.7 Reach the junction with the West Maroon Creek Trail (FT 1970); stay right on the Maroon-Snowmass Trail.

2.5 Turn left at a cairn on the trail crossing Minnehaha Gulch and Minnehaha Creek and enter a scree field.

2.75 Turn left at the base of a rock face.

2.9 Pass under some cliff bands.

3.2 Enter a red rock scree field; climb up a rock glacier.

3.6 At tree line cross to the west side of a grassy gully and begin ascending it.

3.7 Exit the gully on the left side.

3.9 Enter the next gully, ascend diagonally to its west side; turn right and climb out of the gully.

4.1 Reach a ridge crest and ascend to the peak. Return by the same route.

8.2 Arrive back at the trailhead.

Hiking Information

Closest Outfitters

Ute Mountaineer, 210 S. Galena St., Aspen; (970) 925-2849; utemountaineer.com

Bristlecone Mountain Sports, 781 E Valley Rd., Basalt; (970) 927-1492; bristlecone mountainsports.com

Great Pre- or Post-Mountain Spots

Aspen Brewing Co., 304 E Hopkins Ave., Aspen; (970) 920-BREW (2739); aspenbrewing company.com

Woody Creek Tavern, 2858 Upper River Rd., Woody Creek; (970) 923-4585; woody creektavern.com. A favorite haunt of the late Hunter S. Thompson.

Belly Up Aspen, 450 S Galena St. Aspen; (970) 544-9800; bellyupaspen.com

J-Bar at Hotel Jerome, 330 E Main St., Aspen; (970) 925-3721; hoteljerome.auberge resorts.com/dining/

48 Sunlight Peak

14,059' (NGVD29), 14,064' (NAVD88), 39th highest

Sunlight, Mount Eolus (14,084 feet), and Windom (14,087 feet) are climbed via the Chicago Basin. The standard route to the basin is by hiking in from the Durango and Silverton Narrow Gauge Railroad stop at Needleton. From there it is a 6.2-mile hike to the Chicago Basin. Sunlight Peak might be the shortest fourteener in the Needle Mountains, but it's also the toughest fourteener in the range. Some consider it one of the most difficult fourteeners of all—not because of a long stretch of exposed moves but because of the last move, a leap of faith to reach a small summit block. It's been called the most difficult summit move among all the fourteeners in Colorado and earns this peak its Class 4 climbing status.

An alternative route to Windom Peak, Sunlight Peak, and Mount Eolus involves a ride on a narrow-gauge train! These peaks are the furthest from any road—the closest approach by foot via the Purgatory Flats Trailhead requires a 15-mile hike just to get to Chicago Basin. It's a beautiful hike, much of it along the Animas River, but the train offers a unique approach to ascending a peak that's akin to how the miners and settlers of yesteryear did it. Even with the ride in on the train, a 6.2-mile trek still remains—again a beautiful hike—to the start of this hike, the Chicago Basin!

Start: Chicago Basin
Distance: 5.2 miles
Hiking time: 5 to 6 hours
Elevation gain: 2,949 feet
Difficulty: Class 4
Trail surface: Dirt, scree, rock
Trailhead elevation: 11,110 feet
Camping: Backcountry camping in wilderness
Fees: None
Best seasons: Spring through fall
Maps: USGS Columbine Pass, Electra Lake, Engineer Mountain, Mountain View Crest, Snowdon Peak, Storm King Peak, Vallecito Reservoir; National Geographic Trails Illustrated #140: Weminuche Wilderness

Nearest towns: Durango, Silverton
Trail contacts: San Juan National Forest, Columbine Ranger District, (970) 884-2512; La Plata County Sheriff's Office, (970) 247-1157
Trail tips: No dogs are allowed on the train; if bringing a pet, you must hike in. The Chicago Basin is lousy with mountain goats. These goats will approach you. They want your pee (well, the salt in it anyway) and your food. Don't feed them. The more used to humans they become, the more likely they are to eat tents, clothes, and food. Hang a bear bag when camping at night and when climbing in the daytime.

Finding the trailhead: Access to the Needleton/Chicago Basin Trailhead is via the Durango and Silverton Narrow Gauge Railroad. The train picks up passengers at 479 Main Ave. in Durango. That's the main station. It also picks up passengers at 10th St. and Animas St. in Silverton. It drops off hikers at a suspension footbridge across the Animas River. Check the schedule online at www.durangotrain.com. For special pricing check the "Wilderness Access" section under the Ride with Us tab for information. The site also recommends calling for booking information and specials at (888) 872-4607 or (970) 387-5416.

From the drop-off point, hike across the bridge. Straight ahead are some cabins built in the 1950s. Head south on the obvious, excellent dirt trail that turns right from the bridge to follow the river and enter forest. The trail turns to the left moving away from the river at 0.4 mile, at about the same time it hits the first junction. Stay to the left toward Needle Creek as the trail moves away from the river. At 0.5 mile pass the "Weminuche Wilderness" sign and register for the area. From here the trail begins a gradual ascent toward Chicago Basin. It also echoes the southeasterly path of Needle Creek even though the creek is not always visible from the trail. At 1.9 miles the trail crosses over New York Creek on a footbridge. At 4.5 miles and 10,460 feet the forest starts to thin a little and at 5 miles and 10,675 feet the forest is noticeably thinner. At this point the trail turns slightly left and heads around the base of a hill before heading northeast. Look for the remains of old cabins along this stretch. Pass a tan gully on your right with an intermittent stream at 6 miles and 11,000 feet. Chicago Basin is a couple hundred yards beyond that. There is no well-defined trailhead here. But a good reference point is where the trail intersects some old tire ruts near a small stand of trees. GPS: Approach Trailhead at Needleton: N37° 38.01'/W107° 41.57'; Chicago Basin: N37° 36.52'/W107° 37.06'

The Hike

Sunlight Peak and Sunlight Spire bookend a small north–south saddle called The Window that offers, not surprisingly, stunning views of the sun in the morning and evening.

The two peaks—as well as Eolus—are evidence of a period of glaciation that carved away at the 1.6-billion-year-old Precambrian rock that makes up these peaks, leaving them with their needlelike appearance.

Sunlight Peak is among Colorado's toughest fourteeners because of the summit move. The approach to Sunlight is up Red Couloir, a steep, ruddy couloir with no absolute trail that requires Class 2 scrambling; but the haphazard stack of giant's blocks that make up the summit is the real challenge. It requires leaping from one block to another with a gap in between and nothing but air below. There's little ability to anchor another climber on the summit. That's the Class 4 move that elevates this mountain's difficulty level. Once you do ascend, you have to figure out how to get back down. It's a fun puzzle all around. Some may opt to bring climbing gear to belay the final summit and a helmet for the summit block. It's up to your comfort level and ability whether you want to take these precautions.

The US Geological Survey named Sunlight Peak when it mapped the Needles Mountains in 1902.

From the Chicago Basin hike east across the meadow on a solid trail. At 0.4 mile and 11,210 feet stay left at a trail junction heading toward Twin Lakes and enter a stand of trees. Follow the trail as it heads northeast out of the basin through trees and meadows. The path continues northeast as it crosses over a good rock slab at 0.6 mile and 11,400 feet. Exiting the short section of slab and gaining tree line, the trail turns

Sunlight Peak to left, behind Sunlight Spire taken from Windom Peak

left and heads north out of the basin. The excellent trail goes straight up the slope, paralleling a stream to the right. At 0.8 mile and 11,700 feet the trail crosses a tributary to the stream on the left side, just above where it joins the stream. The trail zags to the right and then cuts back to the left. From here it zigzags up the slope, crossing the stream once more before reaching 12,500 feet at 1.5 miles and just south of Twin Lakes. The trail to Eolus heads off to the left.

Turn right (northeast), staying south of the lake. Contour around lower Twin Lake and begin heading right near its southern shore. From here there are numerous ways to begin tackling Sunlight's peak. Climb east and slightly north up a slope with some scree sections. The path comes parallel to a stream that feeds the Twin Lakes.

Enter the upper basin between Sunlight and Windom at 13,000 feet and 1.9 miles. From here the route becomes apparent all the way to the 13,770-foot Window Saddle between Sunlight Peak and Sunlight Spire. Head northeast across the flat basin toward Sunlight's base. Begin cutting across Sunlight Peak's southern slope on a scree-and-dirt trail, following cairns as needed.

Reach the Red Couloir, a gully of ruddy scree in the middle of the saddle, and climb up, zigzagging on trail fragments as needed. The left side of the gully may offer more-solid climbing. Reach the saddle at 2.4 miles and 13,775 feet. Get an awesome view to the east across the San Juans; then turn back to the west and enjoy the view back into the upper basin.

Sunlight Peak's difficult summit block requires some Class 4 moves.

Head left, following cairns toward Sunlight's obvious peak. From here it's a Class 3 climb to the summit block. Climb with care as a trail takes you up to the summit block. The trail threads through the pinnacles of rock and passes under some cliffs. From here scramble to an upper ridge and find a hole, basically a doorframe of piled rocks. It's better to keep left (west) and avoid passing through this hole. Ascend a section of steep rock, using cairns to help guide you as the trail curls around to the right. Turn left at the top and find another, smaller hole. Consider it a rabbit hole to the sky. On the other side find some rock ledges that lead toward the summit. Climb through this chimney to reach some rock ledges on the east side of the summit; follow them to the final summit blocks, which look like a Flintstones-era lean-to.

To get to the very top, climb up and over the large lower block and onto a smaller block to its right. This is the crux. Straddle or reach over to the block in front of you and cross over the gap—there's a 30-foot drop below, which causes most to pause or consider this point on the slabs of rock their summit. Once over the gap, climb up the taller rock to the peak and you're at the top on a peak built for one—maybe two. Getting back down can be just as difficult and requires a long step or leap across to the smaller block.

Another option is to climb straight up the 10- to 15-foot Class 5 slab on the summit's south face. The boulder leans against the summit slab. It's easier to belay on this side than from the Class 4, more exposed route.

Since it's a sheer drop-off in almost every direction from this pinnacle in the sky, the peak offers some of the most dizzying views of any fourteener. The Eolus group is particularly stunning to the west, as are Gray Needle (13,430 feet) and Jagged Mountain (13,824 feet) to the north. Windom's jagged molar dominates the southeastern skyline.

Sunlight Peak

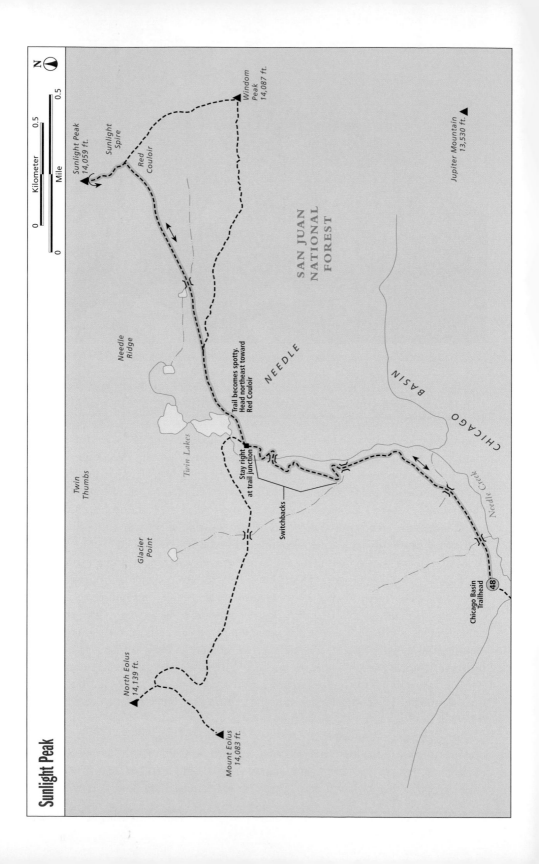

Sunlight Peak
14,059 ft.

Sunlight Spire

Red Couloir

Windom Peak
14,087 ft.

Jupiter Mountain
13,530 ft.

SAN JUAN NATIONAL FOREST

Needle Ridge

Twin Thumbs

Twin Lakes

Glacier Point

NEEDLE

Trail becomes spotty.
Head northeast toward
Red Couloir

Stay right
at trail junction

Switchbacks

CHICAGO BASIN

Needle Creek

North Eolus
14,139 ft.

Mount Eolus
14,083 ft.

48

Chicago Basin
Trailhead

N

Kilometer

0   0.5

0   0.5

Mile

After getting off the summit, carefully rethread your way down from the block and head back down to the saddle. From the saddle you can continue south toward Windom or head back down to the Chicago Basin and save Windom for another day.

Miles and Directions

0.0 Start at the Chicago Basin coordinates above, hiking east.

0.4 Stay left at trail junction, heading toward Twin Lakes.

0.6 Cross over a slab and reach tree line.

0.8 Cross over a stream.

1.25 Cross over another stream.

1.5 A trail leads off to Mount Eolus; stay right on south side of lower Twin Lake, heading northeast.

1.6 At a trail junction continue going straight on the left trail, heading northeast up and out of the Twin Lakes basin.

1.9 Enter the upper basin between Sunlight and Windom.

2.3 Reach the base of Red Couloir and turn left and climb into the couloir.

2.4 Reach top of Red Couloir and head left across Windom Saddle heading northeast toward Sunlight following cairns.

2.6 Reach the crux and climb up through a chimney to reach the final summit blocks. Return via the same route. (**Option:** Return to Windom Saddle, begin heading down Red Couloir and turn left to Windom Peak.)

5.2 Arrive at Chicago Lakes

Hiking Information

Closest Outfitters

Backcountry Experience, 1205 Camino del Rio, Durango; (970) 247-5830; bcexp
.com

Pine Needle Mountaineering, 835 Main Ave., Durango; (970) 247-8728; pineneedle
.com

Great Pre- or Post-Mountain Spots

Avalanche Brewing Company, 1067 Notorious Blair St., Silverton; (970) 387-5282;
avalanchebrewing.com

Brew Pub & Kitchen, 117 West College Drive, Durango; 970-259-5959; brewpub
kitchen.com/

Ska Brewing Co., 225 Girard St., Durango; (970) 247-5792; skabrewing.com

Steamworks Brewing Co., 801 E Second Ave., Durango; (970) 259-9200; steamworks
brewing.com

Handlebars Food & Saloon, 117 W 13th St., Silverton; (970) 387-5395; handlebars
silverton.com

49 Crestone Needle

14,197' (NGVD29), 14,201' (NAVD88), 20th highest

The Crestone Needle is a gorgeous peak of conglomerate rock that's typical of this region of the Sangre de Cristo Mountains in the Rio Grande and San Isabel National Forests. It's next to and almost as hard as Crestone Peak (14,294 feet) and has its own unique challenges. A difficult Class 3 climb with some interesting moves, it was the last of Colorado's fourteeners to be climbed. It's a good peak to bring a helmet on and maybe a rope, particularly if considering the Class 4 saddle between the Crestones. If hiking before July consider bringing a mountaineering ax—some parts of the Needle retain snow into summer.

Start: Lower South Colony Trailhead
Distance: 11.2 miles
Hiking time: About 10 hours
Elevation gain: 4,300 feet
Difficulty: Class 3
Trail surface: Dirt, scree, rock
Trailhead elevation: 9,900 feet
Camping: Multiple spots at 4WD trailhead; backcountry camping
Fees: None
Best seasons: Late spring through fall
Maps: USGS Crestone Peak, Crestone, Beck Mountain; National Geographic Trails Illustrated #138: Sangre de Cristo Mountains

Nearest towns: Westcliffe, Crestone
Trail contacts: Rio Grande National Forest, Saguache Ranger District, (719) 655-2547; San Isabel National Forest, San Carlos Ranger District, (719) 269-8500; Custer County Sheriff's Office, (719) 783-2270; Saguache County Sheriff's Office, (719) 655-2525 (emergencies)
Trail tips: Parts of this trail go through the Sangre de Cristo Wilderness; follow local wilderness rules.

Finding the trailhead: From the junction of CO 69 and CO 96 (6th and Main Streets in town) in Westcliffe, drive south on CO 69 for 4.6 miles. Turn right onto CR 119 (also called Colfax Lane). Drive to the end of Colfax at 10.2 miles and turn right onto CR 120 (South Colony Road). Stay on CR 120 for 1.3 miles and turn right onto Colfax Lane. Drive 5.5 miles to the end of Colfax. Turn right (west) and drive 1.5 miles to a 2WD trailhead on the right at the junction of CR 120 and CR 125. (**Option:** If your vehicle can't go farther, parking and starting your hike here, at 8,800 feet, adds 3 miles to your hike each way: total 17.2 miles round-trip, about 13 hours, elevation gain 5,400 feet.) High-clearance and 4WD vehicles can continue for another 2.4 miles over a rough 4WD road to the upper 4WD trailhead at 9,900 feet. The trailhead is on the southwest side of the parking area next to a kiosk. **Note:** CR 120 used to go farther up into the Crestone Group, but the road was closed in 2009. GPS: 2WD trailhead: N37° 59.61'/W105° 28.36'; 4WD trailhead: N37° 58.59'/W105° 30.34'

Crestone Needle from South Colony Lakes. LEE MAUNEY ▶

The Hike

Crestone Needle was thought unclimbable for a long time. Hence it was one of the last fourteeners to be climbed in the state. Albert Ellingwood and Eleanor Davis took the honor on July 24, 1916. Ellingwood was an accomplished mountaineer who led many first routes in Colorado's and Wyoming's mountains. Davis was the first woman to climb all of Colorado's fourteeners.

Crestone Needle from Crestone Peak. LEE MAUNEY

Ellingwood and Davis climbed the needle when its name was in flux. When trappers and settlers entered the area in the 1850s, they thought the mountains resembled Wyoming's Three Tetons, then the most famous mountains in the Wild West, and called them the Trois Tetons. That name made it into the Wheeler Survey maps of 1877 and 1879. However, the mountains also were known as the Crestones because of their resemblance to a cock's comb or helmet crest. In 1883 the US Land Office Survey named it the "South East Spanish Crag." Ultimately the Colorado Mountain Club named it Crestone Needle, which was later adopted nationally.

From the closure of South Colony Lakes Road (CR 120) at 9,900 feet, head southwest, crossing a footbridge near the closure. Hike through a beautiful forest on the closed road, staying left of a junction and signed trailhead to Humboldt Peak (14,064 feet) at 2.5 miles. Shortly after that cross a log bridge and reach the old 4WD trailhead at 2.75 miles and 11,120 feet. The trail remains nice and wide until about 3.5 miles and 11,400 feet, when it gets narrower.

At 4.0 miles and 11,580 feet the trail comes close to South Colony Lake Creek. Follow the path as it turns left (west) to parallel the stream. At 4.25 miles take the trail to the left at a marked trail junction. Shortly after, the trail makes a sharper left and heads up toward Broken Hand Pass. Let the climbing begin!

The trail enters a patch of large scree at 4.4 miles as it exits tree line at 11,900 feet. The trail becomes much more rugged from here on out. Work your way through a difficult rock section near 12,000 feet and continue up through the bowl toward Broken Hand Pass on a good trail. Reach the southwest side of the bowl and head up a steep couloir to the pass at 4.9 miles and 12,540 feet. Climb out of the bowl,

Crestone Needle

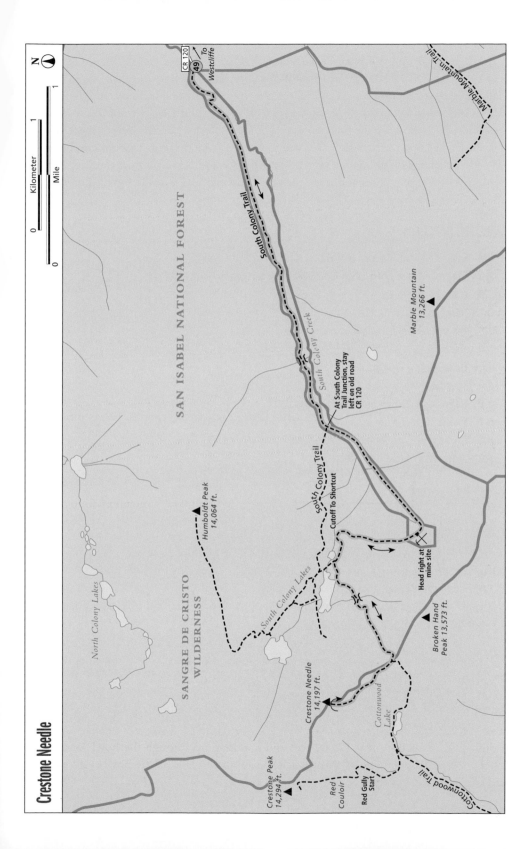

N

Kilometer
0   1

Mile
0   1

SAN ISABEL NATIONAL FOREST

CR 120
49
To
Westcliffe

South Colony Trail

South Colony Creek

South Colony Trail

At South Colony
Trail Junction, stay
left on old road
CR 120

Marble Mountain
13,266 ft.

Marble Mountain Trail

SANGRE DE CRISTO
WILDERNESS

North Colony Lakes

Humboldt Peak
14,064 ft.

South Colony Lakes

South Colony Trail
Cutoff To Shortcut

Head right at
mine site

Broken Hand
Peak 13,573 ft.

Crestone Needle
14,197 ft.

Cottonwood
Lake

Crestone Peak
14,294 ft.

Red
Couloir

Red Gully
Start

Cottonwood Trail

following the trail up and across some ledges, and reach Broken Hand Pass at 12,950 feet and 5.0 miles. Head right (north) toward Crestone Needle's south face. Another trail leads west to Crestone Peak. Follow the trail onto the Needle's south slope. At 12,260 feet downclimb to enter the first of two couloirs that culminate at the Needle's peak. Climb up the first couloir on its west side, looking for a passage on the left close to 13,650 feet that will take you to the next couloir. This requires climbing up onto a rock rib on good rock. Ascend over the rib and down into the next, higher couloir. Ascend the couloir and reach the top. Head northwest to the top of the peak and enjoy the awesome view.

Miles and Directions

0.0 Start at the parking area at the road closure (4WD trailhead).

2.5 Continue on the abandoned road, passing a junction to Humboldt Peak.

2.6 Cross a log bridge.

2.75 Reach the old 4WD trailhead.

3.5 The trail becomes narrower.

4.0 The trail nears South Colony Lake.

4.25 Head left at a trail junction.

4.4 The trail enters a scree field.

4.9 Begin the ascent to Broken Hand Pass.

5.0 Reach the top of the pass and head right. Climb two couloirs.

5.6 Gain the summit. Return via same route.

11.2 Arrive back at the road closure.

Hiking Information

Closest Outfitters

Take a Hike!, 210 Main St., Westcliffe; (719) 783-3771; takeahikewc.com

Chappy's Mountain View Bar & Grill, 213 Main St., Westcliffe; (719) 783-0813; face book.com/ChappybarandgrillwestcliffeCO

Edge Ski Paddle & Pack, 107 N Union Ave., Pueblo; (719) 583-2021; edgeskiand paddle.com

Great Pre- or Post-Mountain Spots

Royal Gorge Brewing Co. & Restaurant, 413 Main St., Cañon City; (719) 345-4141; royalgorgebrewpub.com

Elevation Beer Company, 115 Pahlone Pkwy., Poncha Springs; (719) 539-5258; elevationbeerco.com

50 Crestone Peak

14,294' (NGVD29), 14,298' (NAVD88), 7th highest

At 14,294 feet, Crestone Peak is the tallest in this group of five fourteeners in the Sangre de Cristo Mountains, bordering the Rio Grande and San Isabel National Forests and Custer and Saguache Counties. Unlike some of Colorado's taller peaks, Crestone is not an easy climb. In fact, it's considered one of the most difficult fourteeners in the state, with its long approach and lots of Class 3 moves and a 1,000-foot climb up Red Couloir that leads to its peak. It's a good mountain to bring a helmet on, and since snow can persist in at least one gully into July, consider bringing a mountaineering ax.

Start: Lower South Colony Trailhead
Distance: 13.2 miles
Hiking time: About 10 hours
Elevation gain: 4,300 feet
Difficulty: Class 3
Trail surface: Dirt, scree, rock
Trailhead elevation: 9,900 feet
Camping: Multiple spots at 4WD trailhead; backcountry camping
Fees: None
Best seasons: Late spring through fall
Maps: USGS Crestone Peak, Crestone, Beck Mountain; National Geographic Trails Illustrated #138: Sangre de Cristo Mountains

Nearest towns: Westcliffe, Crestone
Trail contacts: Rio Grande National Forest, Saguache Ranger District, (719) 655-2547; San Isabel National Forest, San Carlos Ranger District, (719) 269-8500; Custer County Sheriff's Office, (719) 783-2270; Saguache County Sheriff's Office, (719) 655-2525 (emergencies)
Trail tips: Parts of this trail go through the Sangre de Cristo Wilderness; follow local wilderness rules.

Finding the trailhead: From the junction of CO 69 and CO 96 (6th and Main Streets in town) in Westcliffe, drive south onto CO 69 for 4.6 miles. Turn right onto CR 119 (also called Colfax Lane). Drive to the end of Colfax at 10.2 miles and turn right onto CR 120 (South Colony Road). Stay on CR 120 for 1.3 miles and turn right onto Colfax Lane. Drive 5.5 miles to the end of Colfax. Turn right (west) and drive 1.5 miles to a 2WD trailhead on the right at the junction of CR 120 and CR 125. (*Option:* If your vehicle can't go farther, parking and starting your hike here, at 8,800 feet, adds 3 miles to your hike each way: total 19.2 miles round-trip, about 15 hours, elevation gain 5,400 feet.) High-clearance and 4WD vehicles can continue for another 2.4 miles over a rough 4WD road to the upper 4WD trailhead at 9,900 feet. The trailhead is on the southwest side of the parking area next to a kiosk. *Note:* CR 120 used to go farther up into the Crestone Group, but the road was closed in 2009. GPS: 2WD trailhead: N37° 59.61'/W105° 28.36'; 4WD trailhead: N37° 58.59'/W105° 30.34'

The Hike

Crestone Peak towers over the other peaks in the range, including Crestone Needle, which is 0.5 mile to the southeast across a steep, forbidding saddle. Crestone is one of Colorado's toughest and most revered peaks. It's also in one of the state's wildest ranges. The first decent topographic maps of the region didn't come out until 1967. In fact, the first climb of Crestone wasn't until July 1916, on the same trip that Albert Ellingwood and Eleanor Davis made the first ascent of Crestone Needle. It's said that Crestone Needle was the last fourteener climbed, but some accounts say Ellingwood and Davis summited the Needle first then climbed across the 0.5-mile ridge to ascend Crestone Peak on the same day.

Like most mountains in this part of the Sangre de Cristos, Crestone Peak is composed of conglomerate rock that offers surprisingly knobby foot- and handholds of rock cemented in place. Most of these are pretty solid, as opposed to the rotten rock that makes up the Maroon Bells in the Elk Range.

Early settlers and trappers who entered the area in the 1850s thought the mountains resembled Wyoming's Three Tetons, then the most famous mountains in the Wild West, and called them the Trois Tetons. That name made it into the Wheeler Survey maps of 1877 and 1879. However, the mountains also were known as the Crestones because of their resemblance to a cock's comb or helmet crest.

From the closure of South Colony Lakes Road (CR 120) at 9,900 feet, head southwest, crossing a footbridge near the closure. Hike through a beautiful forest on the closed road, staying left at a junction and signed trailhead to Humboldt Peak (14,064 feet) at 2.5 miles. Shortly after that cross a log bridge and reach the old 4WD

Climbing down from the Crestones with Crestone Peak in the background. Lee Mauney

Climbing a gully in the Crestones. LEE MAUNEY

trailhead at 2.75 miles and 11,120 feet. The trail remains nice and wide until about 3.5 miles and 11,400 feet, when it gets narrower.

At 4.0 miles and 11,580 feet the trail comes close to South Colony Lake Creek. Follow the path as it turns left (west) to parallel the stream. At 4.25 miles take the trail to the left at a marked trail junction. Shortly after, the trail makes a sharper left and heads up toward Broken Hand Pass. Let the climbing begin!

The trail enters a patch of large scree at 4.4 miles as it exits tree line at 11,900 feet. The trail becomes much more rugged from here on out. Work your way through a difficult rock section near 12,000 feet and continue up through the bowl toward Broken Hand Pass on a good trail. Reach the southwest side of the bowl and head up a steep couloir to the pass at 4.9 miles and 12,540 feet. Climb out of the bowl, following the trail up and across some ledges, and reach Broken Hand Pass at 12,950 feet and 5.0 miles.

Atop the pass, look for a trail that heads left toward Cottonwood Lake in the basin below. Hike down into the alpine meadow in the basin, heading southwest; then turn slightly right. Reach Cottonwood Lake at 5.4 miles and 12,330 feet and skirt around its northern shoreline. Continue hiking west beyond Cottonwood Lake, reaching a low point of 12,240 feet, and look for the bottom of the Red Couloir to the right (north). Follow the trail that parallels the gully until 12,680 feet and 6.1 miles then cut across a rock face to enter the gully at 12,800 feet. Climb the gully on good, stable rock. In early summer the rock may be wet from snowmelt, but climbing up the east

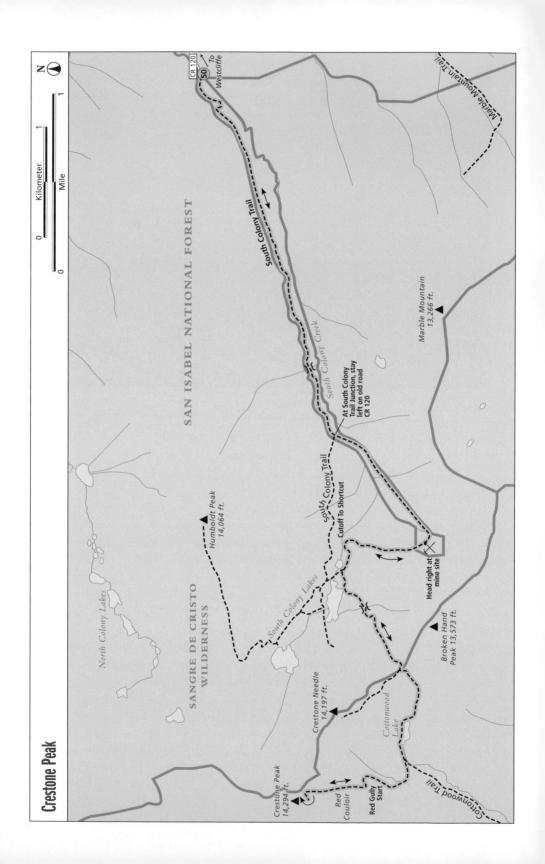

Crestone Peak

N

Kilometer
Mile

SAN ISABEL NATIONAL FOREST

CR 120
50
To Westcliffe

South Colony Trail

South Colony Creek

Marble Mountain Trail

Marble Mountain
13,266 ft.

At South Colony
Trail Junction, stay
left on old road
CR 120

South Colony Trail

South Colony Trail
Cutoff To Shortcut

Humboldt Peak
14,064 ft.

Head right at
mine site

SANGRE DE CRISTO
WILDERNESS

North Colony Lakes

South Colony Lakes

Broken Hand
Peak 13,573 ft.

Crestone Needle
14,197 ft.

Cottonwood
Lake

Crestone Peak
14,294 ft.

Red
Couloir

Red Gully
Start

Cottonwood Trail

side of the gully should be easy enough. At roughly 13,500 feet return to the couloir itself, which becomes wider at this point, and ascend the remaining 700 feet to the red notch at 14,100 feet. The upper portion of the couloir often retains snow through July. Upon reaching the red notch, head left to the taller of Crestone's twin peaks, scrambling and climbing over conglomerate rock. Follow ledges and cairns up the remaining rock to gain the summit of Crestone at 14,294 feet and 6.6 miles. Scramble to the other summit at 14,160 feet on the other side of the notch—or not—and then return via the same route.

Miles and Directions

0.0 Start at the parking area at the road closure (4WD trailhead).

2.5 Continue on the abandoned road, passing a junction to Humboldt Peak.

2.6 Cross a log bridge.

2.75 Reach the old 4WD trailhead.

3.5 The trail becomes narrower.

4.0 The trail nears South Colony Lake.

4.25 Head left at a trail junction.

4.4 The trail enters a scree field.

4.9 Begin the ascent to Broken Hand Pass.

5.0 Reach the top of the pass and head left, climbing down into the basin toward Cottonwood Lake.

5.4 Approach Cottonwood Lake.

6.1 Reach the base of Red Couloir and begin ascending it.

6.6 Exit the couloir, head left, and scramble to the summit. Return by the same route.

13.2 Arrive back at the road closure.

Hiking Information

Closest Outfitters

Take a Hike!, 210 Main St., Westcliffe; (719) 783-3771; takeahikewc.com

Chappy's Mountain View Bar & Grill, 213 Main St., Westcliffe; (719) 783-0813; facebook.com/ChappybarandgrillwestcliffeCO

Edge Ski Paddle & Pack, 107 N Union Ave., Pueblo; (719) 583-2021; edgeskiandpaddle.com

Great Pre- or Post-Mountain Spots

Royal Gorge Brewing Co. & Restaurant, 413 Main St., Cañon City; (719) 345-4141; royalgorgebrewpub.com

Elevation Beer Company, 115 Pahlone Pkwy., Poncha Springs; (719) 539-5258; elevationbeerco.com

51 Little Bear Peak

14,037' (NGVD29), 14,040' (NAVD88), 44th highest

Little Bear, Ellingwood Point (14,042 feet), and Blanca Peak (14,037 feet) share Lake Como Trailhead, which is up the long, gnarled, difficult Lake Como ATV road. Depending on where you park on that road, it will likely add 8 to 10 miles to your adventure. This is definitely a place to camp out for a night or two and do one, two, or all three peaks!

Little Bear is both the shortest peak in the Blanca Group of fourteeners and has the shortest trail to its peak, but it's the hardest of the mountains in the group to climb—indeed it's one of the most dangerous in Colorado, requiring Class 4 climbing. Bring a helmet and consider bringing rope and harnesses. The peak is partially in the Rio Grande National Forest and partially on private land. The border between Alamosa and Castilla Counties also straddles Little Bear's ridge.

The standard route to Ellingwood Point is a Class 2 summit that shares almost all its route with the trail to Blanca. It's a rough push over scree to the peak. The peak shares a short, exciting Class 3 saddle with Ellingwood, and both can be had in a glorious day by adventurous climbers. Snow can persist into summer on this mountain, and a mountaineering ax may come in handy.

If you drive a rock-crawler, extremely modified 4WD, ATV, or perhaps a horse, you may make it up to the Lake Como trailhead (about 10 miles from the highway junction). A 4WD vehicle with high clearance might be able to travel as far as 3.25 miles from the junction with CO 150 at about 8,800 feet. This is a notoriously difficult road with a series of moves called "Jaws" that will chew up and spit out an SUV's undersides.

Start: Lake Como Trailhead
Distance: 3.1 miles
Hiking time: About 7 hours
Elevation gain: 2,287 feet
Difficulty: Class 4
Trail surface: Scree, rock
Trailhead elevation: 11,750 feet at Lake Como
Camping: Backcountry camping
Fees: None
Best seasons: Spring through fall (backcountry winter sports in the area)
Maps: USGS Blanca Peak, Mosca Pass, Twin Peaks; National Geographic Trails Illustrated #138: Sangre de Cristo Mountains

Nearest towns: Fort Garland, Alamosa
Trail contacts: Pike San Isabel National Forest, San Carlos Ranger District, (719) 269-8500; Rio Grande National Forest, Conejos Ranger District, (719) 274-8971; Huerfano County Sheriff, (719) 738-1600; Costilla County Sheriff, (719) 672-3302
Trail tips: Start the hike early as weather can build quickly. It's hard to see it rolling in when lower in the climb.
Special considerations: Summit this peak early. Bad weather can come in quickly, and the Class 4 moves on this mountain's upper portions are slow.

Finding the trailhead: Take CO 150 north toward Great Sand Dunes National Park from the junction of US 160 and CO 150, west of Fort Garland and Blanca and east of Alamosa. Go 3.2 miles on CO 150, passing CR 4S on the left and taking the next right, which becomes Lake Como Road. The Lake Como Trailhead is 7.2 miles from the highway junction along this 4WD road. Most people will have to park their vehicles at about 1.6 to 1.8 miles on Lake Como Road. Those who have a 4WD vehicle with good clearance can make it about 3.25 miles on the road, finding parking along the road or one of the switchbacks—make sure other vehicles can pass your vehicle on the road and that other vehicles can turn around on a switchback. Park your vehicle and begin hiking up the 4WD drive road to Lake Como. If you plan on driving an ATV or rock crawler to Lake Como, check out some videos of the obstacles first. GPS: 2WD Trailhead: N37° 32.27'/W105° 34.64'; 4WD Trailhead: N37° 33.04'/W105° 33.54'; Lake Como: N37° 34.20'/W105° 30.92'

The Hike

Don't be fooled by Little Bear's name. It might lack the height of other fourteeners in Colorado, but this is one of the most—if not the most—dangerous fourteener in Colorado. Surprisingly this Class 4 fourteener's most difficult moves aren't hovering over a sheer thousand-foot drop. Rather they're in the long couloirs that provide access to its west ridge—particularly the "Hourglass" gully, a steep, narrow, scree-filled gully that's further complicated by smooth rock, which is often smooth, wet rock thanks to rain and snowmelt.

While that's enough of a challenge, other climbers pose a distinct threat if they kick a rock loose above. In fact, the gully also is called the "Bowling Alley" because bounding rocks can hurtle toward unsuspecting—or even suspecting—climbers (pins) at speeds upwards of 20 miles an hour. This is a mountain to wear a helmet on and to climb when there's not a lot of traffic, like on a weekday.

The first summit of Little Bear, then West Peak, was actually by mistake. J. R. Edmunds and Charles Fay set out to climb La Blanca in 1888. The two ended up summiting West Peak, which was renamed Little Bear in 1916 by the US Board on Geographic Names. It now shares the name with a creek and lake on its west side.

Hiking to the Lake Como Trailhead is a Class 1 hike on the rutty, dirt Lake Como Road interspersed with some jagged rocks that are easy to hike on but murder on a vehicle. The elevation gain isn't too bad, but it is a pretty steady incline to the lake. The hike itself is lovely too after you reach the shade of trees in Chokecherry Canyon at about 8,800 feet. From there the road heads northeast toward Holbrook Creek, crossing it at 10,700 feet. From there the road parallels the creek until it reaches Lake Como at 11,760 feet.

From the start it's easy to see that Little Bear is difficult to climb. The trail goes straight up a gnarly scree-filled couloir southeast of the lake.

Starting from the Lake Como Trailhead on Lake Como Road, hike around the lake, cross the small meadow, and enter an evergreen forest at 11,760 feet and nearly 0.25 mile. Continue through the forest on the road, passing near some ruins about

The Hourglass. The crux move on Little Bear Peak makes it one of the most difficult fourteeners in the state. CHRIS SEAVER

100 yards into the forest. Exit the forest in 100 more yards. As you exit the forest at 0.5 mile, look to your right for a small trail that leads up to the couloir to your right. Since it's all scree, the trail may be hard to find, but cairns should help guide the way. Begin ascending on a rock pile, following the cairns across the slope below the

couloir. At 12,190 feet and 0.6 mile enter on the right side of the gully. Climb up the gully on loose rock or snow and exit through a notch at the top at 0.7 mile and 12,575 feet. Head left (east) toward Little Bear's summit. On the south (right) side of the ridge, look for a small, cairned trail. Little Bear is directly ahead, but moving off the ridgeline is easier—and safer. The route continues along the south side of ridge and skirts around rocky prominent points. The trekking is relatively flat in this area. At 1.1 miles and 12,880 feet leave the ridge and head toward the center of Little Bear's southern face.

Reach the center of the face and turn left, heading up the infamous Hourglass at 1.4 miles and 13,260 feet. It's an extremely perilous 0.25-mile climb to the top from this point, and it will take a lot longer than expected to climb over this last bit. Climb up the initial Class 3 rock. Sometimes there will be a rope in this area, sometimes not. If there is, don't rely on it totally (it could be rotten), but it can provide some support through this part. The rock wall becomes a Class 4 climb where water has polished the stone face for ages. If water is flowing down the center of the gully, climb left of the gully and up some Class 5 rock to avoid the slick rock. At the top of the gully, roughly 13,560 feet, there's often an anchor set up, allowing climbers to rappel on the way down.

Above The Hourglass the approach gets easier, sort of. You're now on loose scree. Kicking it loose can send rock screaming down the gully. (If you kick any rock loose, yell "Rock" to warn anyone below.) Since the remainder of the trek is on scree, there's no set route to the peak. Pick your route carefully, moving to ledges when you can and staying toward the center of the scree when possible. There are some trail fragments and cairns, but study the pitch to assess and make your moves.

Gain the summit at 1.5 miles and celebrate. You've just made it to the top of one of the toughest mountains in Colorado, and the views from Little Bear's peak are astonishing. The west ridge undulates into the plains below. The ridge that heads north of Little Bear and connects it to Blanca looks as brutal as it is. The western side of Little Bear spreads out into the vast plains of the San Luis Valley.

Keep an eye on the weather while atop. The descent is not any easier, and that scree and polished granite will not make for a pleasant sliding experience in rain or snow.

Miles and Directions

0.0 Start at the trailhead at Lake Como and head east on Lake Como Road.

0.25 Enter an evergreen forest.

0.5 Exit the forest.

0.6 Head south on the trail to start climbing a gully.

0.7 Climb through the notch at the top of the gully and head left (east) toward Little Bear's peak.

1.1 Head toward the center of Little Bear's south slope.

1.4 Reach The Hourglass and start climbing the couloir.

Little Bear Peak

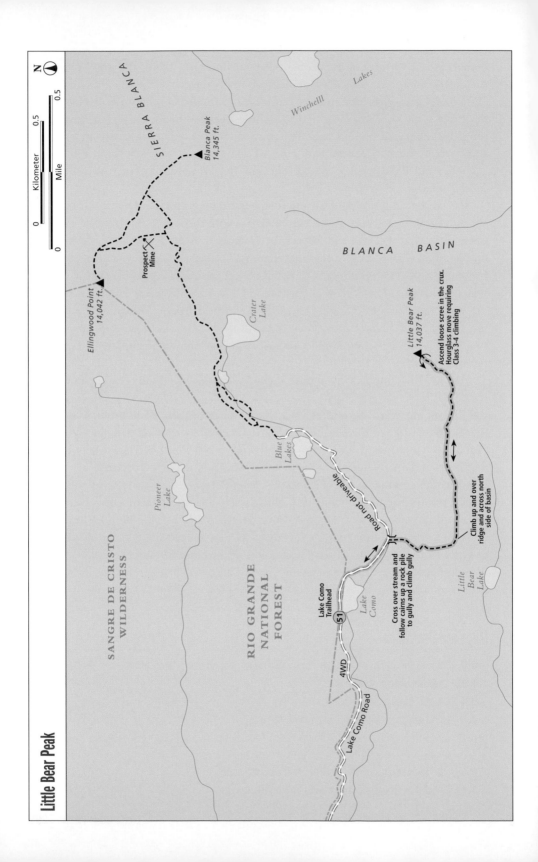

N

0   0.5   Kilometer   0.5
0   Mile   0.5

SANGRE DE CRISTO WILDERNESS

SIERRA BLANCA

Lakes

Winchell

Blanca Peak
14,345 ft.

Prospect
Mine

Ellingwood Point
14,042 ft.

*Crater
Lake*

BLANCA   BASIN

*Pioneer
Lake*

Blue Lakes

RIO GRANDE
NATIONAL
FOREST

Road not driveable

Little Bear Peak
14,037 ft.

Ascend loose scree in the crux.
Hourglass move requiring
Class 3-4 climbing

Climb up and over
ridge and across north
side of basin

Lake Como Trailhead
51

*Lake
Como*

Cross over stream and
follow cairns up a rock pile
to gully and climb gully

*Little
Bear
Lake*

4WD

Lake Como Road

1.55 Climb out of The Hourglass and scramble the last few hundred feet to the obvious summit. Carefully return the same way.

3.1 Arrive back at the trailhead.

Hiking Information

Closest Outfitters

Kristi Mountain Sports, 3223 Main St., Alamosa; (719) 589-9759; kristimountain sports.com

Great Pre- or Post-Mountain Spots

San Luis Valley Brewing Co., 631 Main St., Alamosa; (719) 587-2337; slvbrewco.com

Calvillo's Mexican Restaurant, 400 Main St., Alamosa; (719) 587-5500; calvillos .qwestoffice.net

The Rubi Slipper, 506 State Ave., Alamosa; (719) 589-2641

52 Snowmass Mountain

14,092' (NGVD29), 14,096' (NAVD88), 31st highest

Snowmass is the toughest remote fourteener in Colorado. Like San Luis Peak (14,014 feet) and the Windom Group of fourteeners, the approach to Snowmass is long. In this case the entire trip requires nearly 21 miles of hiking, trekking, and climbing from Class 1 trail to Class 3 scrambling. Consider camping near Snowmass Lake rather than doing this in one day. Unlike its rotten red peers in the Elks, the mountain is composed of relatively solid granite. This mountain has snow year-round, and a mountaineering ax will come in handy on its upper flanks into summer.

Start: Maroon-Snowmass Trailhead (Snowmass Creek Trailhead)
Distance: 20.8 miles
Hiking time: About 15 hours
Elevation gain: 5,700 feet
Difficulty: Class 2, Class 3
Trail surface: Dirt, scree, rock
Trailhead elevation: 8,390 feet
Camping: Backcountry camping
Fees: None
Best seasons: Mid-June through Oct
Maps: USGS Maroon Bells; National Geographic Trails Illustrated #128: Maroon Bells, Redstone, Marble

Nearest town: Aspen
Trail contacts: White River National Forest, Aspen Ranger District, (970) 925-3445; Pitkin County Sheriff's Office, (970) 920-5300
Trail tips: The USDA Forest Service now requires the use of bear canisters for overnight camping in the warmer months. Every person in the party should carry a wilderness tag. Timed right in fall, this route offers not only stunning views of the peaks but also the golden flames of aspen trees changing colors in alpine valleys.

Finding the trailhead: From Marolt Ditch on CO 82, drive northwest for 1.4 miles and take a left on Owl Creek Road passing the Buttermilk ski area, heading west (left from Aspen). Drive 4.4 miles and take a left, staying on Owl Creek Road at the intersection with Highland Road in Snowmass Village. Continue on Owl Creek Road for a total of 5.6 miles. Turn left onto Brush Creek Road for 1 mile then turn right onto Divide Road (CR 10) and drive for 1.8 miles. Take a slight right as the road becomes CR 11, a dirt road that crosses ski slopes as it descends toward the trailhead. After another 0.9 miles reach the trailhead. This route is closed in winter and a bit rougher on vehicles but only takes about 30 minutes. The other route takes nearly an hour from Aspen but is easier on vehicles.

From the intersection of CO 82 West and Watson Divide Road, 13 miles northwest of Aspen and 28 miles south of Glenwood Springs, head west on Watson Divide Road (left from Aspen) and drive 1.9 miles. Turn left onto Snowmass Creek Road, drive 7.9 miles then take a right to stay on Snowmass Creek Road for another 0.9 miles. Park just before the Snowmass Falls Ranch sign. GPS: N39° 11.99' / W106° 59.64'

The Hike

Snowmass is a misty mountain, often hidden among clouds that loom over winsome Snowmass Lake, the best place to see this peak. This mountain has a long, beautiful approach—you get to hike through idyllic forests, across meadows, and past high alpine lakes. You encounter all of that before climbing one of Colorado's largest permanent snowfields and its most remote peak.

When Hayden Survey members William Byers, James Gardner, and W. Rideling made the first summit of Snowmass on August 7, 1873, they had plenty of names to choose from when they put it on the books. The Utes believed that the mountain caused the weather in the region and called it Cold Woman. When pioneers first set their eyes upon its reclusive heights, they called it White House Peak. Noting its two summits, prospectors called it The Twins. The Hayden survey ignored all of these and called it Snowmass Mountain in deference to its permanent snowfields.

The beginning of this epic trip starts at the Maroon-Snowmass Trailhead (FT 1975) near good signage and a trail register. Register here and take a wilderness tag as the regulations describe. Hiking south, immediately enter a thick aspen-and-evergreen forest. The first 1.6 miles pass in and out of land owned by the Snowmass Falls Ranch, and there is no camping for backpackers. Please stay on-trail, follow all signs, and keep the rustic gates closed.

Just after 1.4 miles, pass a small junction to the right for the West Snowmass Trail (FT 1927). At this point the trail comes close to an elbow in Snowmass Creek and begins paralleling the creek as both head gradually south; you find yourself surrounded by growing mountain ridges on both sides. The ruddy top and bottom of Willoughby Mountain to your left have a wide band of gray granite in the middle.

At 4.0 miles cross Bear Creek and get a postcard view of Snowmass to the southwest—if it's not obscured by clouds. The trail has already begun a gradual ascent. Continue on the fantastic trail to a little over 10,000 feet, where it comes to a flat spot at 5.5 miles. You're about to face your first obstacle—the Log Jam. It's essentially a bridge of floating logs at 10,100 feet and 6.0 miles that crosses over Snowmass Creek just below a small lake. It's an easy place to cross if the water's not high and the lake isn't frozen. Still, choose your path carefully; a slip here can result in wet feet or a wet body—not fun. If the water is flowing fast, travel back downstream and look for a place to wade across where it's narrower. On the other side of the lake, follow the trail as it wends past a series of ponds.

On the south side of the ponds, the trail crosses switchbacks twice and reenters forest at 6.75 miles and 10,360 feet. In the spruce-and-fir forest the trail continues gaining altitude, passing through a small meadow at 7.5 miles. Shortly after that pass a trail junction as you reenter the forest. Head straight toward Snowmass Lake, leaving the Maroon-Snowmass Trail.

The trail comes close to Snowmass Creek again and follows it to Snowmass Lake, passing some waterfalls near the lake. The trail reaches the eastern side of the lake at

Shy, yet stately Snowmass Mountain is just right of center, almost overshadowed by its shorter neighbors. Chris Seaver

10,980 feet. Cross over the creek on rocks or some downed trees and follow the trail along the lake's southern shore. There are plenty of wonderful options to camp near the lake, but please follow wilderness rules and stay at least 100 feet from the lakeshore. West, across the lake, the broad granite mass of Snowmass Peak (13,619 feet) dominates the view. Snowmass Mountain is northwest of the imposing rock face, and in summer you can make out parts of the trail as it courses up the gentler slopes.

Follow the trail to the west end of Snowmass Lake, trekking through trees and willows. Turn right at 8.6 miles and left at 8.9 miles to begin ascending Snowmass Mountain on the southwest side of the lake.

The trail chases a line of vegetation along a gully and up a cairned, scree-covered slope to 11,900 feet. Find a good place to cross over the gully and continue on the trail at 12,000 feet. The trail passes through waning vegetation in summer. It's snow covered earlier in the year and may be easier to climb on the firm snow then, but the trail is relatively easy, despite its steepness through this part.

Hike around some cliffs near the ridge at 10 miles and 13,540 feet. Climb over some rocks to gain the ridge crest just above a low point in the saddle between Snowmass Peak to the left and Snowmass Mountain to the right. Reach the ridge crest at 13,740 feet and scramble the remaining 0.25 mile to the top over some Class 3 rock.

Snowmass Mountain

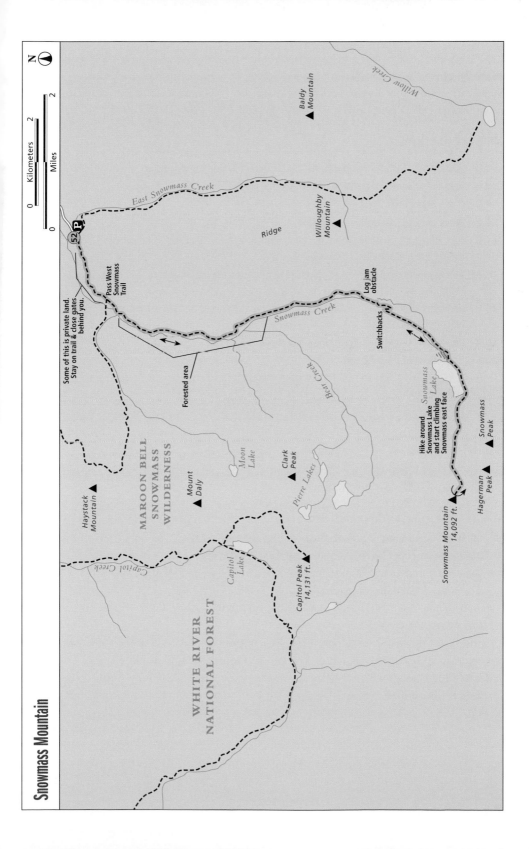

N

Kilometers
0   2

Miles
0   2

Willow Creek

Baldy Mountain ▲

East Snowmass Creek

Ridge

Willoughby Mountain ▲

52 P

Pass West Snowmass Trail

Some of this is private land. Stay on trail & close gates behind you.

Snowmass Creek

Log jam obstacle

Switchbacks

Forested area

Bear Creek

MAROON BELL SNOWMASS WILDERNESS

Haystack Mountain ▲

Mount Daly ▲

Moon Lake

Clark Peak ▲

Pierre Lakes

Snowmass Lake

Hike around Snowmass Lake and start climbing Snowmass east face

WHITE RIVER NATIONAL FOREST

Capitol Creek

Capitol Lake

Capitol Peak 14,131 ft. ▲

Snowmass Mountain 14,092 ft. ▲

Hagerman Peak ▲

Snowmass Peak ▲

Reach the peak of Snowmass Mountain at 14,092 feet and embrace the wonder of the Maroon–Snowmass Wilderness in a veritable ocean of mountain peaks. Capitol Peak is the most prominent, and the two can be connected, albeit by a long (4.0-mile), rough ridge climb, as Glen Dunny and Bill Forest first did in 1966.

Miles and Directions

0.0   Start at the Maroon-Snowmass Trailhead (FT 1975) near a trail register.

1.4   Pass the junction for the West Snowmass Trail (FT 1927) on the right.

4.0   Cross Bear Creek.

6.0   Cross the Log Jam below a small lake.

7.5   Pass through a small meadow and head straight at a trail junction to Snowmass Lake, leaving the Maroon-Snowmass Trail.

8.6   Turn right and then turn left at 8.9 miles to begin ascending Snowmass Mountain on the southwest side of the lake.

10.0 Hike around some cliffs near the ridge. Gain the ridge crest and do some Class 3 scrambling to gain the peak.

10.4 Reach the summit. Return via the same route.

20.8 Arrive back at the trailhead.

Hiking Information

Closest Outfitters

Ute Mountaineer, 210 S. Galena St., Aspen; (970) 925-2849; utemountaineer.com

Bristlecone Mountain Sports, 781 E Valley Rd., Basalt; (970) 927-1492; bristlecone mountainsports.com

Great Pre- or Post-Mountain Spots

Big Hoss Grill, 45 Village Square Store #1, Snowmass Village; (970) 923-2597; eatsnow mass.com/snowmass/restaurants/1298/big-hoss-grill

Venga Venga Cantina and Tequila Bar, 105 Daly Ln., Snowmass Village; (970) 923-7777; richardsandoval.com/vengavenga/

Aspen Brewing Co., 304 E Hopkins Ave., Aspen; (970) 920-BREW (2739); aspenbrewing company.com

Woody Creek Tavern, 2858 Upper River Rd., Woody Creek; (970) 923-4585; woody creektavern.com. A favorite haunt of the late Hunter S. Thompson.

J-Bar at Hotel Jerome, 330 E Main St., Aspen; (970) 925-3721; hoteljerome.auberge resorts.com/dining/

53 Capitol Peak

14,130' (NGVD29), 14,141' (NAVD88), 29th highest

Capitol Peak is perhaps the most dangerous fourteener in Colorado. Its standard route includes the infamous Knife Edge, an exposed Class 4 ridge. The ridge is breathtaking, but thankfully Capitol is one of the two difficult fourteeners in the Elk Range and the Maroon-Snowmass Wilderness that's not made of crumbly red rock. Still, many people rope up for the Knife Edge of Capitol, and it's a smart idea to wear a helmet on this challenging peak.

Start: Capitol Creek Trailhead
Distance: 16.2 miles
Hiking time: About 15 hours
Elevation gain: 4,670 feet
Difficulty: Class 4
Trail surface: Dirt, scree, rock
Trailhead elevation: 9,460 feet
Camping: Backcountry camping; great spots near Capitol Lake
Fees: None
Best seasons: Spring through fall
Maps: USGS Capitol Peak, Highland Peak; National Geographic Trails Illustrated #128: Maroon Bells, Redstone, Marble

Nearest town: Aspen
Trail contacts: White River National Forest, Aspen Ranger District, (970) 925-3445; Pitkin County Sheriff's Office, (970) 920-5300
Trail tips: The USDA Forest Service now requires the use of bear canisters for overnight camping in the warmer months. Every person in the party should carry a wilderness tag. Timed right in fall, this route offers not only stunning views of the peaks but also the golden flames of aspen trees changing colors in alpine valleys.

Finding the trailhead: From the intersection of CO 82 and Snowmass Creek Road (CR 11) (not to be confused with the road to Snowmass Village), 28 miles southeast of Glenwood Springs and 14 miles northwest of Aspen, head south on Snowmass Creek Road for 1.7 miles; it's a right from Glenwood Springs. Turn right onto Capitol Creek Road (CR 9) and stay on the road for 8.1 miles (The last 2 miles, shortly after passing Snowmass Creek Outfitters, are on rough dirt road). The well-marked trailhead is above Capitol Creek. GPS: N39° 14.06'/W107° 04.77'

The Hike

When the Hayden Survey encountered and named Capitol Peak in 1874, geographer Henry Gannett remarked that Capitol Mountain was: "One of the crowning summits of the range, whose gray, prism-shaped top and precipitous sides forbid access." Indeed, this massive peak named in honor of the US Capitol's dome must have looked imposing in more than a Mr. Smith Goes to Washington sort of way. It remained indomitable until Harold Clark and Percy Hagerman summited the peak, traversing the knife edge on August 22, 1909.

Climbing across the infamous Knife Edge with Capitol Peak in the background. CHRIS SEAVER

Capitol looms above the alpine forests and meadows that surround it, and the peak's solid block is visible from the trailhead. From the trailhead take the Capitol Ditch Trail, a jeep road that avoids 400 feet of additional elevation gain on the way back on Capitol Creek Trail by skirting a hill. The road heads west as it parallels a water ditch used by roaming cattle in the area. (***Note:*** Cattle do roam the area, particularly in summer. They have created offshoots from the Ditch Trail here and there.) Stay on the main trail and cross Capitol Creek for the first of many times at 0.6 mile. At 1.2 miles and 9,500 feet reach a signed trail junction to the right. Cross over the ditch and hike on a good trail. The forest empties into a meadow dotted with tree clusters, entering the Maroon-Snowmass Wilderness. From here the trail contours along the eastern side of a hill and then down slightly. Closer to the creek, leave the jeep road on a trail to the left at 3.2 miles. Cross Capitol Creek and turn right as you rejoin the Capitol Creek Trail. At this point Capitol's peak is already visible.

Follow this good dirt trail as it rises gradually, bordering swaths of evergreens and aspens until 10,500 feet and 4.1 miles, when it enters a thick grove of trees. The trail continues meandering in and out of forest as it gains altitude. At 10,800 feet and 5.1 miles the trail makes a sharp right into a patch of forest, climbing a hill before it turns left to resume its southern trajectory. Once again the trail crosses Capitol Creek below Capitol Lake at 5.5 miles and 11,080 feet. It parallels the creek until 11,550 feet, when it cuts to the left before reaching Capitol Lake—a good place to camp if you plan an overnight trip. If you're not camping, or the next morning, head left (southeast) on a trail that climbs up toward the saddle between Capitol and Mount Daly. At 6.25 miles and 11,800 feet the trail begins switchbacking up the steep slope. Gain the saddle at 12,500 feet and 6.7 miles and turn right, heading southeast.

Climb into the basin, crossing two small couloirs and head toward the middle of the slope under Capitol's northern ridge. There's no good trail here, so follow trail fragments and try not to lose too much elevation as you cross to the eastern side of the slope, staying under a cliff face. At 7.1 miles and 12,630 feet the trail begins to arc around a rocky bulkhead; at 7.3 miles and 13,110 feet it takes a more direct right turn close to a notch. K2's distant anthill of a peak is ahead to the southwest. Climb over the broken rock, following cairns as you can, aiming for K2's northwestern side and skirting its summit. (K2 offers a great view of Capitol and the surrounding peaks and basins, but you don't need to climb this Class 4 peak; after all, the next part is the Class 4 Knife Edge!)

K2 is a good time to assess the weather, as well as the health and readiness of your group to summit. The remainder of the route is tough and eats up time, starting with the Knife Edge directly ahead.

From the west side of K2 the trail dips into a notch and then climbs up a small tower. The Knife Edge begins at 7.6 miles and 13,580 feet and continues for a vertiginous, heart-thumping 100 feet. You can traverse this section in a number of ways, including by straddling it or by grasping the ridge with your hands and walking your feet under it. Adventurous, surf-footed climbers can walk across the knife's edge— thanks to the solid granite of the ridge—but remember, you've got to make it back on the same route! It's easiest to traverse the last bit of the edge on the south side.

The remaining 0.25 mile doesn't get much easier as you gain about 400 feet from the edge to the summit over craggy, broken granite. Climb the left side of the ridge, crossing over a notch just after the edge and following cairns roughly 80 to 100 feet below the ridge crest. At 8.0 miles and 13,900 feet climb up the steep rock to gain the short southeast-facing ridge; follow it 0.1 mile to the top of this difficult peak.

The summit offers a gorgeous view of Snowmass Mountain (14,092 feet) to the south, with the Pierre Lakes in the basin on the east side of the ridge that connects

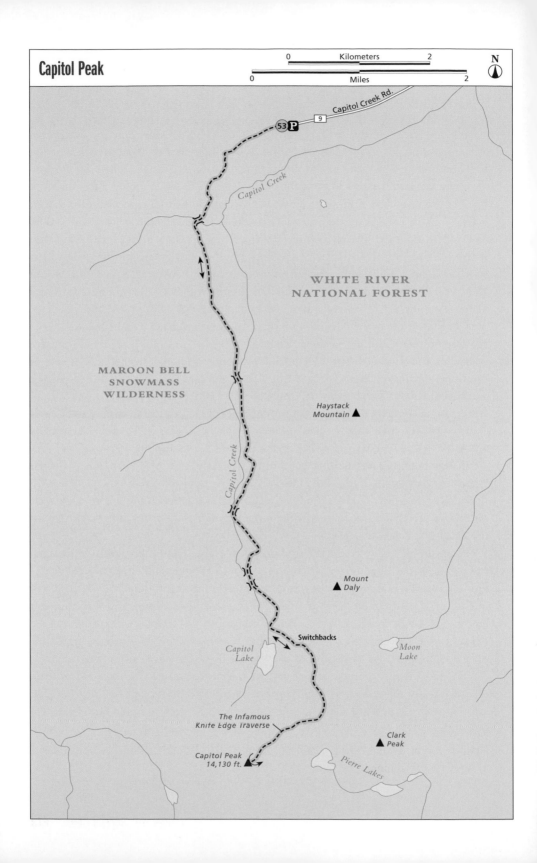

0   Kilometers   2

0   Miles   2

N

Capitol Creek Rd.

53 P 9

Capitol Creek

WHITE RIVER
NATIONAL FOREST

MAROON BELL
SNOWMASS
WILDERNESS

Capitol Creek

Haystack
Mountain ▲

Mount
Daly ▲

Switchbacks

Capitol
Lake

Moon
Lake

The Infamous
Knife Edge Traverse

Clark
Peak ▲

Capitol Peak
14,130 ft. ▲

Pierre Lakes

these two giants. The Maroon Bells are just left of Snowmass in the distance. The north offers an awesome expanse of verdant rolling hills and valleys. If the weather's good, enjoy the peak as long as you want—or at least until your nerves are steeled for the descent—and return via the same route. If clouds are on the horizon or closer, start your descent ASAP.

Miles and Directions

0.0 Start at the Capitol Creek Trailhead and go west on the Capitol Ditch Trail.

0.6 Cross Capitol Creek.

1.2 Head right at the signed trail junction.

3.2 Find a trail to the left of the main trail. Follow it to Capitol Creek and rejoin the Capitol Creek Trail, heading to the right.

5.1 Take a sharp right, heading into a grove of trees, and climb a steep hill.

5.5 Cross Capitol Creek again.

6.25 Switchback up a steep slope.

6.7 Gain the saddle and head right, climbing into a basin.

7.1 The trail curls around a rocky bulkhead.

7.3 Turn right, heading toward K2's peak.

7.6 Skirt around K2 to reach the 100-foot-long Knife Edge and cross it.

7.7 On the other side of Capitol, stay on the south side of a ridge and head for the peak, climbing over Class 3 rock.

8.0 Climb steep rock to gain the southeast ridge to the top of Capitol Peak.

8.1 Reach the peak. Return via same route.

16.2 Arrive at the trailhead.

Hiking Information

Closest Outfitters

Ute Mountaineer, 210 S. Galena St., Aspen; (970) 925-2849; utemountaineer.com

Bristlecone Mountain Sports, 781 E Valley Rd., Basalt; (970) 927-1492; bristlecone mountainsports.com

Great Pre- or Post-Mountain Spots

Aspen Brewing Co., 304 E Hopkins Ave., Aspen; (970) 920-BREW (2739); aspenbrewing company.com

Woody Creek Tavern, 2858 Upper River Rd., Woody Creek; (970) 923-4585; woody creektavern.com. A favorite haunt of the late Hunter S. Thompson.

Belly Up Aspen, 450 S Galena St. Aspen; (970) 544-9800; bellyupaspen.com

J-Bar at Hotel Jerome, 330 E Main St., Aspen; (970) 925-3721; hoteljerome.auberge resorts.com/dining/

Appendix A: Mountain Clubs, Organizations, and Resources

The Colorado Fourteeners Initiative (CFI) is the organization that works with land managers and owners throughout Colorado to ensure access to the mountains; 710 Tenth St., Suite 220, Golden 80401; (303) 278-7650; 14ers.org

14ers.com is a great reference that's regularly updated by thousands of members. It has weather forecasts, maps, trip reports, and more for each fourteener.

SummitPost.org is another great resource for climbing fourteeners in Colorado and across the United States. The website has trip reports and other information about the mountains.

The Hiking Project has trip reports, maps, pictures, and more for fourteeners and other hikes in Colorado and across the United States. hikingproject.com

The Colorado Mountain Club, headquartered in Golden at the American Mountaineering Center, has chapters throughout Colorado. It's a great resource and coordinates hikes, mountaineering adventures, and classes throughout the state. 710 10th St., Suite 200, Golden 80401; (303) 279-3080; cmc.org

The AdAmAn Club is a long-standing organization that helps with trail maintenance on and near Pikes Peak. It's most famous for its New Year's Eve ascent of Pikes Peak to light fireworks. The name is a take on "add a man," and each year the number of people ascending the mountain for the event grows. 392 Cobblestone Dr., Colorado Springs 80906; adaman.org

American Mountaineering Center, 710 10th St., Suite 200, Golden 80401; (303) 996-2760; americanmountaineeringcenter.org

Colorado Canyons Association, 543 Main St., Suite 4, Grand Junction 81501; (970) 623-7902; coloradocanyonsassociation.org

Colorado Trail Foundation, 710 10th St., Suite 210, Golden 80401; (303) 384-3729; coloradotrail.org

Friends of the Dillon Ranger District, PO Box 1648, Silverthorne 80498; (970) 262-3449; fdrd.org

Friends of Cheyenne Mountain State Park, 410 JL Ranch Heights, Colorado Springs 80926; friendsofcmsp.org

Friends of the Dunes, 11500 Hwy. 150, Mosca 81146; (719) 378-6381; friendsof greatsanddunes.org

Friends of Mount Evans & Lost Creek Wilderness, PO Box 3431, Evergreen 80439; (303) 670-3853; fomelc.org

Friends of the Eagles Nest Wilderness, PO Box 4504, Frisco 80443; (970) 468-5400; fenw.org

Friends of Larimer County Parks and Open Lands, 1800 S CR 31, Loveland 80537; (970) 679-4570; larimer.org/friends

Friends of the Peak (Pikes Peak), PO Box 2494, Colorado Springs 80901; (719) 527-1384; fotp.com

The Rocky Mountain Field Institute, 815 S 25th St. #101, Colorado Springs 80904; (719) 471-7736; rmfi.org

San Juan Mountains Association, 15 Burnett Ct., Durango 81301; (970) 385-1210; sjma.org

Volunteers for Outdoor Colorado, 600 S Marion Pkwy, Denver 80209; (303) 715-1010; voc.org

Wilderness Workshop, Third Street Center, Suite 27, 520 S 3rd St., Carbondale 81623; (970) 963-3977; wildernessworkshop.org

Conservation Groups

Colorado Wildlife Federation, 1410 Grant St., Suite C-313, Denver 80203; (303) 987-0400, ext. 1; coloradowildlife.org

Conservation Colorado, 1536 Wynkoop St. 5C, Denver 80202; (303) 333-7846; conservationco.org

Environment Colorado, 1536 Wynkoop St. #400, Denver 80202; (303) 573-3871; environmentcolorado.org

High Country Conservation Advocates, PO Box 1066, Crested Butte 81224; (970) 349-7104; hccacb.org

Leave No Trace Center for Outdoor Ethics, 1000 North St., Boulder 80304; (303) 442-8222; LNT.org

The Nature Conservancy, 2424 Spruce St., Boulder 80302; (303) 444-2950; nature.org

Rocky Mountain Wild, 1536 Wynkoop St., Suite 900, Denver 80202; (303) 546-0214; rockymountainwild.org

Sierra Club, Rocky Mountain Chapter, 1536 Wynkoop St., Suite 200, Denver 80202; (303) 861-8819; rmc.sierraclub.org

Appendix B: Further Reading

Roach, Gerry. *Colorado's Fourteeners: From Hikes to Climbs*. Golden, CO: Fulcrum Publishing, 2011. *Colorado's Fourteeners* is the most comprehensive fourteener guidebook and covers multiple routes up each mountain, not just the standard approaches.

Arps, Louisa Ward, and Elinor Eppich Kingery. *High Country Names: Rocky Mountain National Park and the Indian Peaks*. Boulder, CO: Johnson Books, 1994.

Borneman, Marlene, and James Ells. *Rocky Mountain Wildflowers*. Golden, CO: The Colorado Mountain Club Press, 2012.

Buchholtz, C. W. *Rocky Mountain National Park: A History*. Niwot: University Press of Colorado, 1983.

Bueler, William. *Roof of the Rockies: A History of Colorado Mountaineering*. Golden, CO: The Colorado Mountain Club Press, 2000.

The Colorado Mountain Club Foundation. *The Colorado 14ers; The Standard Routes*. Golden, CO: The Colorado Mountain Club Press, 2010.

Gilliland, Mary Ellen. *Summit: A Gold Rush History of Summit County, Colorado*. Silverthorne, CO: Alpenrose Press, 2006.

Jacobs, Randy, and Robert Ormes. *Guide to the Colorado Mountains*, 10th edition. Golden, CO: The Colorado Mountain Club Press, 2003.

Lichter, Justin. *Trail-Tested: A Thru-Hiker's Guide to Ultralight Hiking and Backpacking*. Guilford, CT: FalconGuides, 2013. A great reference for hiking and climbing tips.

Robertson, Jan, Jay Fell, David Hite, Chris Case, and Walt Borneman. *100 Years Up High: Colorado Mountains and Mountaineers*. Golden, CO: The Colorado Mountain Club Press, 2011.

About the Author

Chris Meehan grew up in the shadows of the Appalachians, where he cultivated a love of the outdoors. He has written for *Outdoor USA* magazine, *Westword*, and *Sun & Wind Energy*, among other publications. A former Colorado mountain guide, he has taken children as young as twelve and people in their seventies to the top of Colorado's fourteeners and has hiked some of Colorado's toughest mountains, including Little Bear, Longs Peak, and Sunlight Peak.

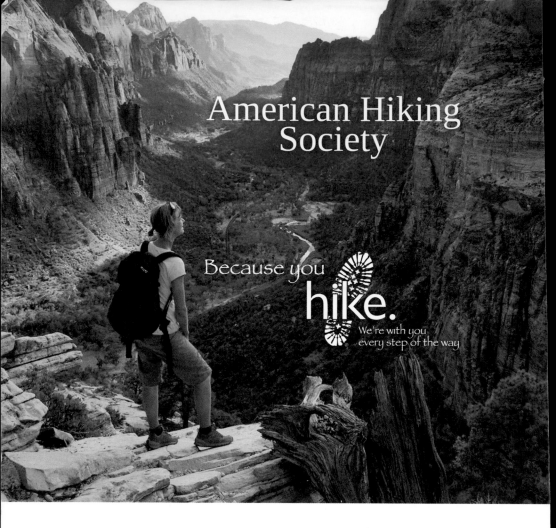

American Hiking Society

Because you

hike.

We're with you every step of the way

As a national voice for hikers, **American Hiking Society** works every day:

- Building and maintaining hiking trails
- Educating and supporting hikers by providing information and resources
- Supporting hiking and trail organizations nationwide
- Speaking for hikers in the halls of Congress and with federal land managers

Whether you're a casual hiker or a seasoned backpacker, become a member of American Hiking Society and join the national hiking community! You'll enjoy great member benefits and help preserve the nation's hiking trails, so tomorrow's hike is even better than today's. We invite you to join us now!

American Hiking Society